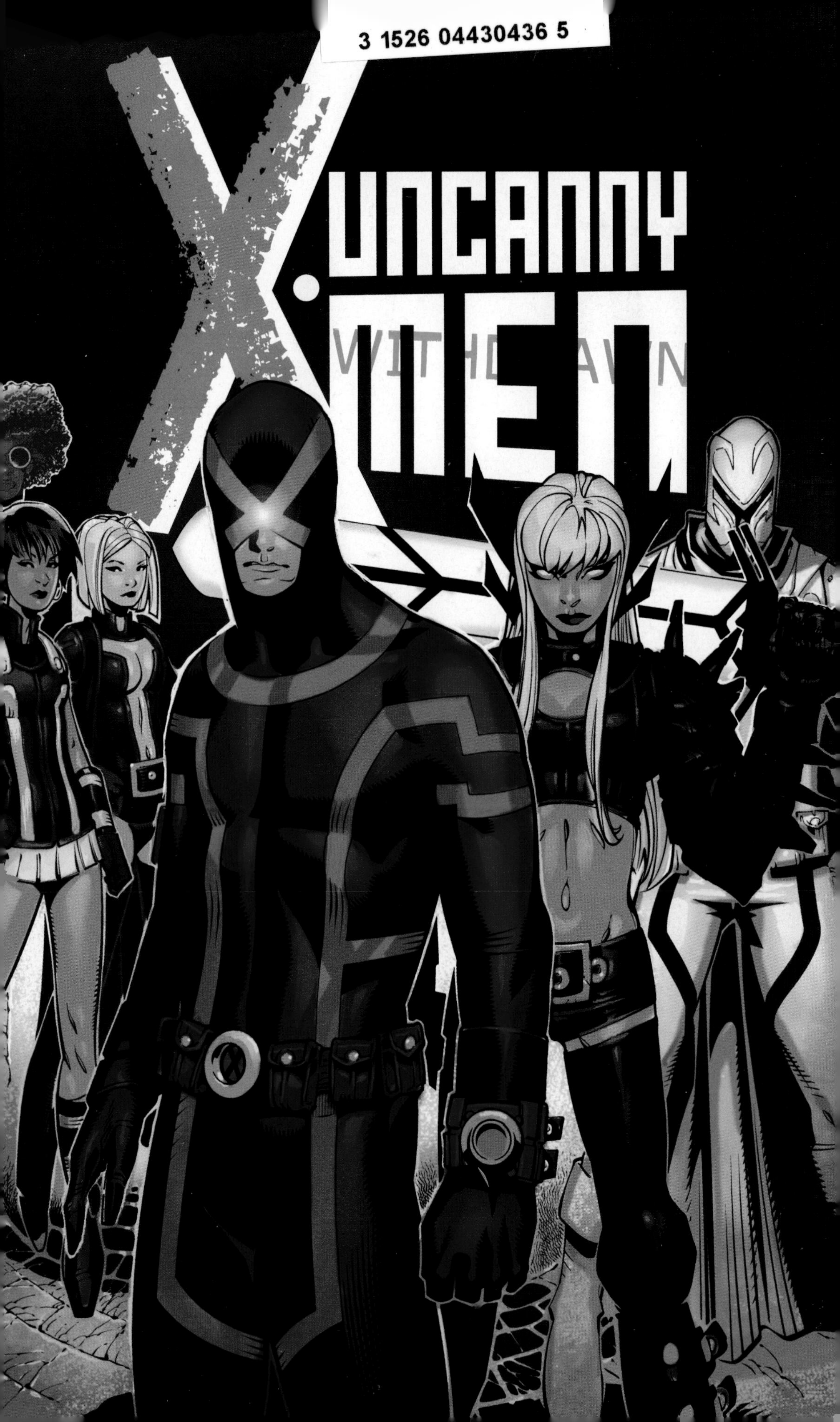
X
UNCANNY
MEN

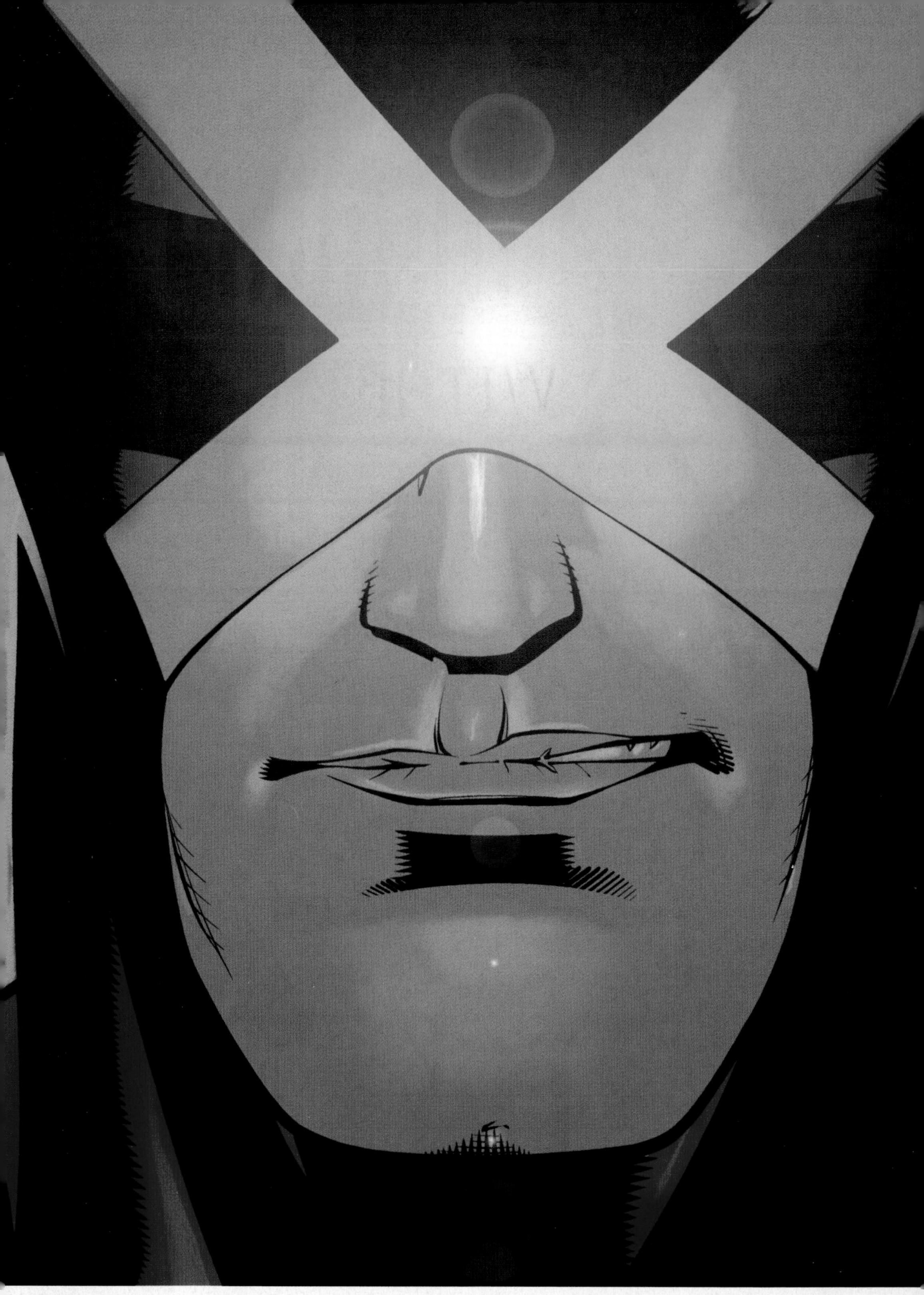

REVOLUTION

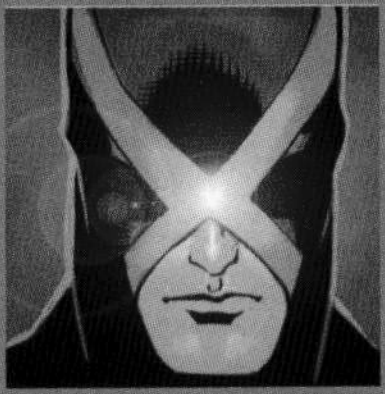

CYCLOPS
SCOTT SUMMERS

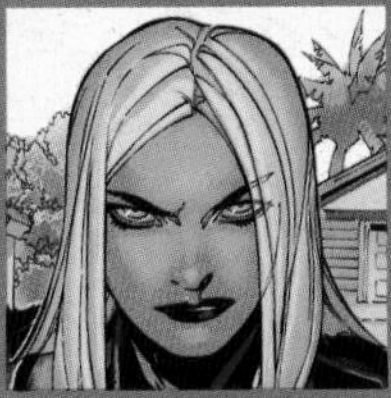

EMMA FROST

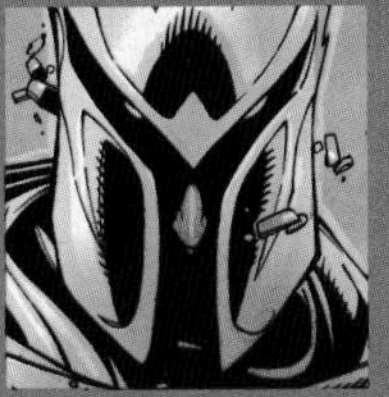

MAGNETO
ERIK LEHNSHERR

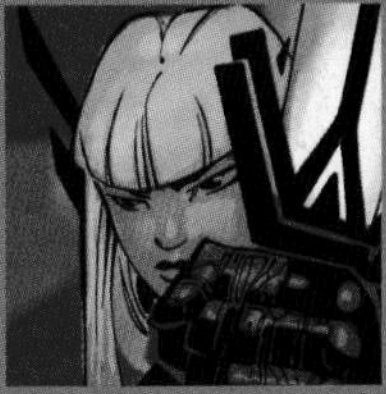

MAGIK
ILLYANA RASPUTINA

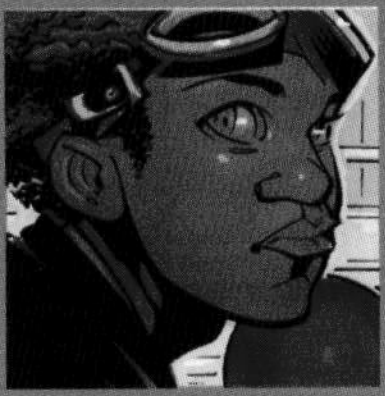

TRIAGE
CHRISTOPHER MUSE

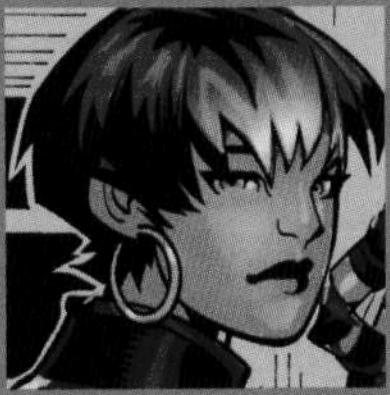

TEMPUS
EVA BELL

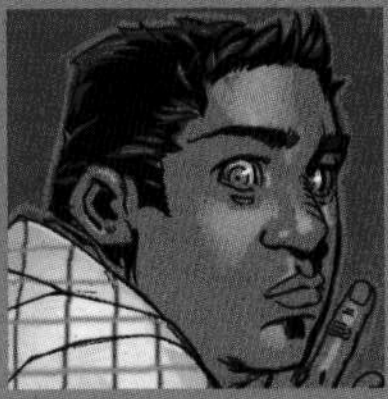

FABIO MEDIA

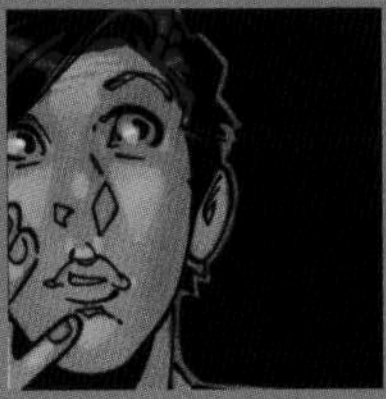

BENJAMIN DEEDS

BRIAN MICHAEL
BENDIS
WRITER

CHRIS
BACHALO
PENCILER/COLORIST, #1-4

FRAZER
IRVING
ARTIST, #5

TIM
TOWNSEND

JAIME
MENDOZA

AL
VEY

VICTOR
OLAZABA

INKERS, #1-4

COVER ART: **CHRIS BACHALO & TIM TOWNSEND (#1-4) AND FRAZER IRVING (#5)**

VC'S JOE
CARAMAGNA
LETTERER

JORDAN D.
WHITE
ASSISTANT EDITOR

NICK
LOWE
EDITOR

COLLECTION EDITOR: **JENNIFER GRÜNWALD**
ASSISTANT EDITORS: **ALEX STARBUCK & NELSON RIBEIRO**
EDITOR, SPECIAL PROJECTS: **MARK D. BEAZLEY**
SENIOR EDITOR, SPECIAL PROJECTS: **JEFF YOUNGQUIST**
SVP OF PRINT & DIGITAL PUBLISHING SALES: **DAVID GABRIEL**
BOOK DESIGN: **JEFF POWELL**

EDITOR IN CHIEF: **AXEL ALONSO**
CHIEF CREATIVE OFFICER: **JOE QUESADA**
PUBLISHER: **DAN BUCKLEY**
EXECUTIVE PRODUCER: **ALAN FINE**

UNCANNY X-MEN VOL. 1: REVOLUTION. Contains material originally published in magazine form as UNCANNY X-MEN #1-5. First printing 2013. ISBN# 978-0-7851-6846-1. Published by MARVEL WORLDWIDE, INC., a subsidiary of MARVEL ENTERTAINMENT, LLC. OFFICE OF PUBLICATION: 135 West 50th Street, New York, NY 10020. **Printed in the U.S.A.** ALAN FINE, EVP - Office of the President, Marvel Worldwide, Inc. and EVP & CMO Marvel Characters B.V.; DAN BUCKLEY, Publisher & President - Print, Animation & Digital Divisions; JOE QUESADA, Chief Creative Officer; TOM BREVOORT, SVP of Publishing; DAVID BOGART, SVP of Operations & Procurement, Publishing; C.B. CEBULSKI, SVP of Creator & Content Development; DAVID GABRIEL, SVP of Print & Digital Publishing Sales; JIM O'KEEFE, VP of Operations & Logistics; DAN CARR, Executive Director of Publishing Technology; SUSAN CRESPI, Editorial Operations Manager; ALEX MORALES, Publishing Operations Manager; STAN LEE, Chairman Emeritus. For information regarding advertising in Marvel Comics or on Marvel.com, please contact Niza Disla, Director of Marvel ... **Manufactured between 5/6/2013 and 6/17/2013 by R.R. DONNELLEY, INC., SALEM, VA, USA.**

Born with genetic mutations that gave them abilities beyond those of normal humans, mutants are the next stage in evolution. As such, they are feared and hated by humanity. A group of mutants known as the X-Men fight for peaceful coexistence between mutants and humankind. But not all mutants see peaceful coexistence as a reality.

X. UNCANNY MEN

Cyclops, one of the original X-Men, is the public face of the new mutant revolution and he and his teammates are gathering new mutants as fast as they appear.

Privately, Scott is battling demons — having once been possessed by a cosmic force that drove him to do things he will always regret.

1

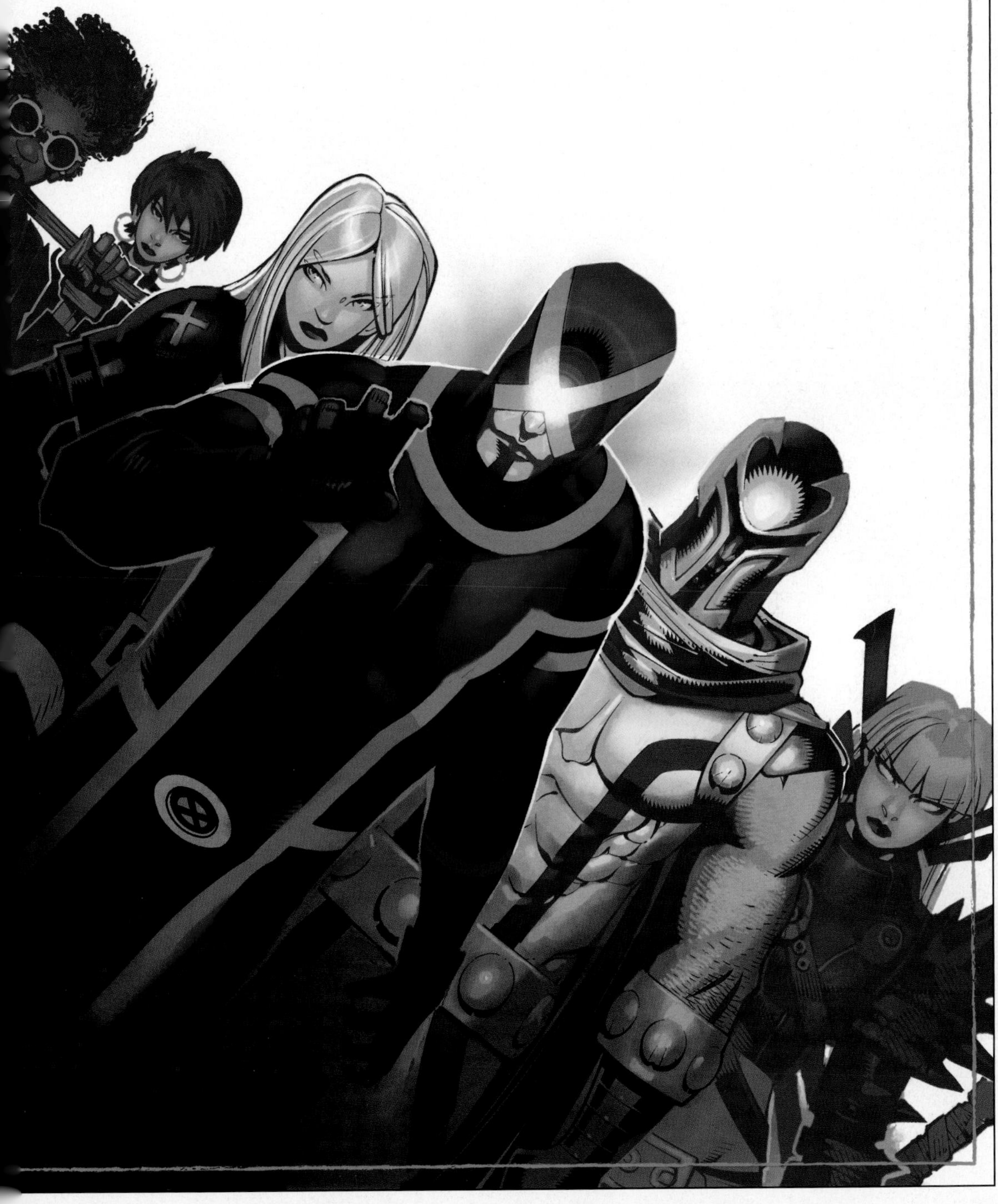

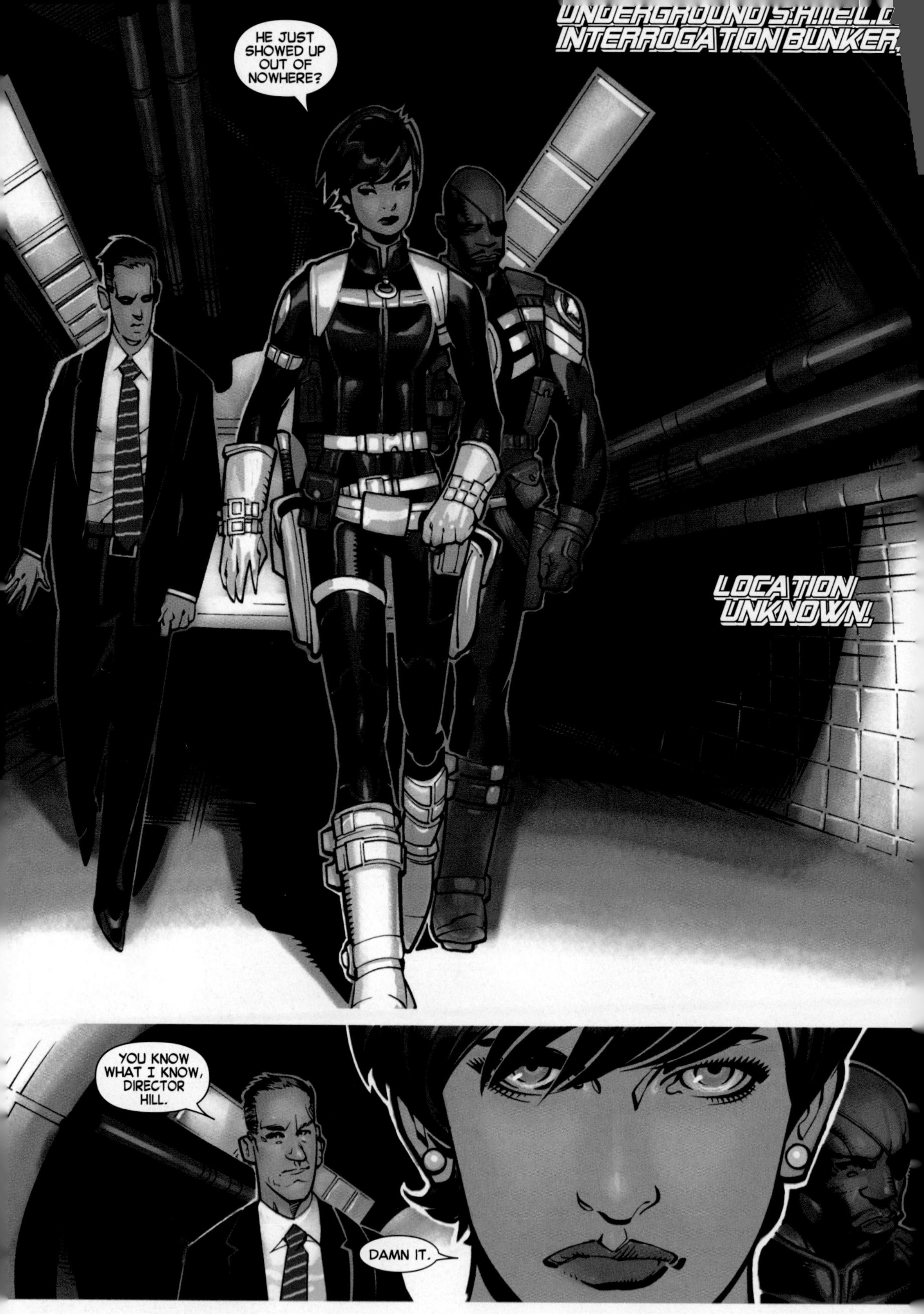
UNDERGROUND S.H.I.E.L.
INTERROGATION BUNKER.
HE JUST SHOWED UP OUT OF NOWHERE?
LOCATION UNKNOWN.
YOU KNOW WHAT I KNOW, DIRECTOR HILL.
DAMN IT.

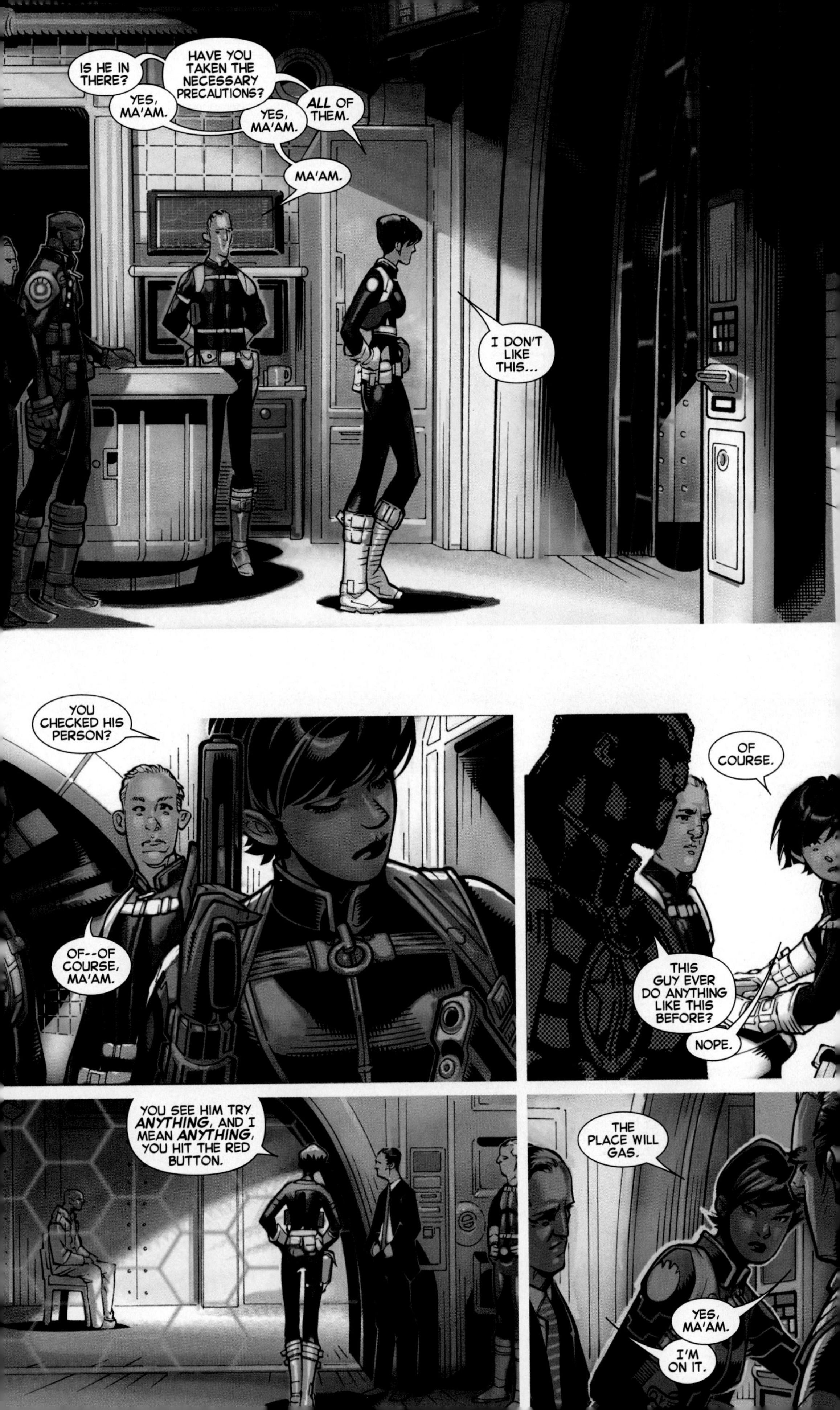
IS HE IN THERE?
YES, MA'AM.
HAVE YOU TAKEN THE NECESSARY PRECAUTIONS?
YES, MA'AM.
ALL OF THEM.
MA'AM.
I DON'T LIKE THIS...
YOU CHECKED HIS PERSON?
OF--OF COURSE, MA'AM.
OF COURSE.
THIS GUY EVER DO ANYTHING LIKE THIS BEFORE?
NOPE.
YOU SEE HIM TRY ANYTHING, AND I MEAN ANYTHING, YOU HIT THE RED BUTTON.
THE PLACE WILL GAS.
YES, MA'AM.
I'M ON IT.

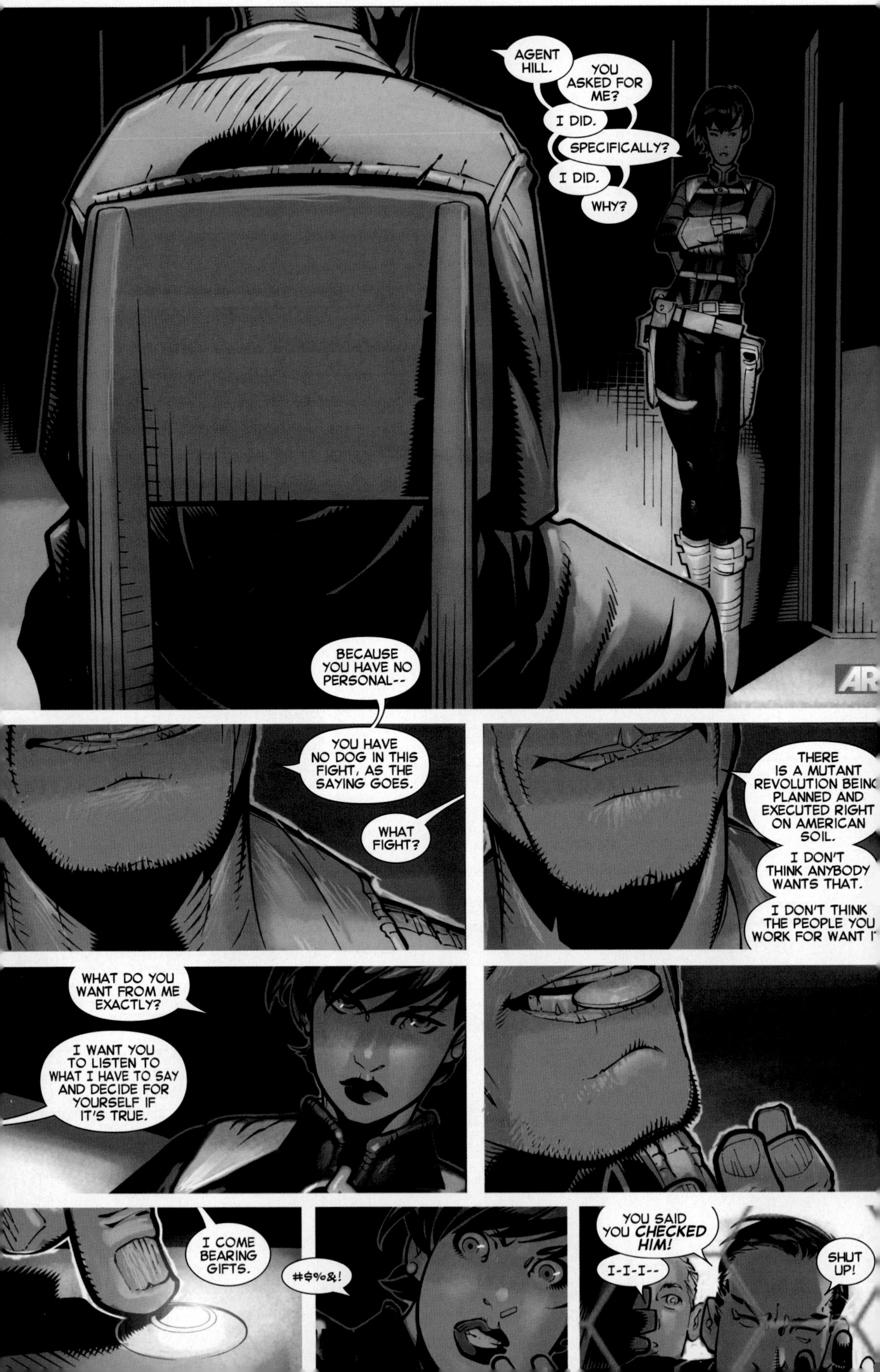
AGENT HILL.
YOU ASKED FOR ME?
I DID.
SPECIFICALLY?
I DID.
WHY?
BECAUSE YOU HAVE NO PERSONAL--
YOU HAVE NO DOG IN THIS FIGHT, AS THE SAYING GOES.
WHAT FIGHT?
THERE IS A MUTANT REVOLUTION BEIN PLANNED AND EXECUTED RIGHT ON AMERICAN SOIL.
I DON'T THINK ANYBODY WANTS THAT.
I DON'T THINK THE PEOPLE YOU WORK FOR WANT I
WHAT DO YOU WANT FROM ME EXACTLY?
I WANT YOU TO LISTEN TO WHAT I HAVE TO SAY AND DECIDE FOR YOURSELF IF IT'S TRUE.
I COME BEARING GIFTS.
#$%&!
YOU SAID YOU *CHECKED HIM!*
I-I-I--
SHUT UP!

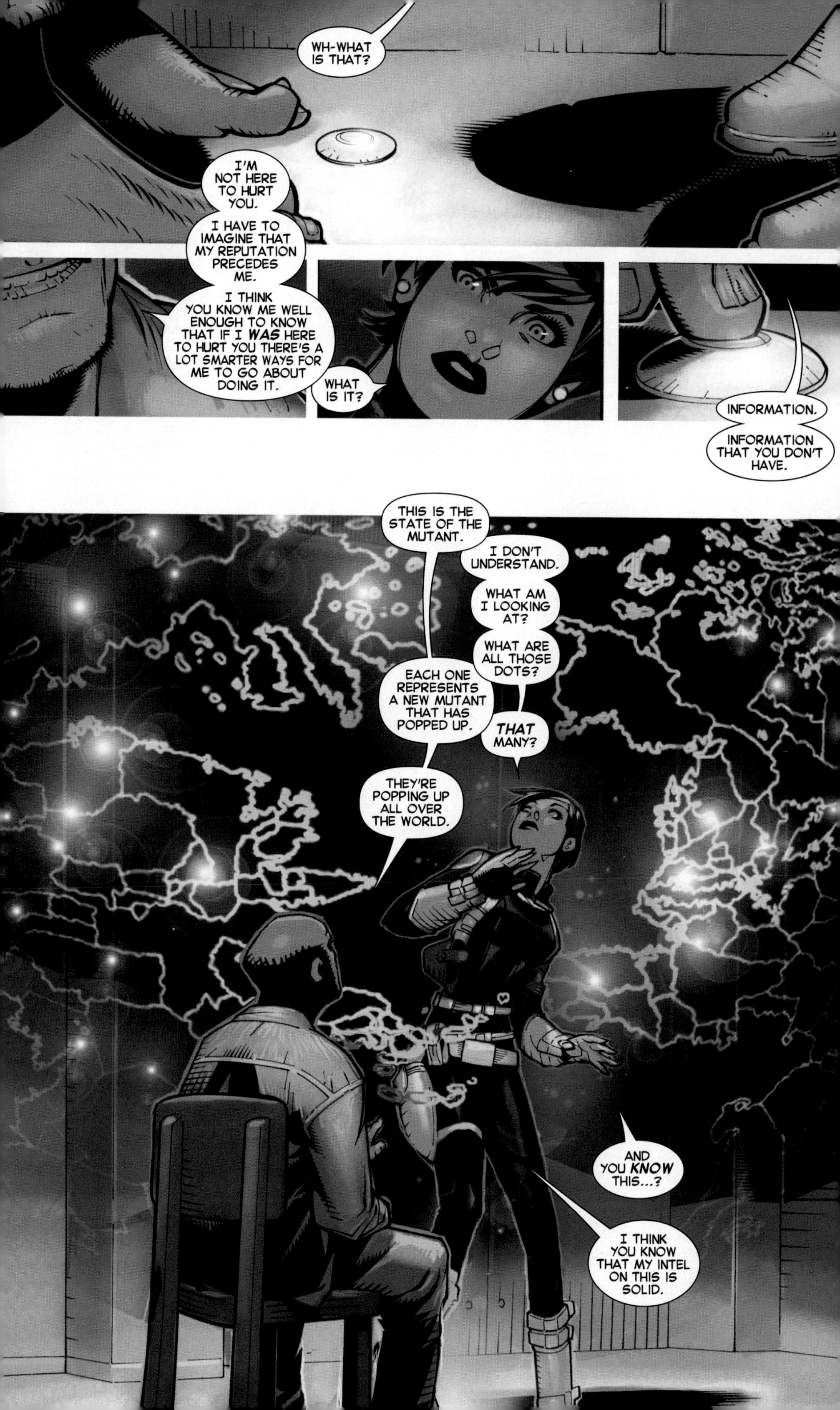
WH-WHAT IS THAT?
I'M NOT HERE TO HURT YOU.
I HAVE TO IMAGINE THAT MY REPUTATION PRECEDES ME.
I THINK YOU KNOW ME WELL ENOUGH TO KNOW THAT IF I WAS HERE TO HURT YOU THERE'S A LOT SMARTER WAYS FOR ME TO GO ABOUT DOING IT.
WHAT IS IT?
INFORMATION.
INFORMATION THAT YOU DON'T HAVE.
THIS IS THE STATE OF THE MUTANT.
I DON'T UNDERSTAND.
WHAT AM I LOOKING AT?
WHAT ARE ALL THOSE DOTS?
EACH ONE REPRESENTS A NEW MUTANT THAT HAS POPPED UP.
THAT MANY?
THEY'RE POPPING UP ALL OVER THE WORLD.
AND YOU KNOW THIS...?
I THINK YOU KNOW THAT MY INTEL ON THIS IS SOLID.

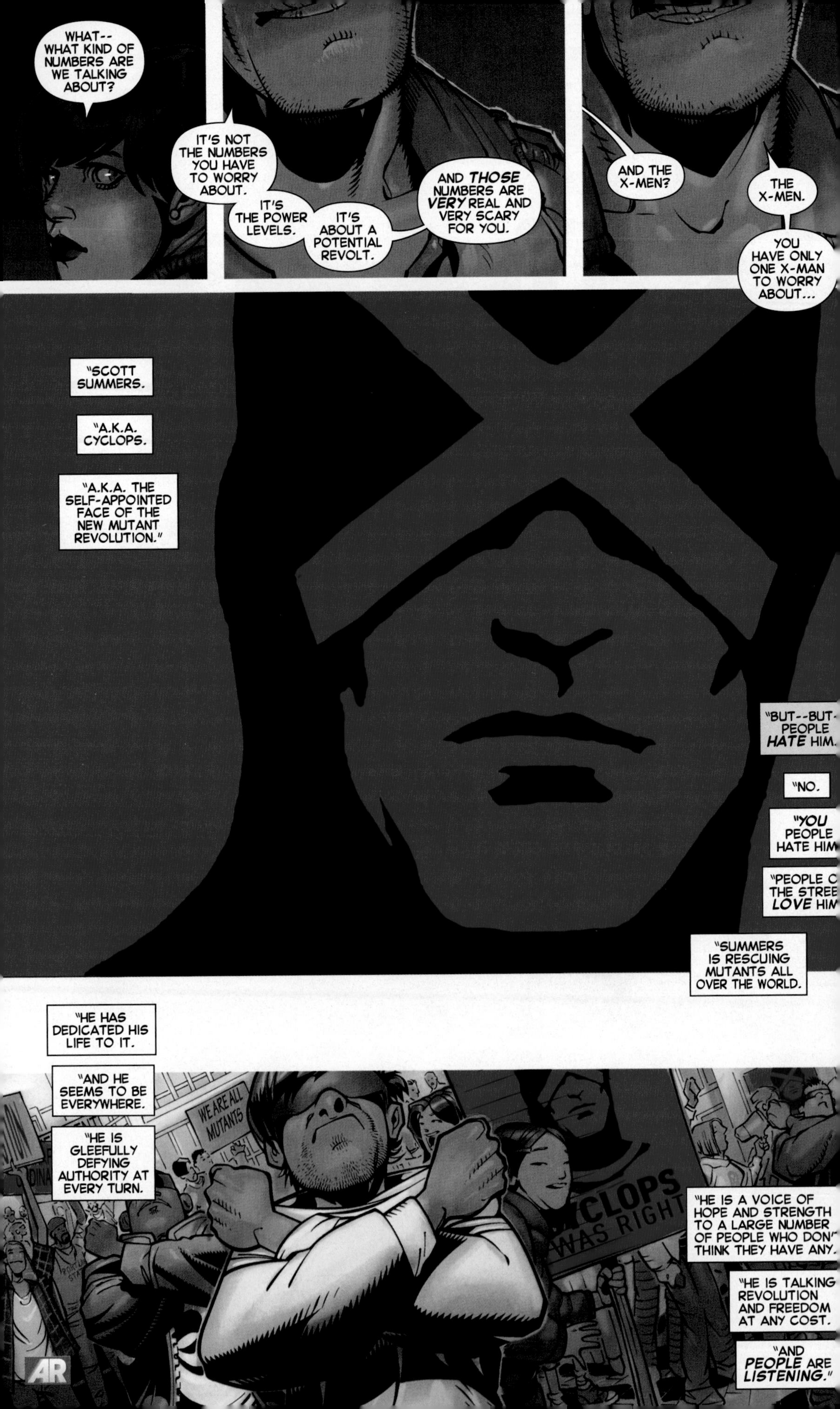

WHAT-- WHAT KIND OF NUMBERS ARE WE TALKING ABOUT?
IT'S NOT THE NUMBERS YOU HAVE TO WORRY ABOUT.
IT'S THE POWER LEVELS.
IT'S ABOUT A POTENTIAL REVOLT.
AND THOSE NUMBERS ARE VERY REAL AND VERY SCARY FOR YOU.
AND THE X-MEN?
THE X-MEN.
YOU HAVE ONLY ONE X-MAN TO WORRY ABOUT...
"SCOTT SUMMERS.
"A.K.A. CYCLOPS.
"A.K.A. THE SELF-APPOINTED FACE OF THE NEW MUTANT REVOLUTION."
"BUT--BUT- PEOPLE HATE HIM.
"NO.
"YOU PEOPLE HATE HIM
"PEOPLE O THE STREE LOVE HIM
"SUMMERS IS RESCUING MUTANTS ALL OVER THE WORLD.
"HE HAS DEDICATED HIS LIFE TO IT.
"AND HE SEEMS TO BE EVERYWHERE.
"HE IS GLEEFULLY DEFYING AUTHORITY AT EVERY TURN.
WE ARE ALL MUTANTS
CYCLOPS WAS RIGHT
"HE IS A VOICE OF HOPE AND STRENGTH TO A LARGE NUMBER OF PEOPLE WHO DON' THINK THEY HAVE ANY.
"HE IS TALKING REVOLUTION AND FREEDOM AT ANY COST.
"AND PEOPLE ARE LISTENING."

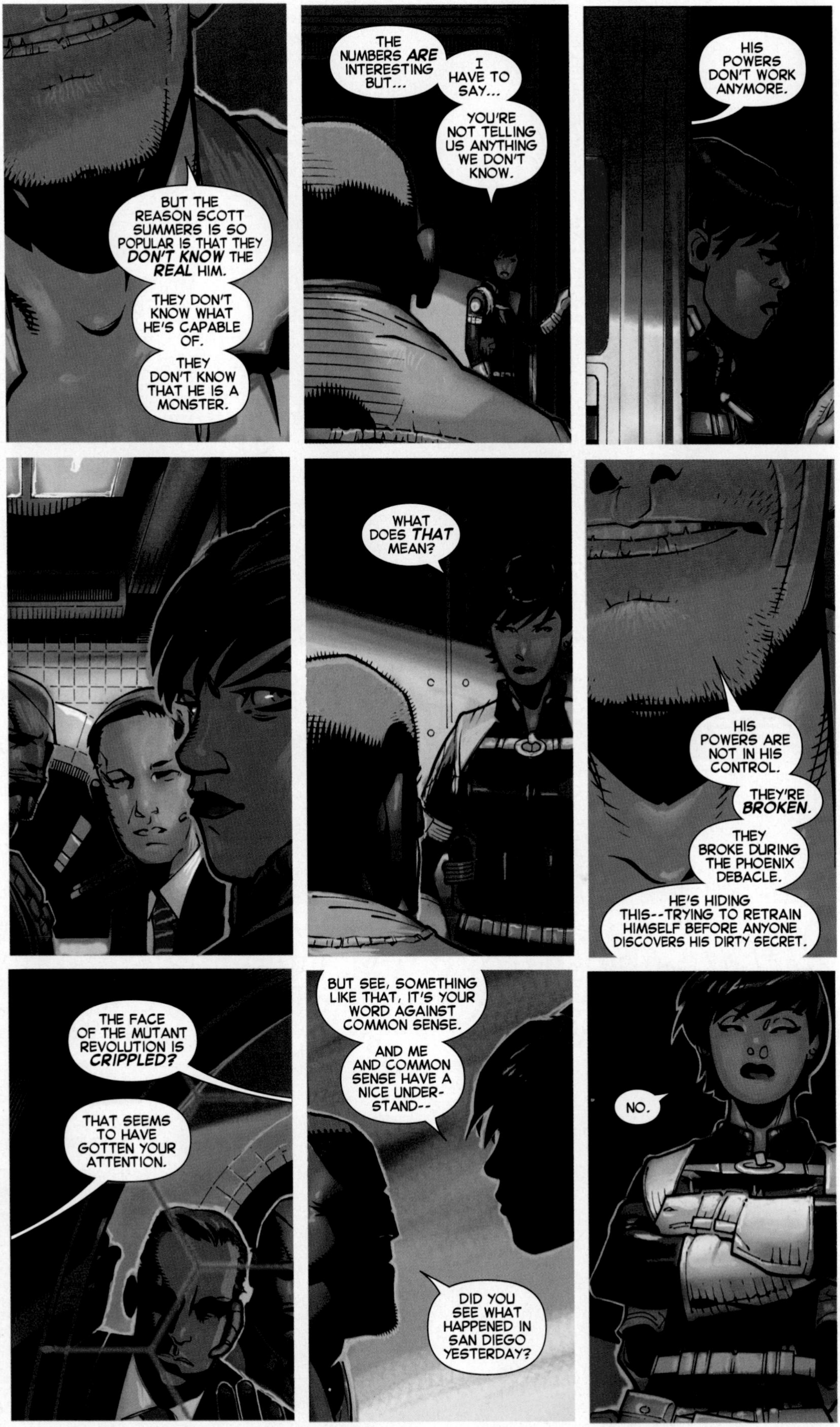
BUT THE REASON SCOTT SUMMERS IS SO POPULAR IS THAT THEY *DON'T KNOW* THE *REAL* HIM.
THEY DON'T KNOW WHAT HE'S CAPABLE OF.
THEY DON'T KNOW THAT HE IS A MONSTER.
THE NUMBERS *ARE* INTERESTING BUT...
I HAVE TO SAY...
YOU'RE NOT TELLING US ANYTHING WE DON'T KNOW.
HIS POWERS DON'T WORK ANYMORE.
WHAT DOES *THAT* MEAN?
HIS POWERS ARE NOT IN HIS CONTROL.
THEY'RE *BROKEN*.
THEY BROKE DURING THE PHOENIX DEBACLE.
HE'S HIDING THIS--TRYING TO RETRAIN HIMSELF BEFORE ANYONE DISCOVERS HIS DIRTY SECRET.
THE FACE OF THE MUTANT REVOLUTION IS *CRIPPLED?*
THAT SEEMS TO HAVE GOTTEN YOUR ATTENTION.
BUT SEE, SOMETHING LIKE THAT, IT'S YOUR WORD AGAINST COMMON SENSE.
AND ME AND COMMON SENSE HAVE A NICE UNDER-STAND--
DID YOU SEE WHAT HAPPENED IN SAN DIEGO YESTERDAY?
NO.

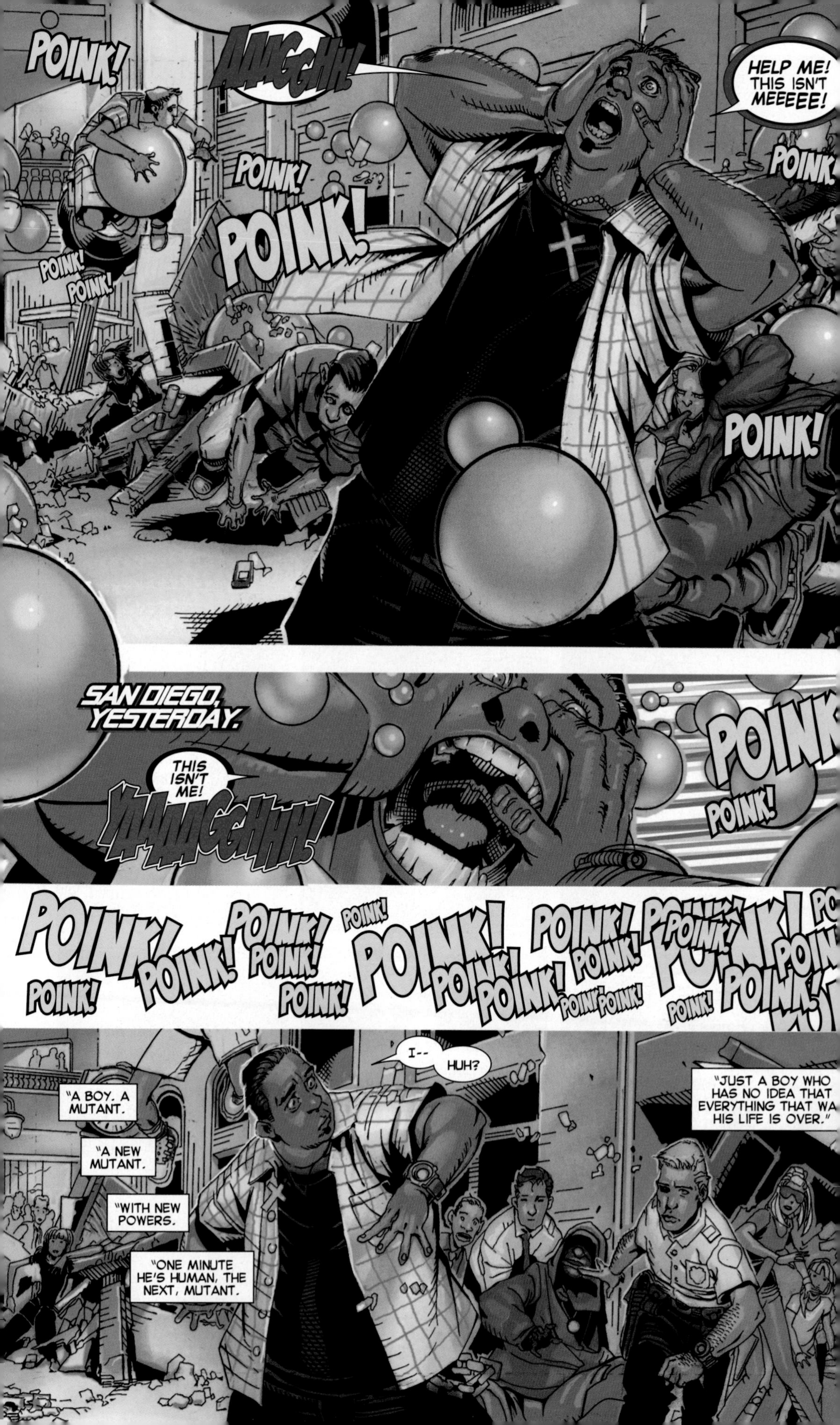
POINK!
AAAGGHH!
HELP ME! THIS ISN'T MEEEEE!
POINK!
POINK!
POINK!
POINK!
POINK!
POINK!
POINK!
SAN DIEGO, YESTERDAY.
THIS ISN'T ME!
YAAAGGHHH!
POINK
POINK!
POINK! POINK! POINK! POINK! POINK! POINK! POINK! POINK! POINK! POINK! POINK! POINK! POINK! POINK! POINK!
I--
HUH?
"A BOY. A MUTANT.
"A NEW MUTANT.
"WITH NEW POWERS.
"ONE MINUTE HE'S HUMAN, THE NEXT, MUTANT.
"JUST A BOY WHO HAS NO IDEA THAT EVERYTHING THAT WA
HIS LIFE IS OVER."

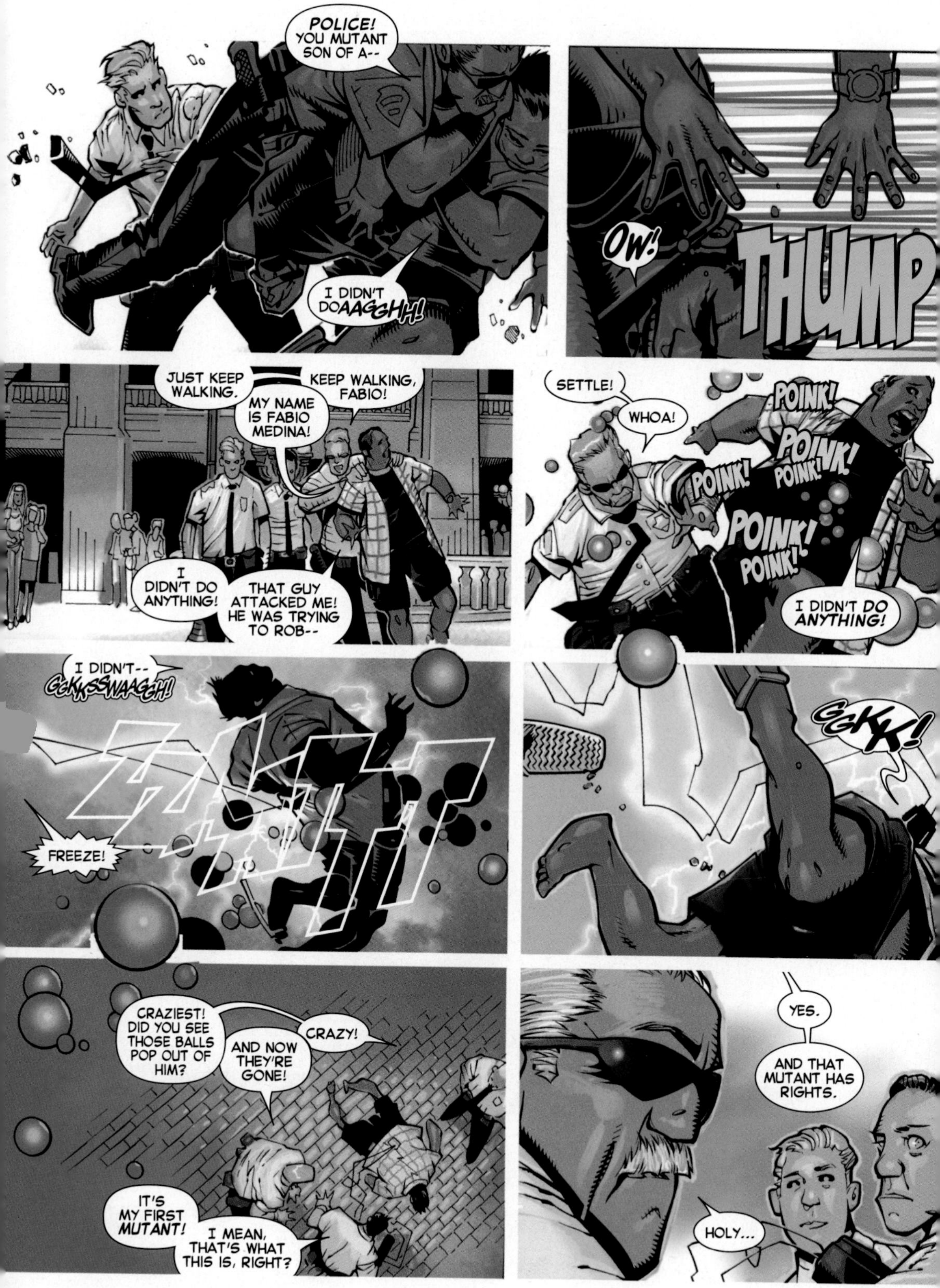
POLICE! YOU MUTANT SON OF A--
I DIDN'T DOAAGGHH!
OW!
THUMP
JUST KEEP WALKING.
KEEP WALKING, FABIO!
MY NAME IS FABIO MEDINA!
I DIDN'T DO ANYTHING!
THAT GUY ATTACKED ME! HE WAS TRYING TO ROB--
SETTLE!
WHOA!
POINK!
POINK!
POINK!
POINK!
POINK!
POINK!
I DIDN'T DO ANYTHING!
I DIDN'T-- GGKKSSWAAGGH!
FREEZE!
GGKK!
CRAZIEST! DID YOU SEE THOSE BALLS POP OUT OF HIM?
CRAZY!
AND NOW THEY'RE GONE!
IT'S MY FIRST MUTANT!
I MEAN, THAT'S WHAT THIS IS, RIGHT?
YES.
AND THAT MUTANT HAS RIGHTS.
HOLY...

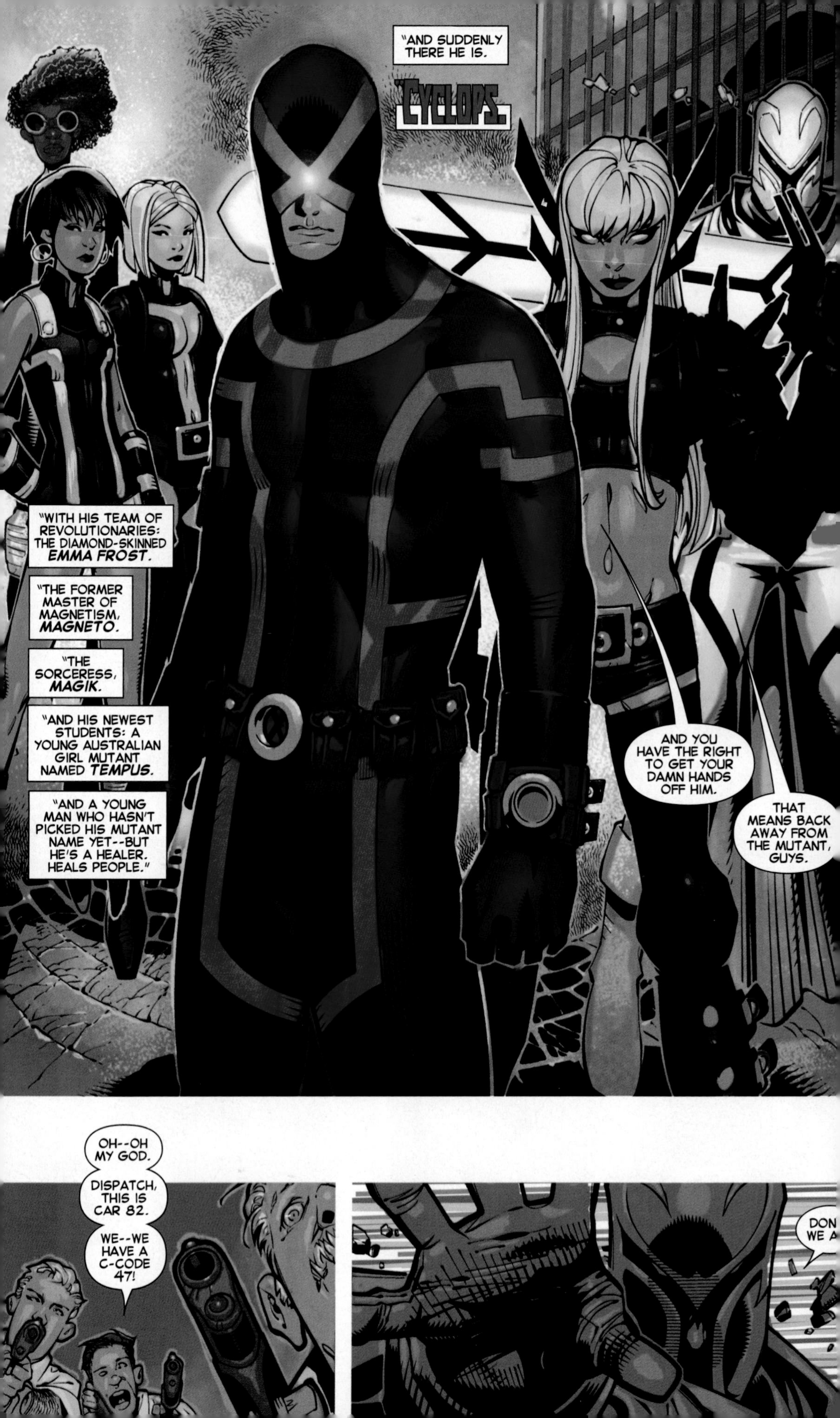
"AND SUDDENLY THERE HE IS.
"CYCLOPS.
"WITH HIS TEAM OF REVOLUTIONARIES: THE DIAMOND-SKINNED EMMA FROST.
"THE FORMER MASTER OF MAGNETISM, MAGNETO.
"THE SORCERESS, MAGIK.
"AND HIS NEWEST STUDENTS: A YOUNG AUSTRALIAN GIRL MUTANT NAMED TEMPUS.
"AND A YOUNG MAN WHO HASN'T PICKED HIS MUTANT NAME YET--BUT HE'S A HEALER. HEALS PEOPLE."
AND YOU HAVE THE RIGHT TO GET YOUR DAMN HANDS OFF HIM.
THAT MEANS BACK AWAY FROM THE MUTANT, GUYS.
OH--OH MY GOD.
DISPATCH, THIS IS CAR 82.
WE--WE HAVE A C-CODE 47!

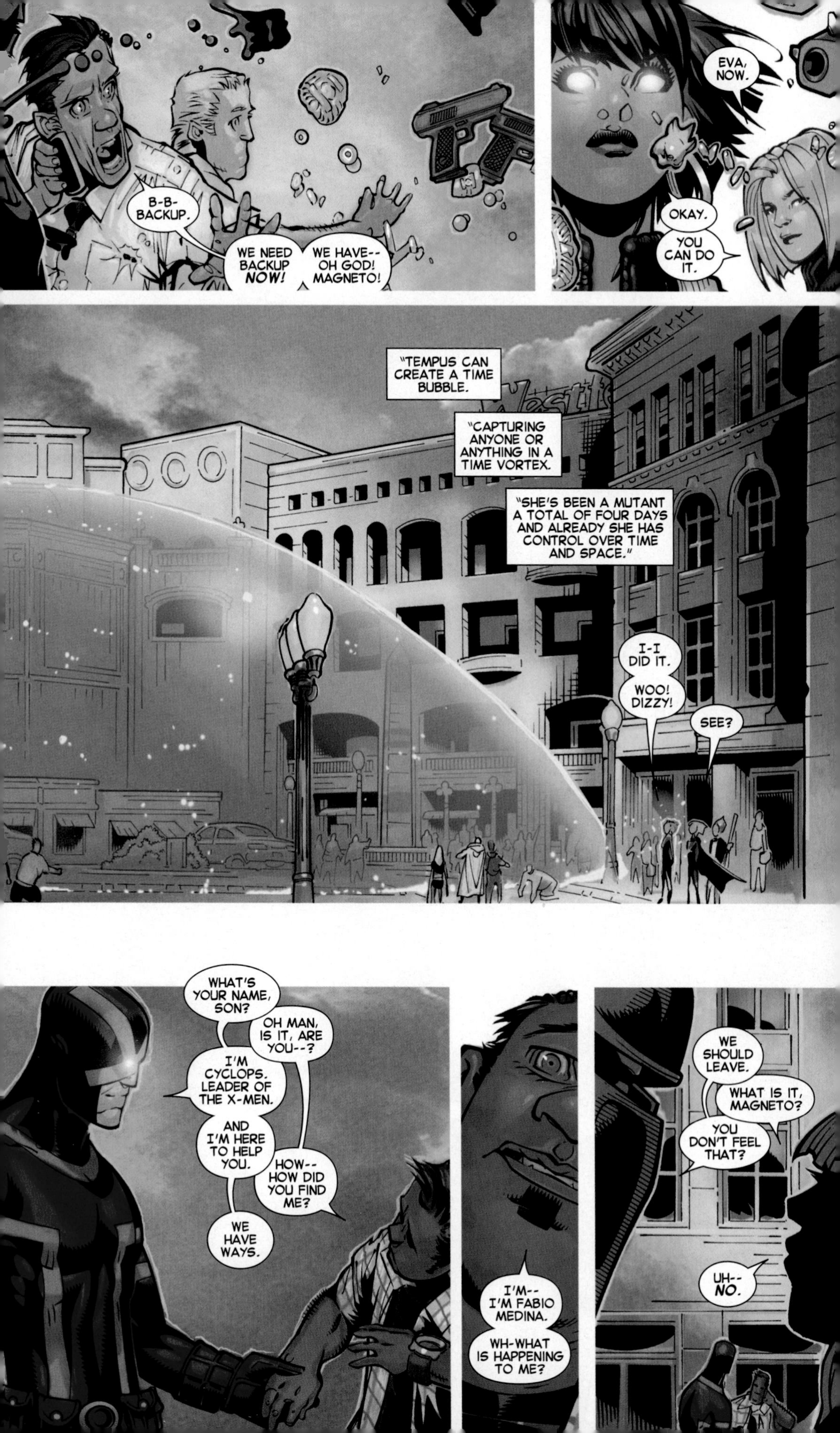
B-B-BACKUP.
WE NEED BACKUP NOW!
WE HAVE-- OH GOD! MAGNETO!
EVA, NOW.
OKAY.
YOU CAN DO IT.
"TEMPUS CAN CREATE A TIME BUBBLE.
"CAPTURING ANYONE OR ANYTHING IN A TIME VORTEX.
"SHE'S BEEN A MUTANT A TOTAL OF FOUR DAYS AND ALREADY SHE HAS CONTROL OVER TIME AND SPACE."
I-I DID IT.
WOO! DIZZY!
SEE?
WHAT'S YOUR NAME, SON?
OH MAN, IS IT, ARE YOU--?
I'M CYCLOPS. LEADER OF THE X-MEN.
AND I'M HERE TO HELP YOU.
HOW-- HOW DID YOU FIND ME?
WE HAVE WAYS.
I'M-- I'M FABIO MEDINA.
WH-WHAT IS HAPPENING TO ME?
WE SHOULD LEAVE.
WHAT IS IT, MAGNETO?
YOU DON'T FEEL THAT?
UH-- NO.

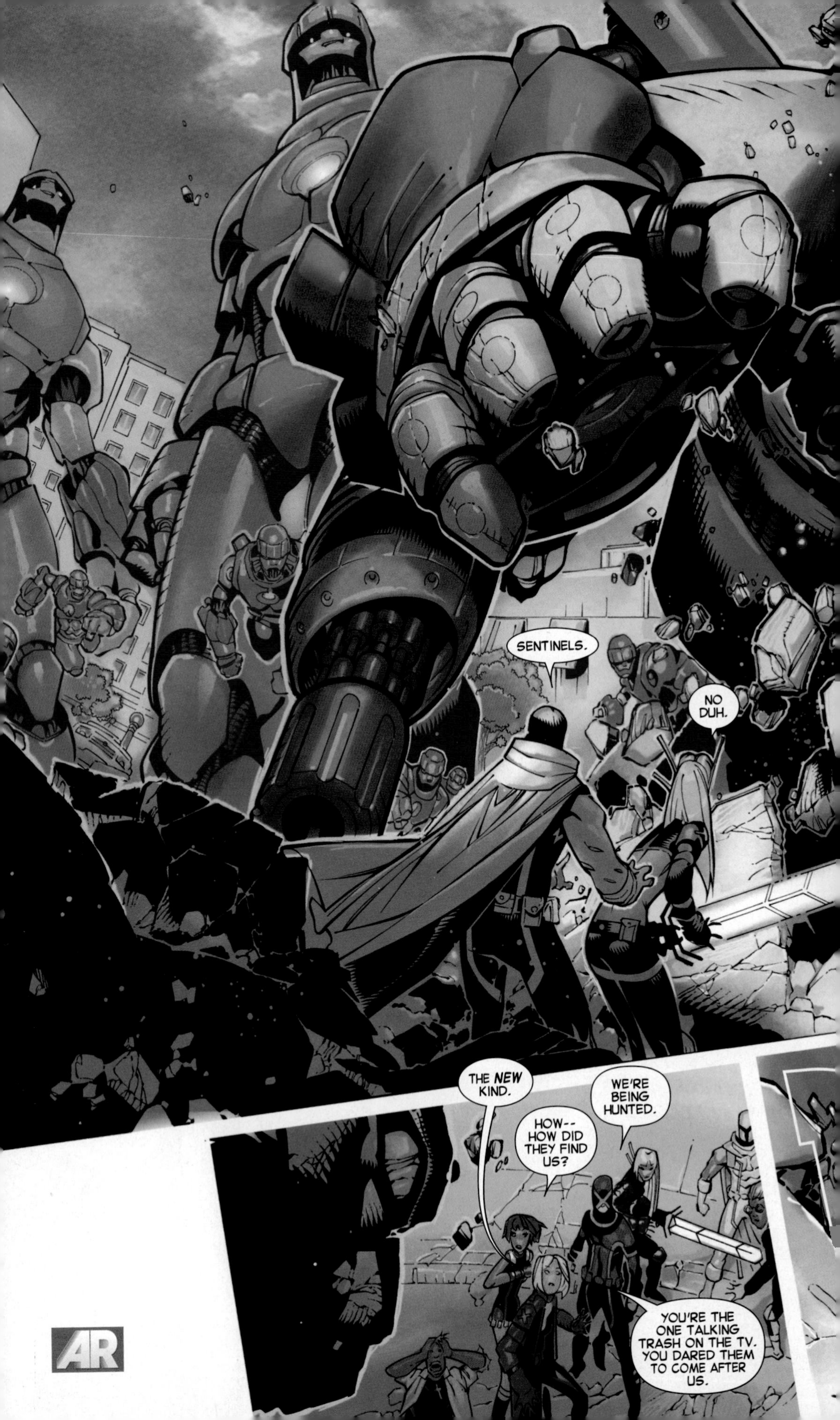
SENTINELS.
NO DUH.
THE *NEW* KIND.
WE'RE BEING HUNTED.
HOW-- HOW DID THEY FIND US?
YOU'RE THE ONE TALKING TRASH ON THE TV. YOU DARED THEM TO COME AFTER US.

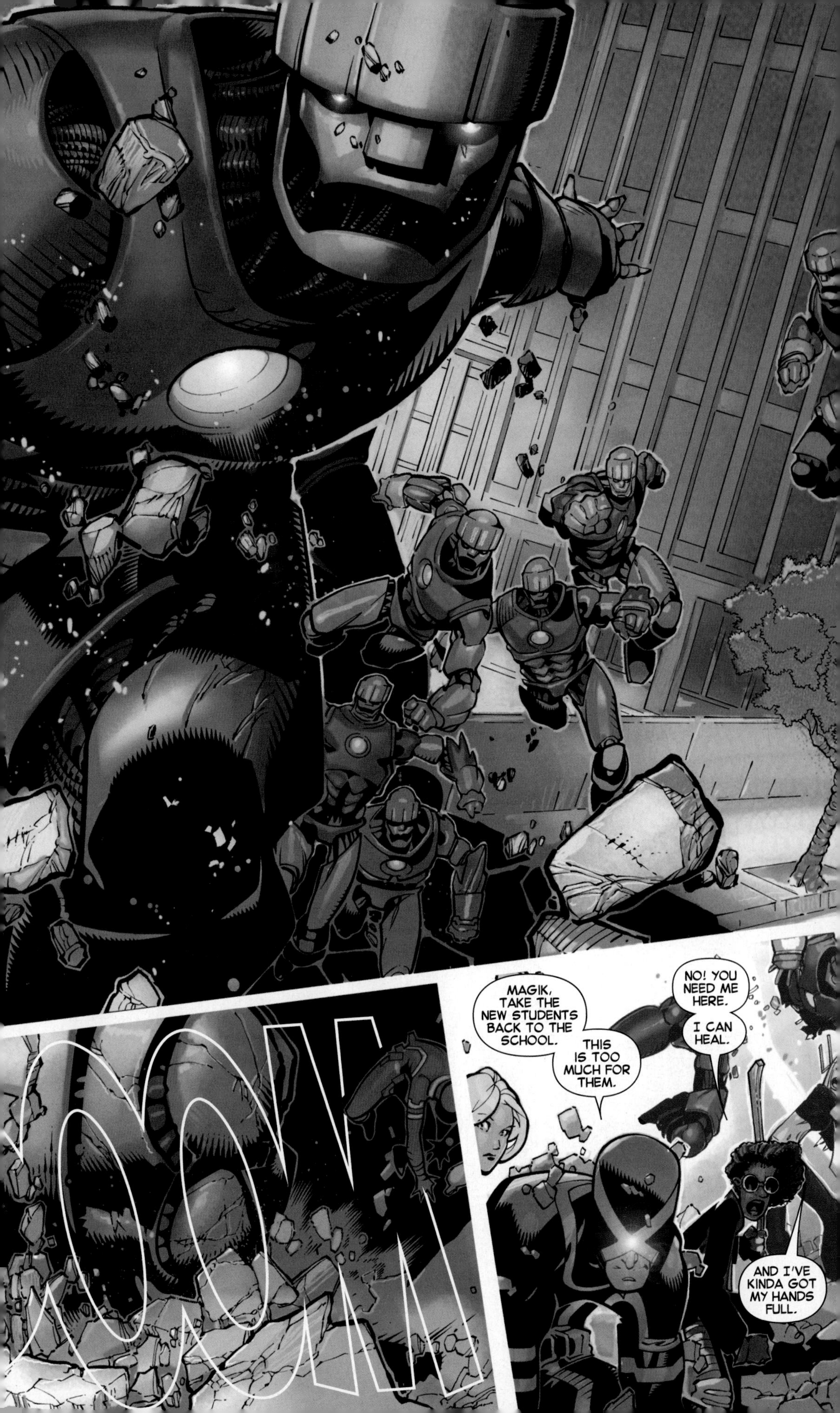

MAGIK, TAKE THE NEW STUDENTS BACK TO THE SCHOOL.
THIS IS TOO MUCH FOR THEM.
NO! YOU NEED ME HERE.
I CAN HEAL.
AND I'VE KINDA GOT MY HANDS FULL.

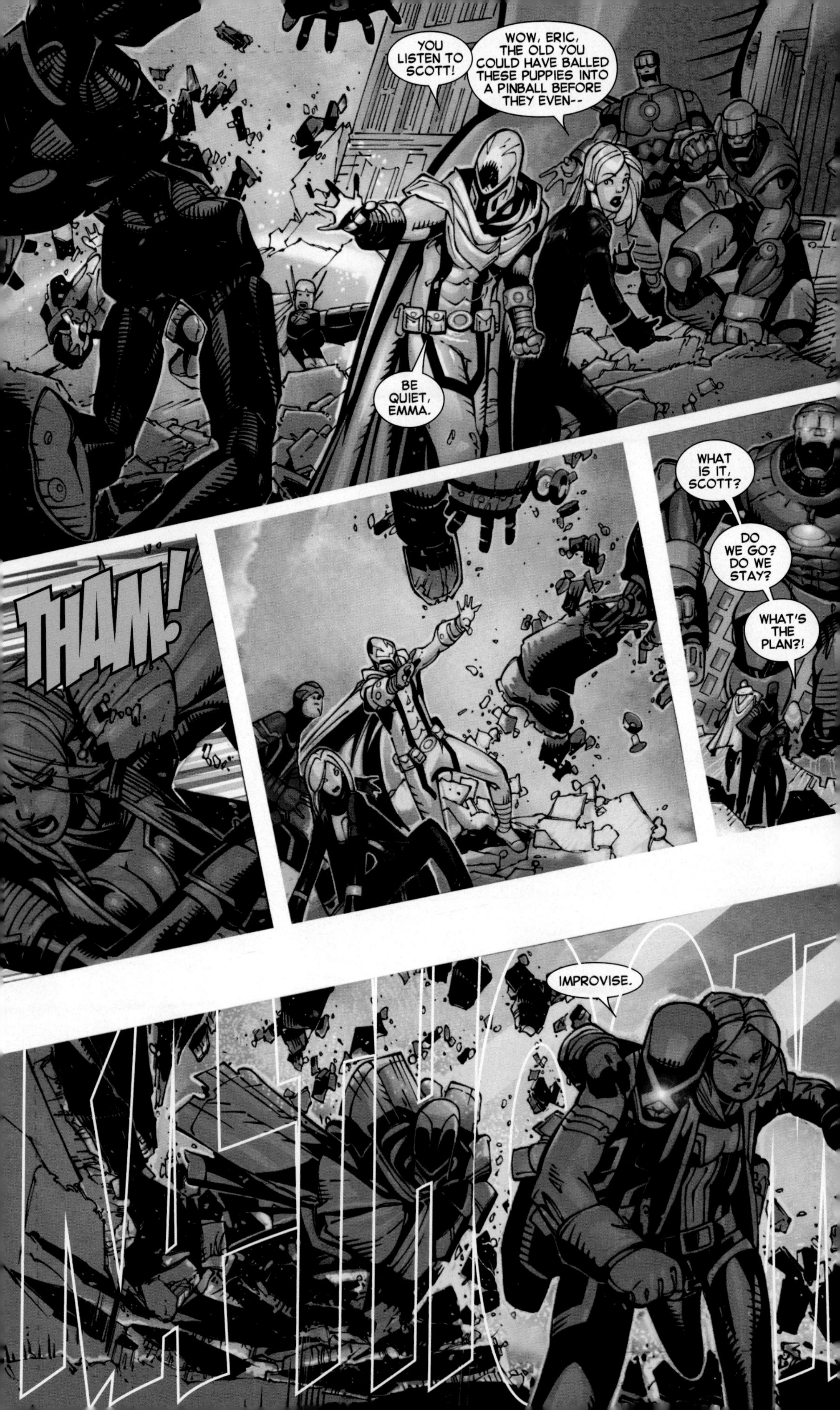
YOU LISTEN TO SCOTT!
WOW, ERIC, THE OLD YOU COULD HAVE BALLED THESE PUPPIES INTO A PINBALL BEFORE THEY EVEN--
BE QUIET, EMMA.
THAM!
WHAT IS IT, SCOTT?
DO WE GO? DO WE STAY?
WHAT'S THE PLAN?!
IMPROVISE.

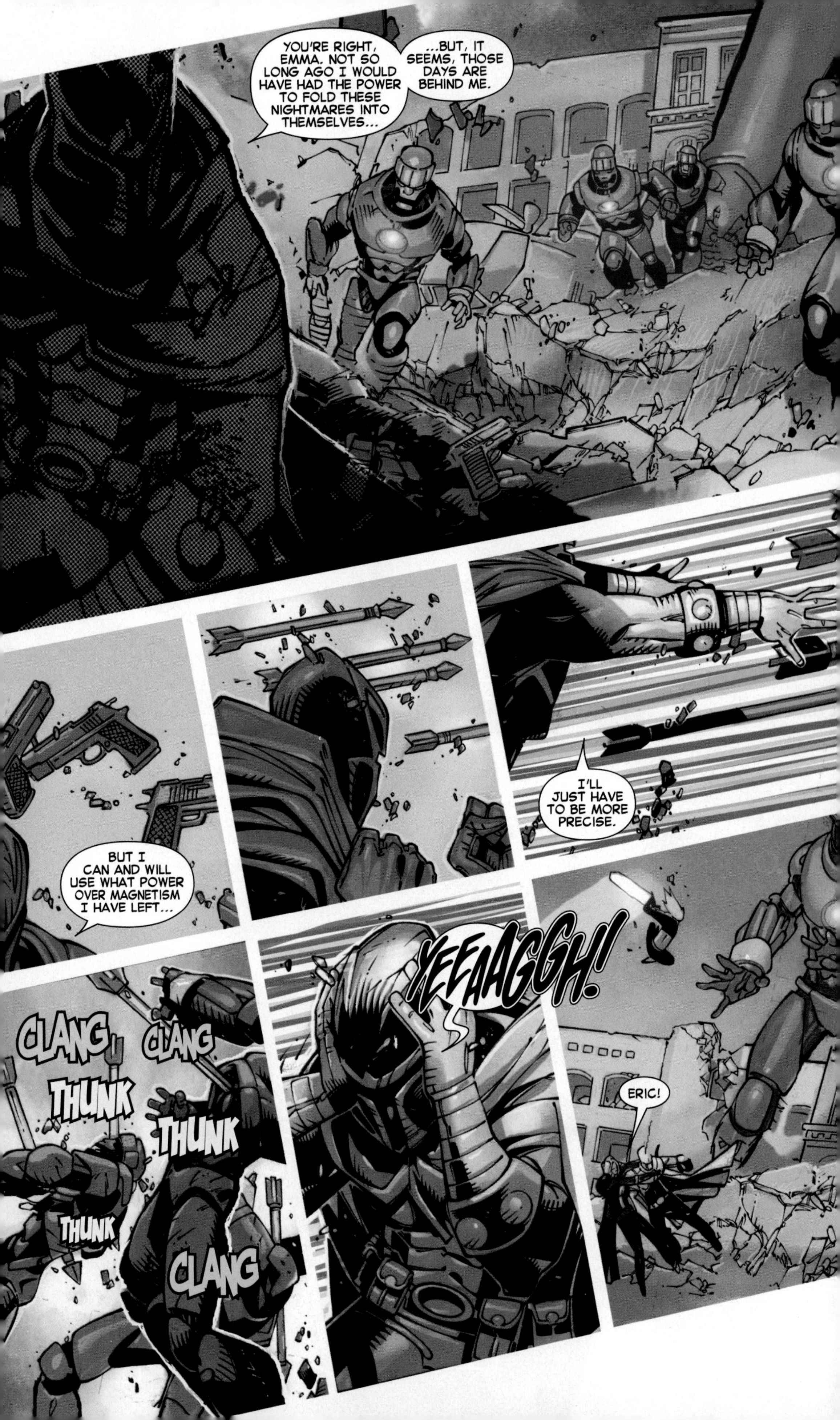
YOU'RE RIGHT, EMMA. NOT SO LONG AGO I WOULD HAVE HAD THE POWER TO FOLD THESE NIGHTMARES INTO THEMSELVES...
...BUT, IT SEEMS, THOSE DAYS ARE BEHIND ME.
BUT I CAN AND WILL USE WHAT POWER OVER MAGNETISM I HAVE LEFT...
I'LL JUST HAVE TO BE MORE PRECISE.
CLANG
CLANG
THUNK
THUNK
THUNK
CLANG
YEEAAGGH!
ERIC!

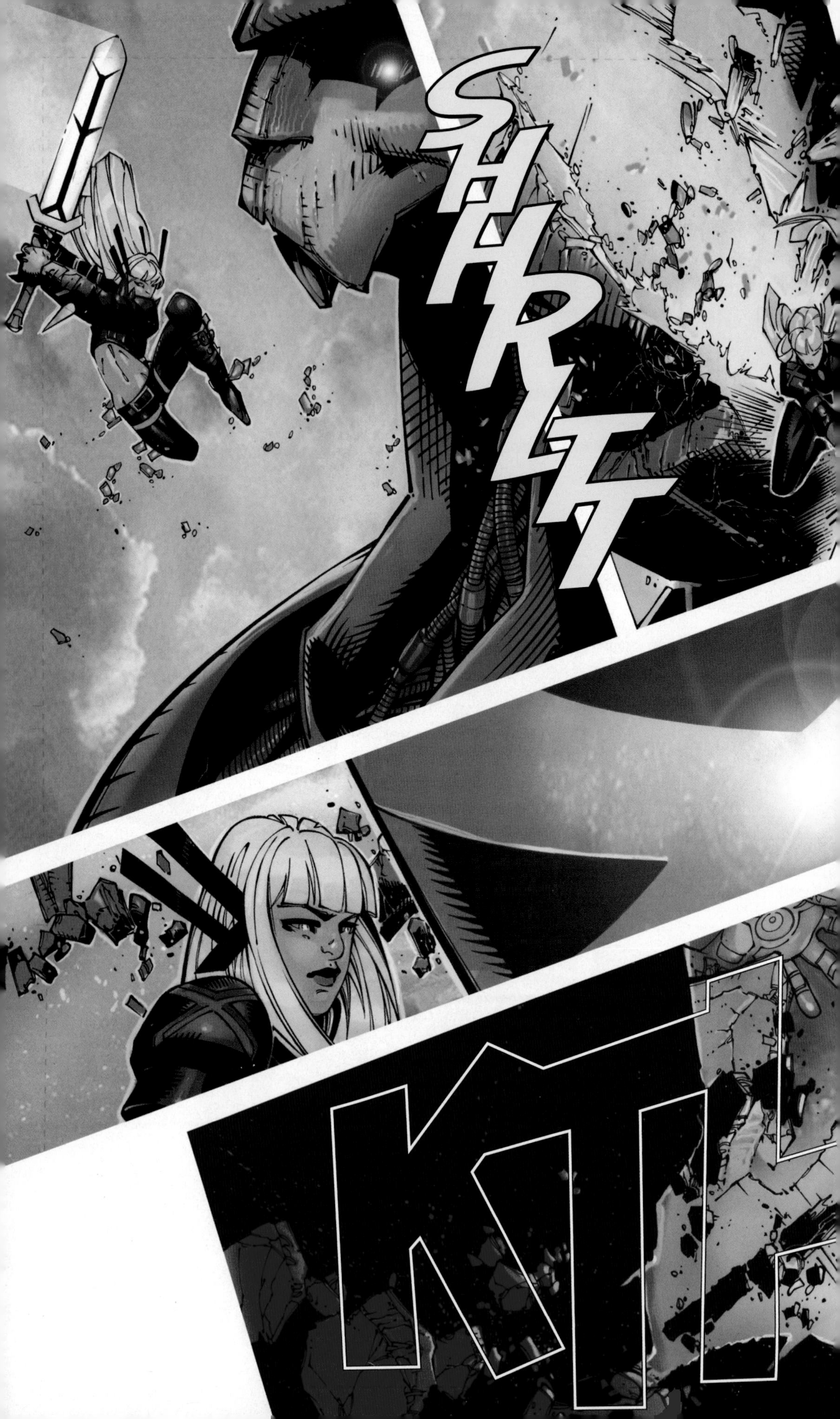
SHRLTT
KT

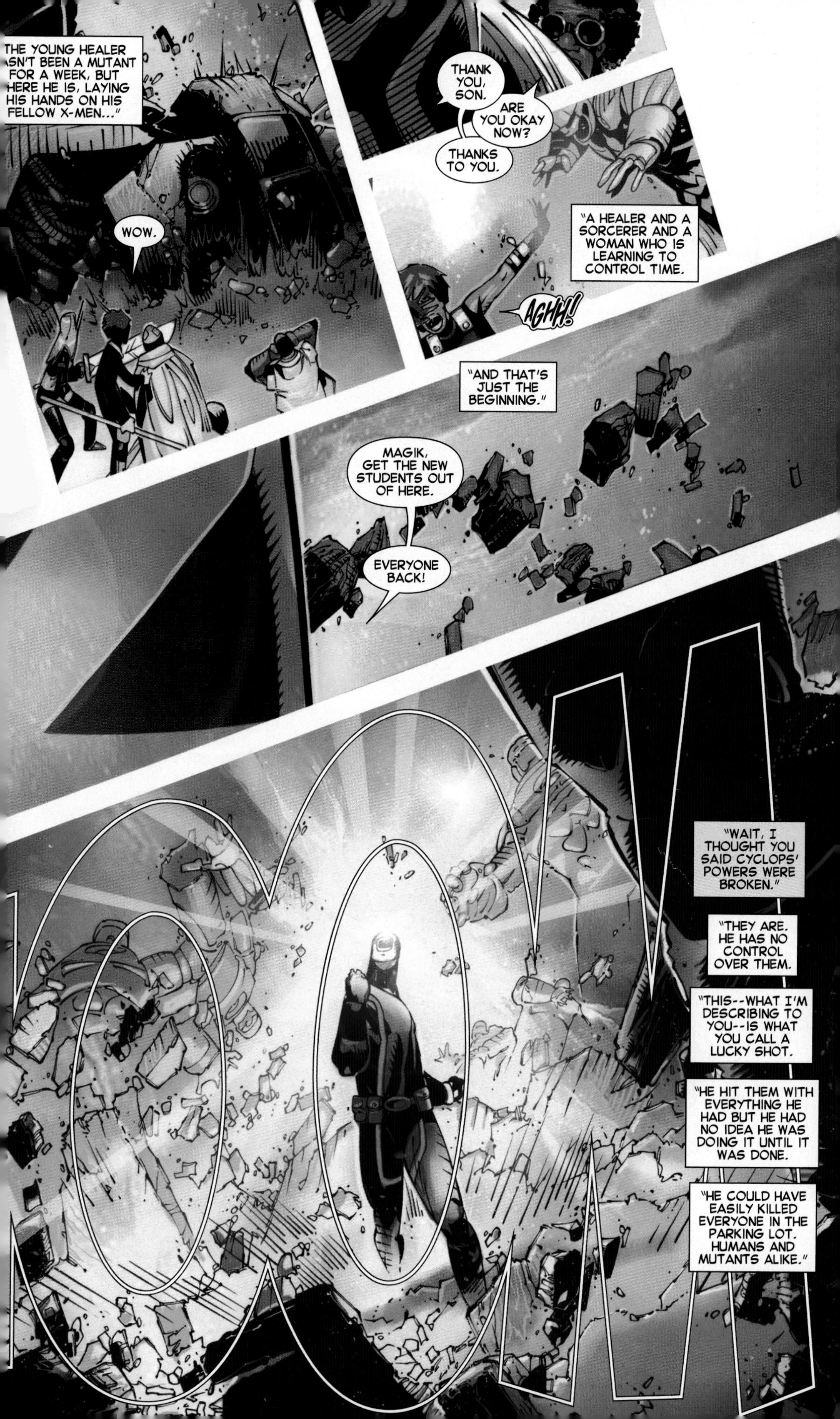
"THE YOUNG HEALER HASN'T BEEN A MUTANT FOR A WEEK, BUT HERE HE IS, LAYING HIS HANDS ON HIS FELLOW X-MEN..."
WOW.
THANK YOU, SON.
ARE YOU OKAY NOW?
THANKS TO YOU.
"A HEALER AND A SORCERER AND A WOMAN WHO IS LEARNING TO CONTROL TIME.
AGHH!
"AND THAT'S JUST THE BEGINNING."
MAGIK, GET THE NEW STUDENTS OUT OF HERE.
EVERYONE BACK!
"WAIT, I THOUGHT YOU SAID CYCLOPS' POWERS WERE BROKEN."
"THEY ARE. HE HAS NO CONTROL OVER THEM.
"THIS--WHAT I'M DESCRIBING TO YOU--IS WHAT YOU CALL A LUCKY SHOT.
"HE HIT THEM WITH EVERYTHING HE HAD BUT HE HAD NO IDEA HE WAS DOING IT UNTIL IT WAS DONE.
"HE COULD HAVE EASILY KILLED EVERYONE IN THE PARKING LOT. HUMANS AND MUTANTS ALIKE."

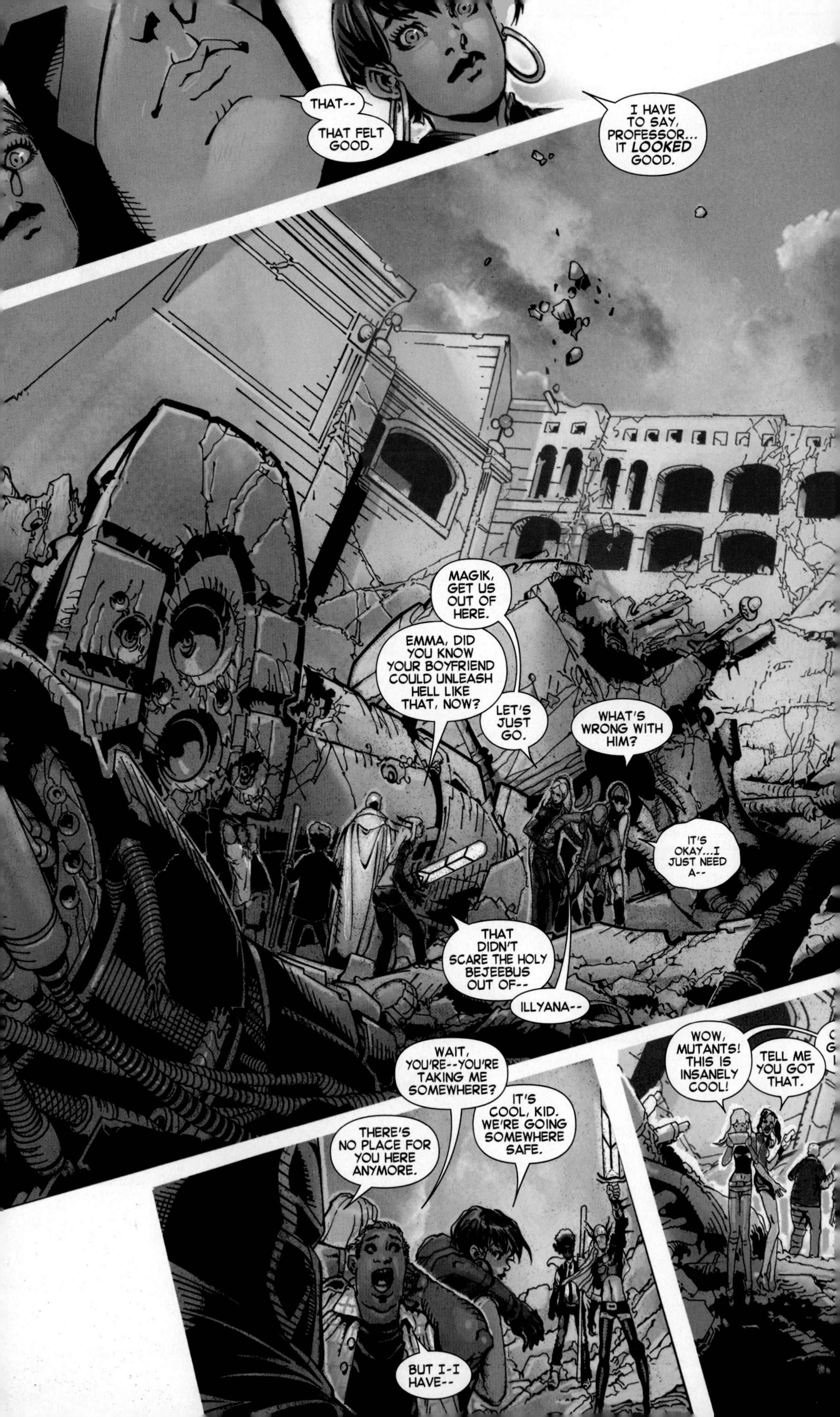
THAT--
THAT FELT GOOD.
I HAVE TO SAY, PROFESSOR... IT *LOOKED* GOOD.
MAGIK, GET US OUT OF HERE.
EMMA, DID YOU KNOW YOUR BOYFRIEND COULD UNLEASH HELL LIKE THAT, NOW?
LET'S JUST GO.
WHAT'S WRONG WITH HIM?
IT'S OKAY...I JUST NEED A--
THAT DIDN'T SCARE THE HOLY BEJEEBUS OUT OF--
ILLYANA--
WAIT, YOU'RE--YOU'RE TAKING ME SOMEWHERE?
IT'S COOL, KID. WE'RE GOING SOMEWHERE SAFE.
THERE'S NO PLACE FOR YOU HERE ANYMORE.
BUT I-I HAVE--
WOW, MUTANTS! THIS IS INSANELY COOL!
TELL ME YOU GOT THAT.

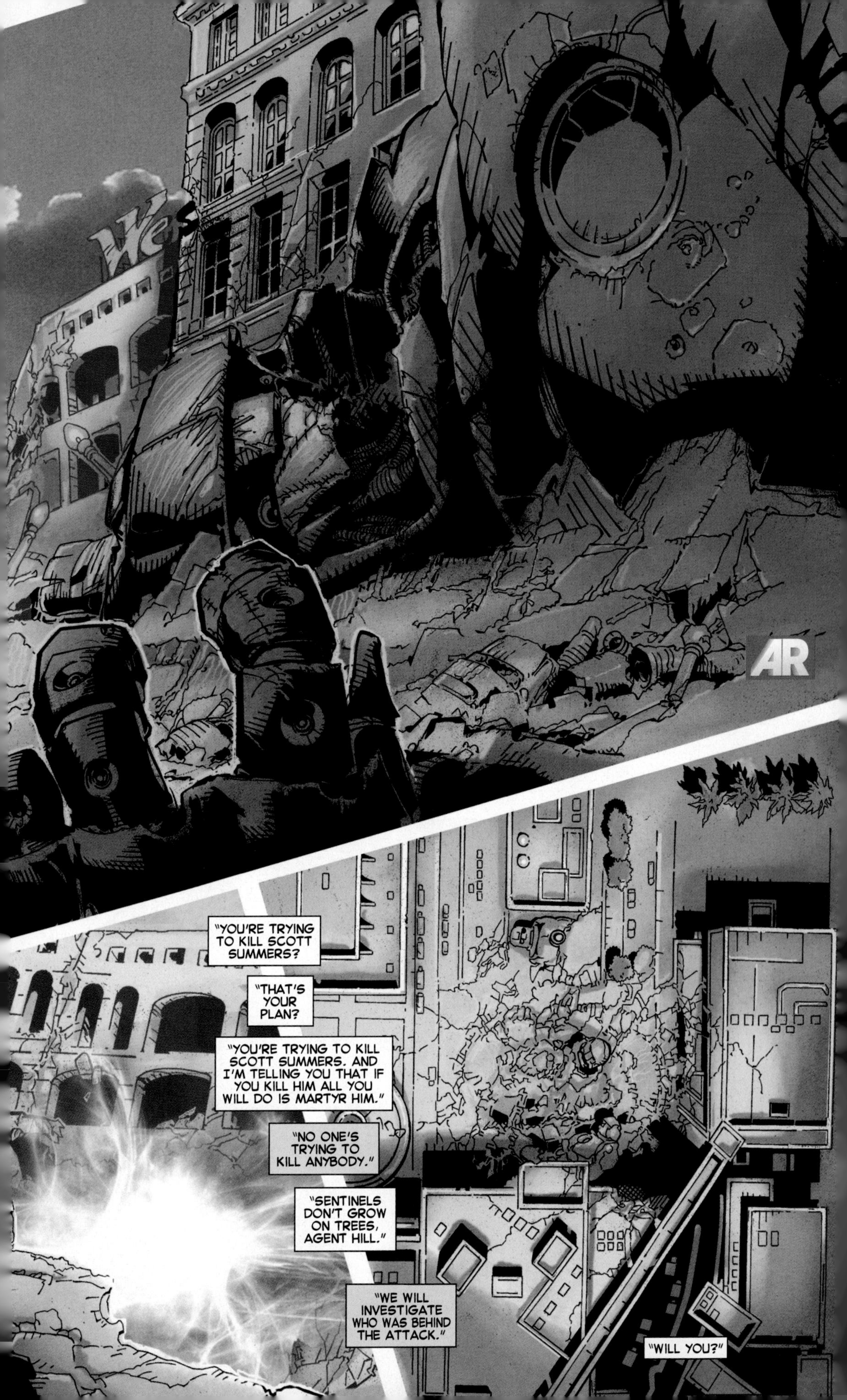

"YOU'RE TRYING TO KILL SCOTT SUMMERS?
"THAT'S YOUR PLAN?
"YOU'RE TRYING TO KILL SCOTT SUMMERS. AND I'M TELLING YOU THAT IF YOU KILL HIM ALL YOU WILL DO IS MARTYR HIM."
"NO ONE'S TRYING TO KILL ANYBODY."
"SENTINELS DON'T GROW ON TREES, AGENT HILL."
"WE WILL INVESTIGATE WHO WAS BEHIND THE ATTACK."
"WILL YOU?"

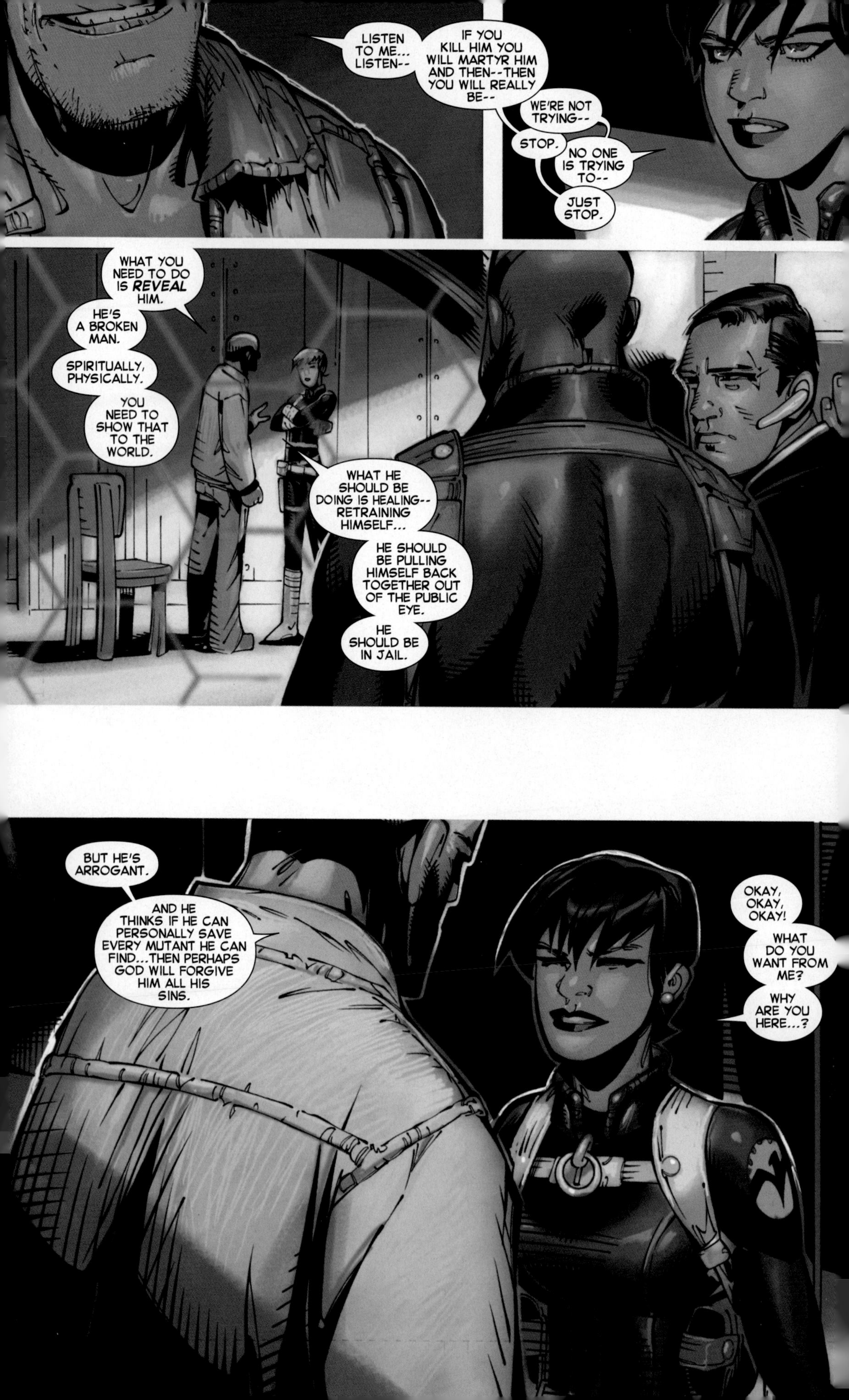

LISTEN TO ME... LISTEN--
IF YOU KILL HIM YOU WILL MARTYR HIM AND THEN--THEN YOU WILL REALLY BE--
WE'RE NOT TRYING--
STOP.
NO ONE IS TRYING TO--
JUST STOP.
WHAT YOU NEED TO DO IS REVEAL HIM.
HE'S A BROKEN MAN.
SPIRITUALLY, PHYSICALLY.
YOU NEED TO SHOW THAT TO THE WORLD.
WHAT HE SHOULD BE DOING IS HEALING--RETRAINING HIMSELF...
HE SHOULD BE PULLING HIMSELF BACK TOGETHER OUT OF THE PUBLIC EYE.
HE SHOULD BE IN JAIL.
BUT HE'S ARROGANT.
AND HE THINKS IF HE CAN PERSONALLY SAVE EVERY MUTANT HE CAN FIND...THEN PERHAPS GOD WILL FORGIVE HIM ALL HIS SINS.
OKAY, OKAY, OKAY!
WHAT DO YOU WANT FROM ME?
WHY ARE YOU HERE...?

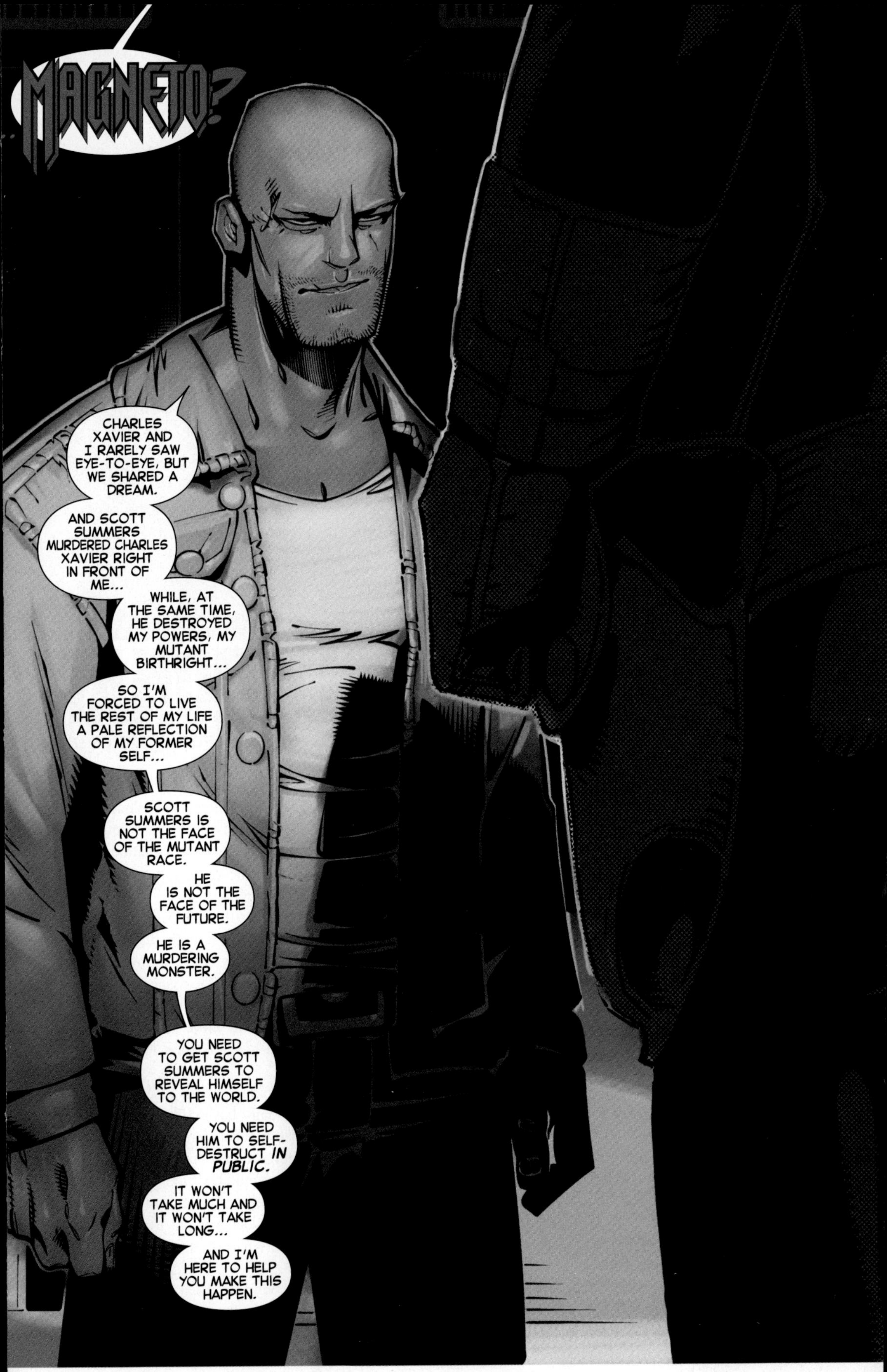
MAGNETO?
CHARLES XAVIER AND I RARELY SAW EYE-TO-EYE, BUT WE SHARED A DREAM.
AND SCOTT SUMMERS MURDERED CHARLES XAVIER RIGHT IN FRONT OF ME...
WHILE, AT THE SAME TIME, HE DESTROYED MY POWERS, MY MUTANT BIRTHRIGHT...
SO I'M FORCED TO LIVE THE REST OF MY LIFE A PALE REFLECTION OF MY FORMER SELF...
SCOTT SUMMERS IS NOT THE FACE OF THE MUTANT RACE.
HE IS NOT THE FACE OF THE FUTURE.
HE IS A MURDERING MONSTER.
YOU NEED TO GET SCOTT SUMMERS TO REVEAL HIMSELF TO THE WORLD.
YOU NEED HIM TO SELF-DESTRUCT IN PUBLIC.
IT WON'T TAKE MUCH AND IT WON'T TAKE LONG...
AND I'M HERE TO HELP YOU MAKE THIS HAPPEN.

Photo: C. Bachalo, A

TERRORIST X REVOLUTIONARY

HOW CYCLOPS' MUTANT "REVOLUTION" IS EVOLVING THE WORLD...FOR GOOD OR FOR ILL

By: FRANK ALLEN   *February 13, 2013*

Those who fear mutants have had plenty to be scared of in recent months. The mutant species, thought near extinction not long ago, has undergone a very high-profile and dangerous resurgence. There are those who would call anyone afraid of *homo sapiens superior* racists, bigots or hate-mongers. That may remain for history to judge, but when one examines the recent actions of mutantkind, actions mostly taken by or under the direction of mutant leader Scott Summers (who also goes by the "mutant name" Cyclops), it's hard not to fear for humanity.

It was not long ago that the "mutant problem" seemed managed. With the worldwide population counting at under 200 by some estimates, the mutants seemed content to segregate themselves to the artificial island of Utopia off the shore of San Francisco. The fact that they had illegally declared their home an autonomous nation-state was a small price to pay for having essentially the entire race contained in one place. It was there that Cyclops cemented himself as the de facto ruler of the mutants. Even known mutant terrorist Magneto (whose crimes are so numerous and well-documented elsewhere as to not bear listing here) fell into lock-step behind him. The defection of the group who founded the mutant-friendly Jean Grey School in New York aside, Cyclops spoke with authority as the voice of his people.

Then came the Phoenix. Outside of the offices of Theoretical Celestial Metaphysics professors, very little is known about this strange, alien force. What we do know is that Cyclops and a handful of his fellow mutants wielded this force and that, through some violation of the natural laws of the universe, the mutant species was restarted.

We also know that in the aftermath of that debacle, Cyclops was put in prison. Exactly what he was charged with has been classified by the government, giving those on the pro-mutant side of the issue the opportunity to claim that the US had no justification for holding him. The point soon became moot as the aforementioned Magneto led a team to break their leader out of prison.

Now, with new mutants being discovered around the world on a nearly daily basis, Cyclops has slipped back into his role as leader, the difference being that he's taken his operation underground. Popping up around the world wherever these new mutants emerge, Cyclops appears, fights against local authorities and/or other super heroes, makes his little public declarations to the news crews and poof! Disappears to whatever spider-hole he calls home.

If these tactics sound familiar, they should—they're the same that have been used by terrorists and other guerilla forces for hundreds of years. Of course, those organizations didn't have T-Shirts. They didn't have Facebook "likes" and Twitter followers and rubber wristlets. They didn't snare the minds of the youth like mutantkind has...and that makes *(cont. on pg. 32)*

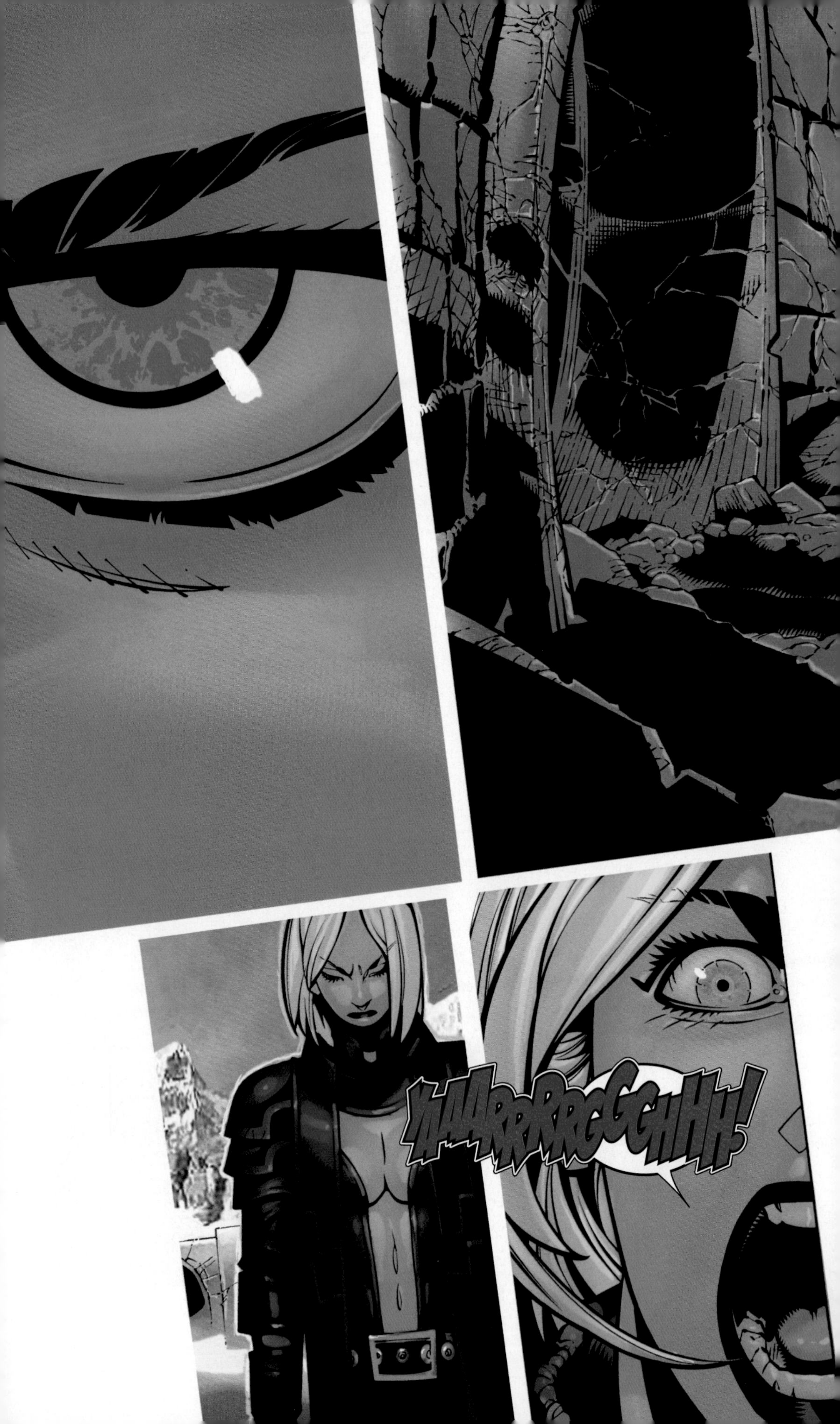
YAARRRRRGGGHHH!

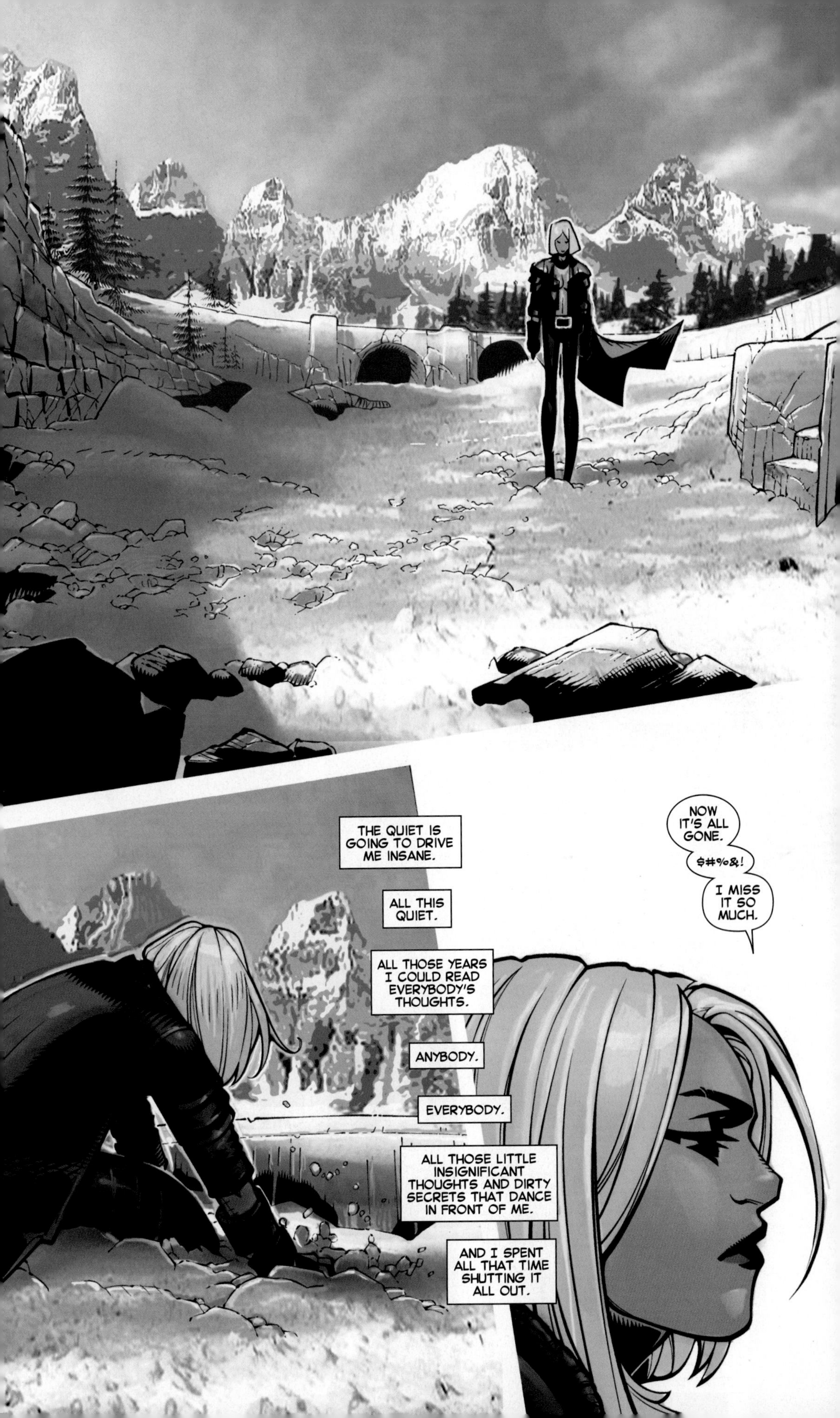
THE QUIET IS GOING TO DRIVE ME INSANE.
ALL THIS QUIET.
ALL THOSE YEARS I COULD READ EVERYBODY'S THOUGHTS.
ANYBODY.
EVERYBODY.
ALL THOSE LITTLE INSIGNIFICANT THOUGHTS AND DIRTY SECRETS THAT DANCE IN FRONT OF ME.
AND I SPENT ALL THAT TIME SHUTTING IT ALL OUT.
NOW IT'S ALL GONE.
$#%&!
I MISS IT SO MUCH.

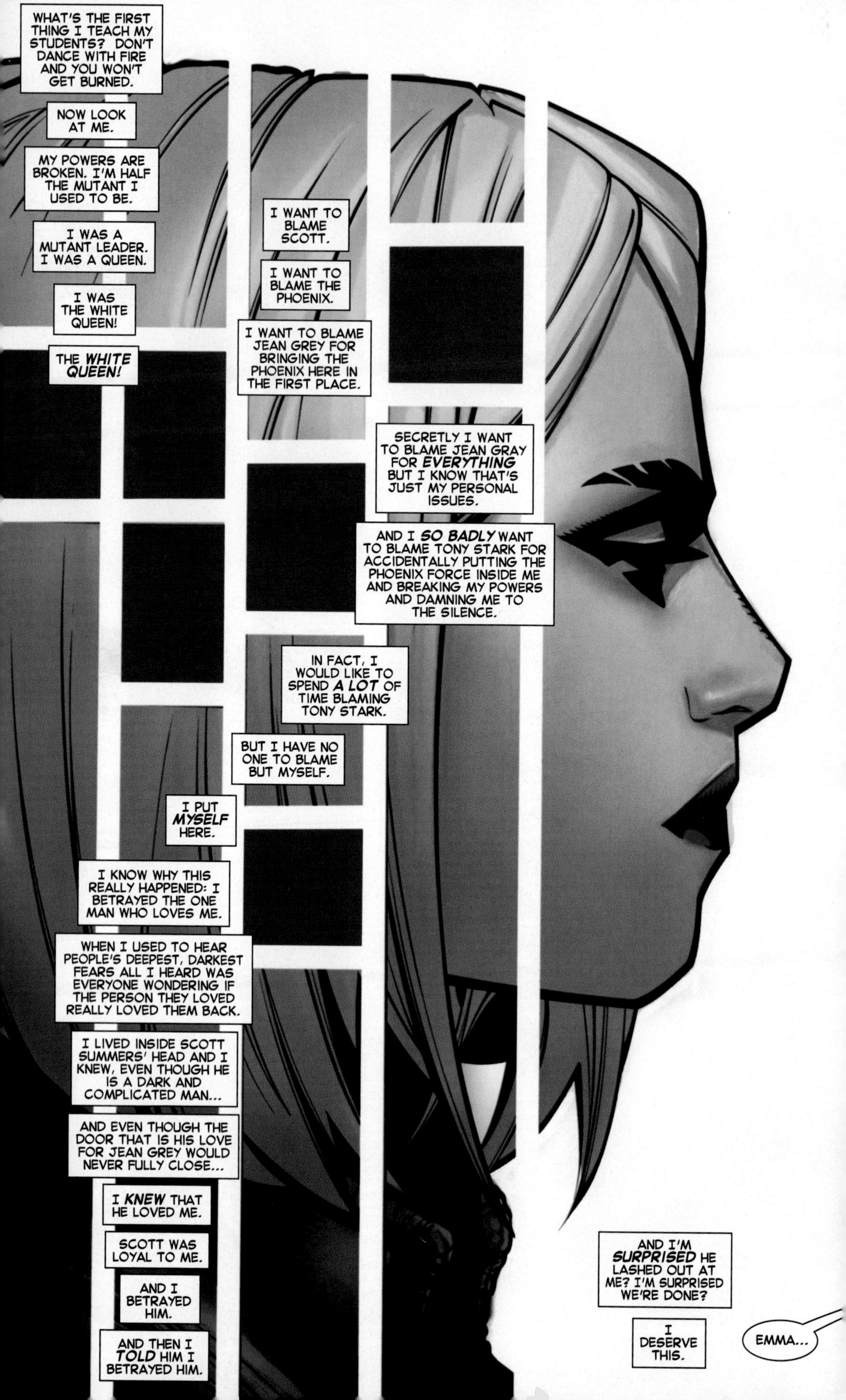
WHAT'S THE FIRST THING I TEACH MY STUDENTS? DON'T DANCE WITH FIRE AND YOU WON'T GET BURNED.
NOW LOOK AT ME.
MY POWERS ARE BROKEN. I'M HALF THE MUTANT I USED TO BE.
I WAS A MUTANT LEADER. I WAS A QUEEN.
I WAS THE WHITE QUEEN!
THE *WHITE QUEEN!*
I WANT TO BLAME SCOTT.
I WANT TO BLAME THE PHOENIX.
I WANT TO BLAME JEAN GREY FOR BRINGING THE PHOENIX HERE IN THE FIRST PLACE.
SECRETLY I WANT TO BLAME JEAN GRAY FOR *EVERYTHING* BUT I KNOW THAT'S JUST MY PERSONAL ISSUES.
AND I *SO BADLY* WANT TO BLAME TONY STARK FOR ACCIDENTALLY PUTTING THE PHOENIX FORCE INSIDE ME AND BREAKING MY POWERS AND DAMNING ME TO THE SILENCE.
IN FACT, I WOULD LIKE TO SPEND *A LOT* OF TIME BLAMING TONY STARK.
BUT I HAVE NO ONE TO BLAME BUT MYSELF.
I PUT *MYSELF* HERE.
I KNOW WHY THIS REALLY HAPPENED: I BETRAYED THE ONE MAN WHO LOVES ME.
WHEN I USED TO HEAR PEOPLE'S DEEPEST, DARKEST FEARS ALL I HEARD WAS EVERYONE WONDERING IF THE PERSON THEY LOVED REALLY LOVED THEM BACK.
I LIVED INSIDE SCOTT SUMMERS' HEAD AND I KNEW, EVEN THOUGH HE IS A DARK AND COMPLICATED MAN...
AND EVEN THOUGH THE DOOR THAT IS HIS LOVE FOR JEAN GREY WOULD NEVER FULLY CLOSE...
I *KNEW* THAT HE LOVED ME.
SCOTT WAS LOYAL TO ME.
AND I BETRAYED HIM.
AND THEN I *TOLD* HIM I BETRAYED HIM.
AND I'M *SURPRISED* HE LASHED OUT AT ME? I'M SURPRISED WE'RE DONE?
I DESERVE THIS.
EMMA...

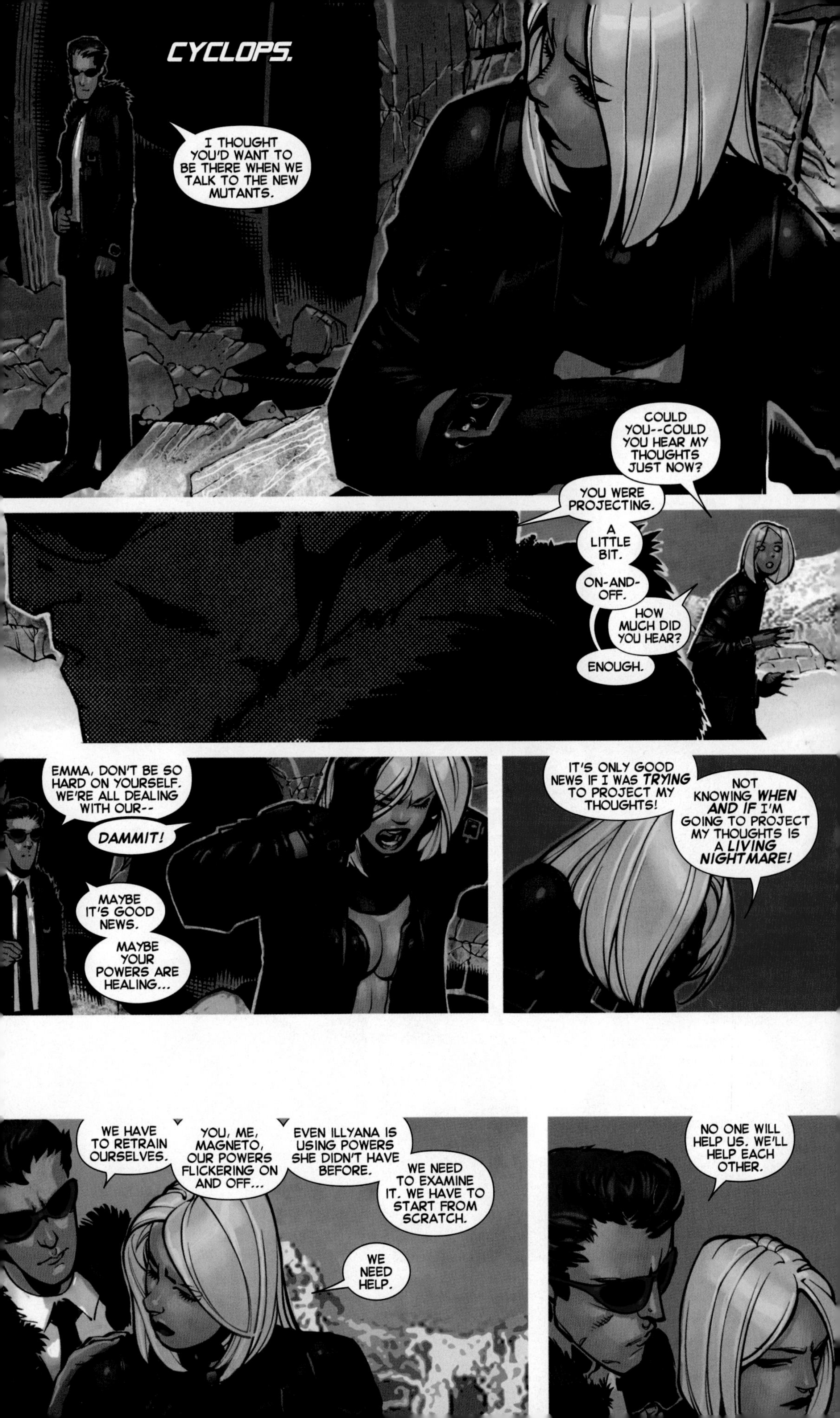
CYCLOPS.
I THOUGHT YOU'D WANT TO BE THERE WHEN WE TALK TO THE NEW MUTANTS.
COULD YOU--COULD YOU HEAR MY THOUGHTS JUST NOW?
YOU WERE PROJECTING.
A LITTLE BIT.
ON-AND-OFF.
HOW MUCH DID YOU HEAR?
ENOUGH.
EMMA, DON'T BE SO HARD ON YOURSELF. WE'RE ALL DEALING WITH OUR--
DAMMIT!
MAYBE IT'S GOOD NEWS.
MAYBE YOUR POWERS ARE HEALING...
IT'S ONLY GOOD NEWS IF I WAS TRYING TO PROJECT MY THOUGHTS!
NOT KNOWING WHEN AND IF I'M GOING TO PROJECT MY THOUGHTS IS A LIVING NIGHTMARE!
WE HAVE TO RETRAIN OURSELVES.
YOU, ME, MAGNETO, OUR POWERS FLICKERING ON AND OFF...
EVEN ILLYANA IS USING POWERS SHE DIDN'T HAVE BEFORE.
WE NEED TO EXAMINE IT. WE HAVE TO START FROM SCRATCH.
WE NEED HELP.
NO ONE WILL HELP US. WE'LL HELP EACH OTHER.

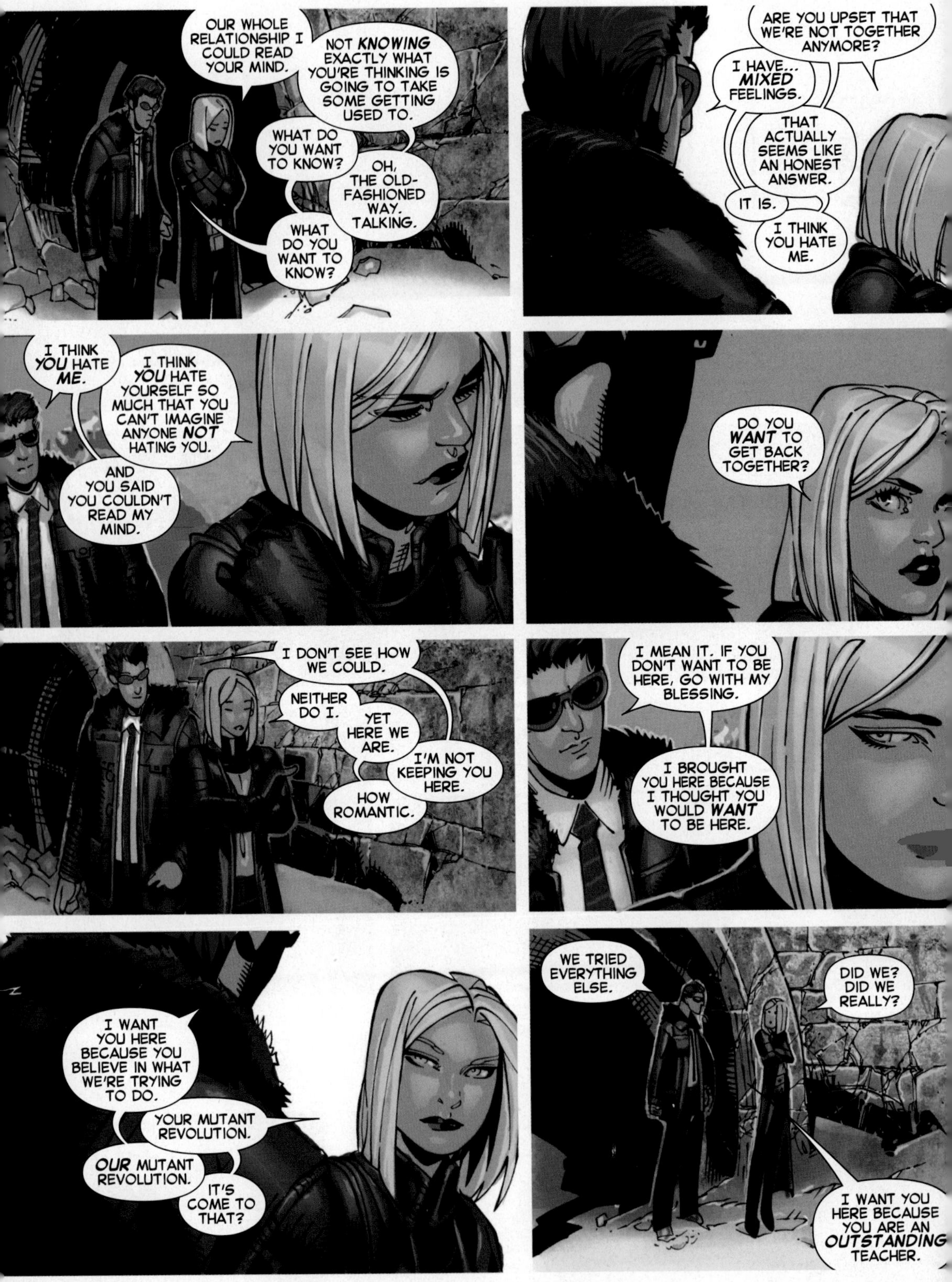
OUR WHOLE RELATIONSHIP I COULD READ YOUR MIND.
NOT KNOWING EXACTLY WHAT YOU'RE THINKING IS GOING TO TAKE SOME GETTING USED TO.
WHAT DO YOU WANT TO KNOW?
OH, THE OLD-FASHIONED WAY. TALKING.
WHAT DO YOU WANT TO KNOW?
ARE YOU UPSET THAT WE'RE NOT TOGETHER ANYMORE?
I HAVE... MIXED FEELINGS.
THAT ACTUALLY SEEMS LIKE AN HONEST ANSWER.
IT IS.
I THINK YOU HATE ME.
I THINK YOU HATE ME.
I THINK YOU HATE YOURSELF SO MUCH THAT YOU CAN'T IMAGINE ANYONE NOT HATING YOU.
AND YOU SAID YOU COULDN'T READ MY MIND.
DO YOU WANT TO GET BACK TOGETHER?
I DON'T SEE HOW WE COULD.
NEITHER DO I.
YET HERE WE ARE.
I'M NOT KEEPING YOU HERE.
HOW ROMANTIC.
I MEAN IT. IF YOU DON'T WANT TO BE HERE, GO WITH MY BLESSING.
I BROUGHT YOU HERE BECAUSE I THOUGHT YOU WOULD WANT TO BE HERE.
I WANT YOU HERE BECAUSE YOU BELIEVE IN WHAT WE'RE TRYING TO DO.
YOUR MUTANT REVOLUTION.
OUR MUTANT REVOLUTION.
IT'S COME TO THAT?
WE TRIED EVERYTHING ELSE.
DID WE? DID WE REALLY?
I WANT YOU HERE BECAUSE YOU ARE AN OUTSTANDING TEACHER.

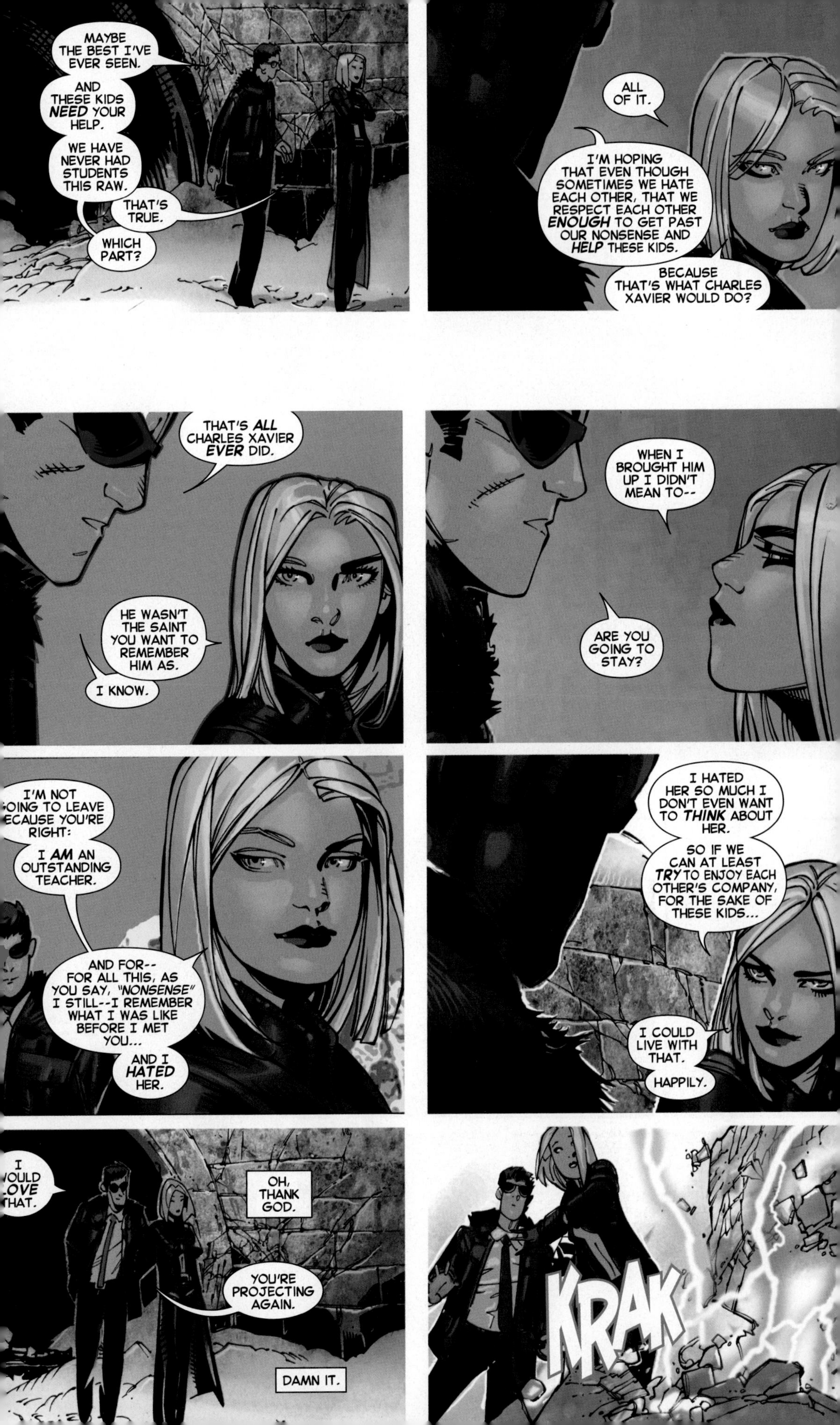
MAYBE THE BEST I'VE EVER SEEN.
AND THESE KIDS NEED YOUR HELP.
WE HAVE NEVER HAD STUDENTS THIS RAW.
THAT'S TRUE.
WHICH PART?
ALL OF IT.
I'M HOPING THAT EVEN THOUGH SOMETIMES WE HATE EACH OTHER, THAT WE RESPECT EACH OTHER ENOUGH TO GET PAST OUR NONSENSE AND HELP THESE KIDS.
BECAUSE THAT'S WHAT CHARLES XAVIER WOULD DO?
THAT'S ALL CHARLES XAVIER EVER DID.
HE WASN'T THE SAINT YOU WANT TO REMEMBER HIM AS.
I KNOW.
WHEN I BROUGHT HIM UP I DIDN'T MEAN TO--
ARE YOU GOING TO STAY?
I'M NOT GOING TO LEAVE BECAUSE YOU'RE RIGHT:
I AM AN OUTSTANDING TEACHER.
AND FOR-- FOR ALL THIS, AS YOU SAY, "NONSENSE" I STILL--I REMEMBER WHAT I WAS LIKE BEFORE I MET YOU...
AND I HATED HER.
I HATED HER SO MUCH I DON'T EVEN WANT TO THINK ABOUT HER.
SO IF WE CAN AT LEAST TRY TO ENJOY EACH OTHER'S COMPANY, FOR THE SAKE OF THESE KIDS...
I COULD LIVE WITH THAT.
HAPPILY.
I WOULD LOVE THAT.
OH, THANK GOD.
YOU'RE PROJECTING AGAIN.
DAMN IT.
KRAK

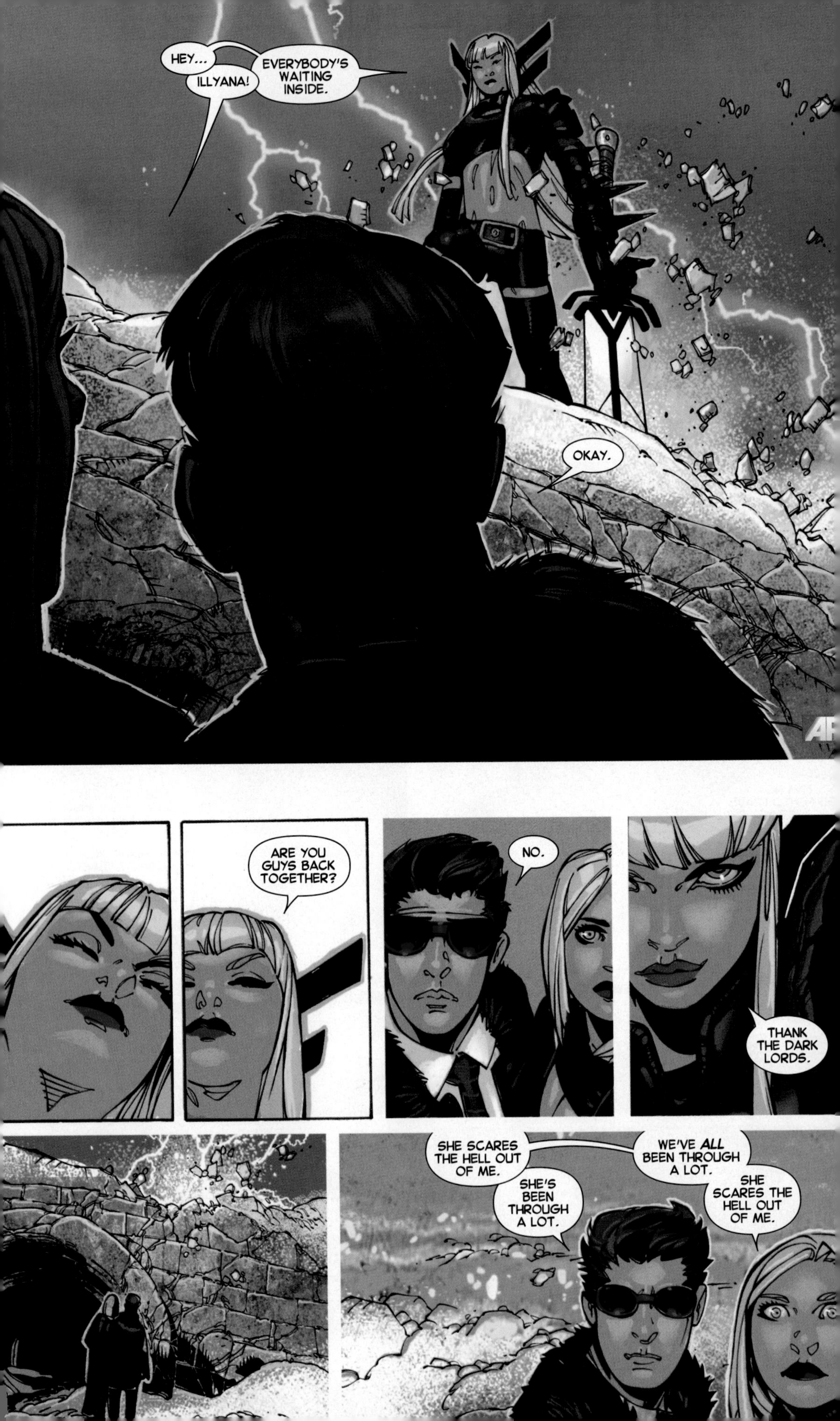
HEY...
ILLYANA!
EVERYBODY'S WAITING INSIDE.
OKAY.
ARE YOU GUYS BACK TOGETHER?
NO.
THANK THE DARK LORDS.
SHE SCARES THE HELL OUT OF ME.
SHE'S BEEN THROUGH A LOT.
WE'VE ALL BEEN THROUGH A LOT.
SHE SCARES THE HELL OUT OF ME.

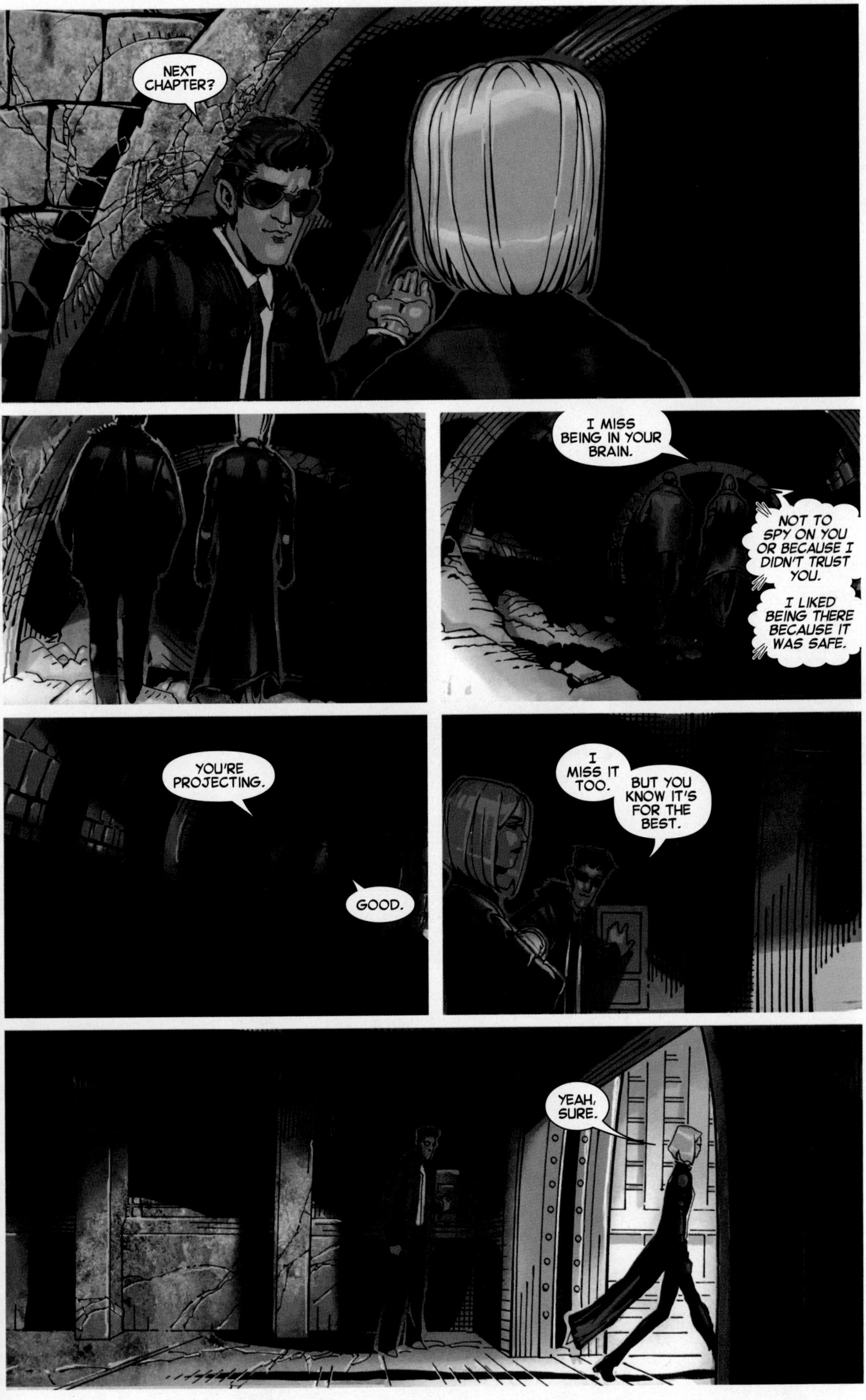
NEXT CHAPTER?
I MISS BEING IN YOUR BRAIN.
NOT TO SPY ON YOU OR BECAUSE I DIDN'T TRUST YOU.
I LIKED BEING THERE BECAUSE IT WAS SAFE.
YOU'RE PROJECTING.
GOOD.
I MISS IT TOO.
BUT YOU KNOW IT'S FOR THE BEST.
YEAH, SURE.

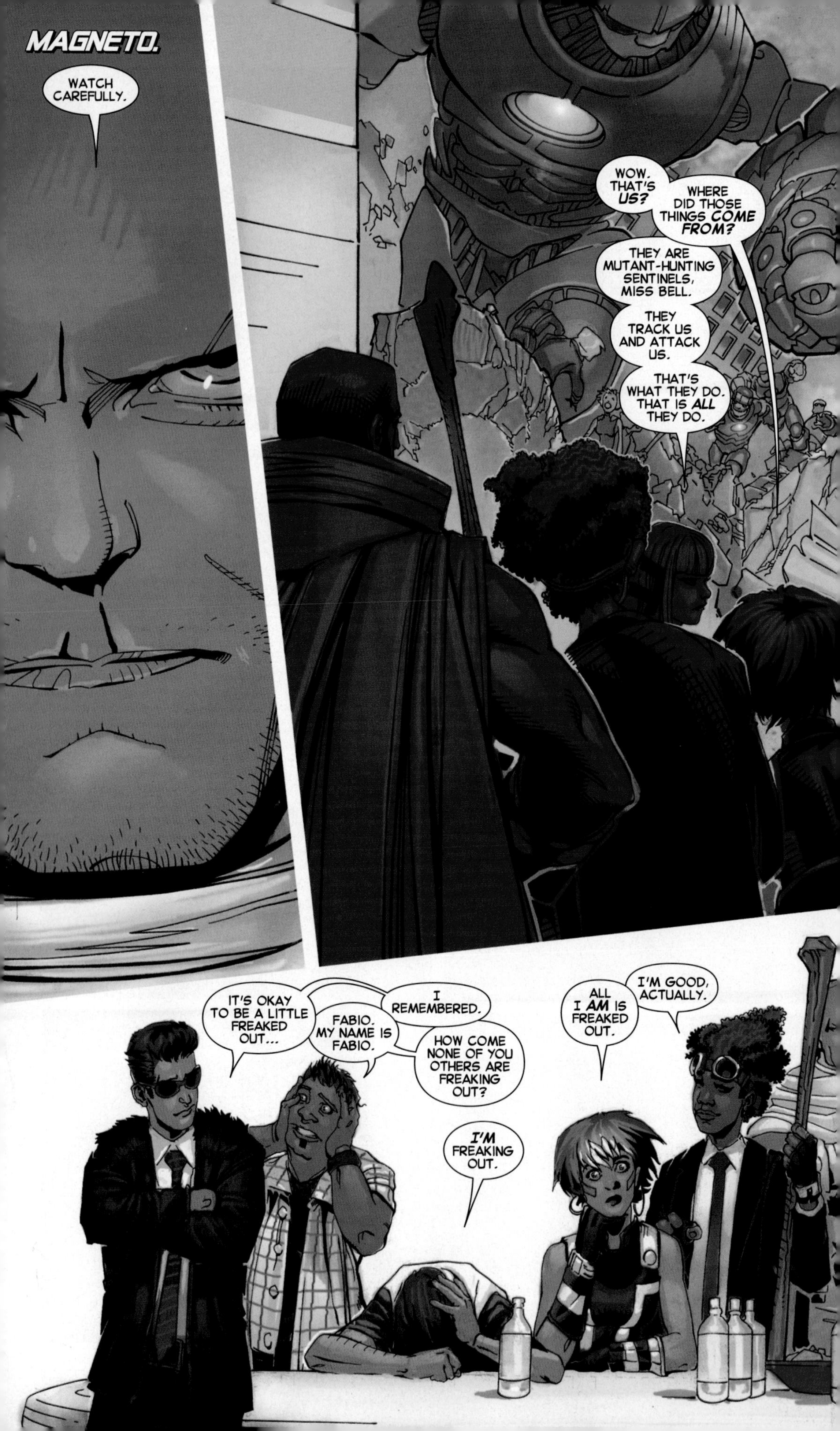

MAGNETO.
WATCH CAREFULLY.
WOW. THAT'S US?
WHERE DID THOSE THINGS COME FROM?
THEY ARE MUTANT-HUNTING SENTINELS, MISS BELL.
THEY TRACK US AND ATTACK US.
THAT'S WHAT THEY DO. THAT IS ALL THEY DO.
IT'S OKAY TO BE A LITTLE FREAKED OUT...
FABIO. MY NAME IS FABIO.
I REMEMBERED.
HOW COME NONE OF YOU OTHERS ARE FREAKING OUT?
I'M FREAKING OUT.
ALL I AM IS FREAKED OUT.
I'M GOOD, ACTUALLY.

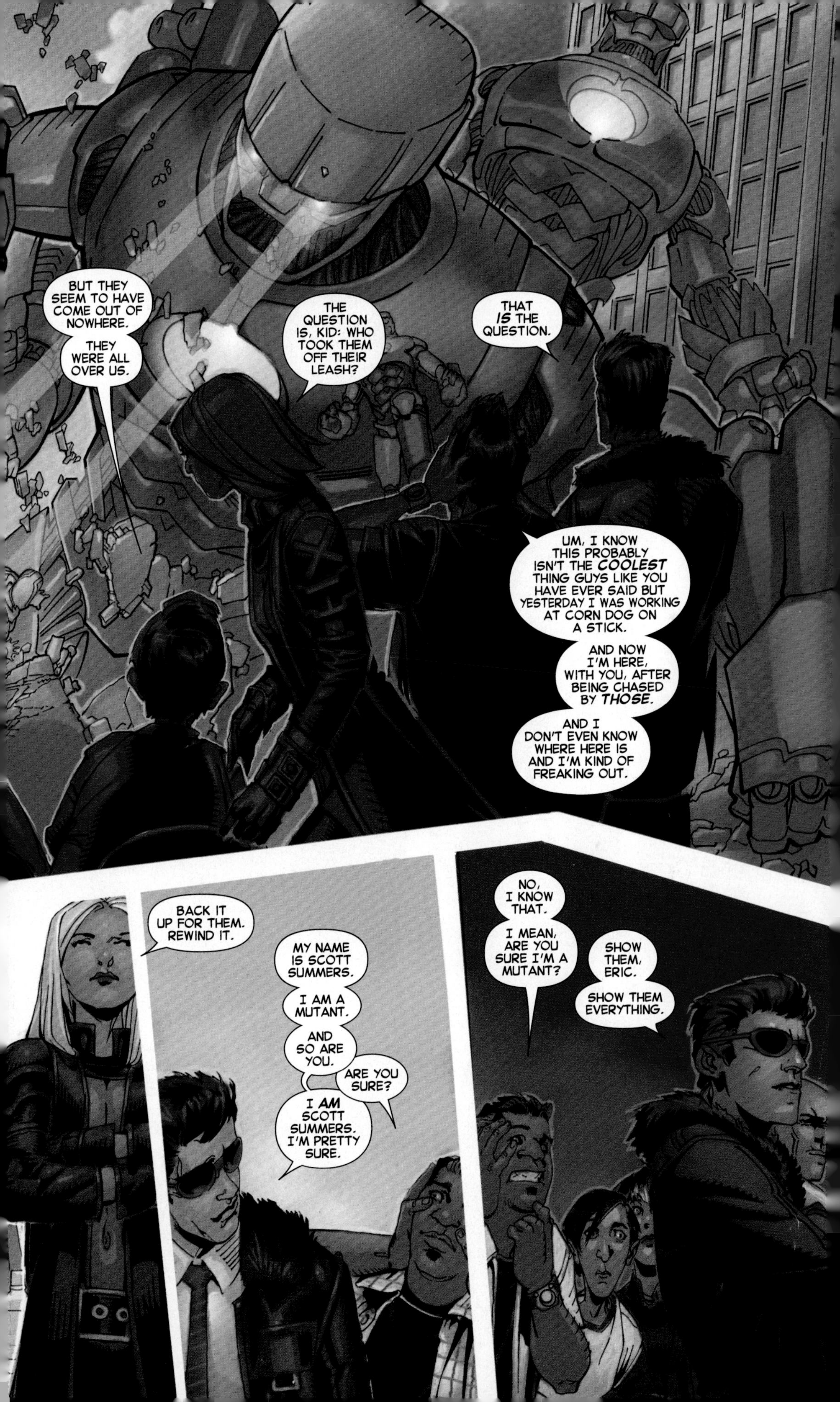

BUT THEY SEEM TO HAVE COME OUT OF NOWHERE.
THEY WERE ALL OVER US.
THE QUESTION IS, KID: WHO TOOK THEM OFF THEIR LEASH?
THAT *IS* THE QUESTION.
UM, I KNOW THIS PROBABLY ISN'T THE **COOLEST** THING GUYS LIKE YOU HAVE EVER SAID BUT YESTERDAY I WAS WORKING AT CORN DOG ON A STICK.
AND NOW I'M HERE, WITH YOU, AFTER BEING CHASED BY ***THOSE***.
AND I DON'T EVEN KNOW WHERE HERE IS AND I'M KIND OF FREAKING OUT.
BACK IT UP FOR THEM. REWIND IT.
MY NAME IS SCOTT SUMMERS.
I AM A MUTANT.
AND SO ARE YOU.
ARE YOU SURE?
I **AM** SCOTT SUMMERS. I'M PRETTY SURE.
NO, I KNOW THAT.
I MEAN, ARE YOU SURE I'M A MUTANT?
SHOW THEM, ERIC.
SHOW THEM EVERYTHING.

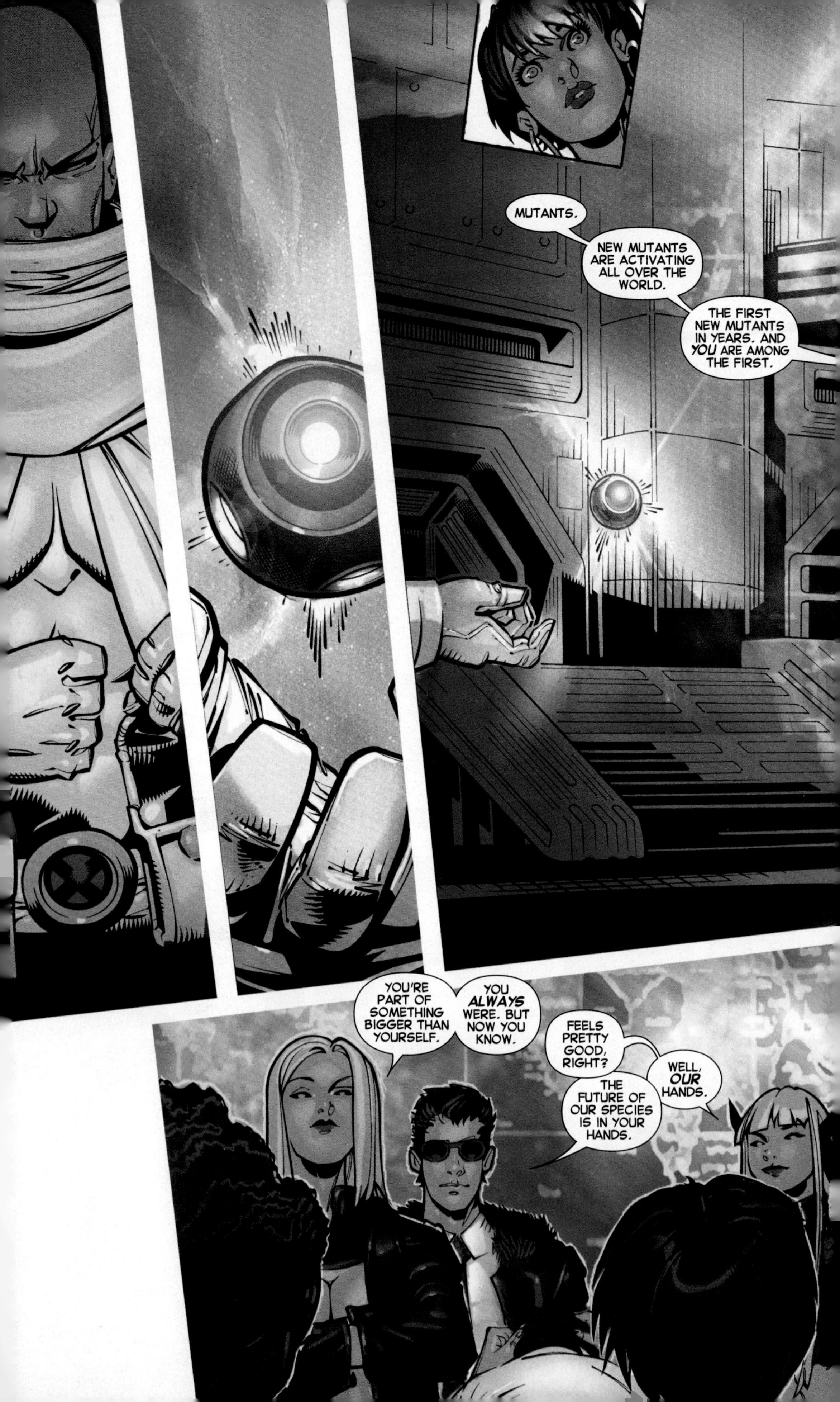
MUTANTS.
NEW MUTANTS ARE ACTIVATING ALL OVER THE WORLD.
THE FIRST NEW MUTANTS IN YEARS. AND YOU ARE AMONG THE FIRST.
YOU'RE PART OF SOMETHING BIGGER THAN YOURSELF.
YOU ALWAYS WERE. BUT NOW YOU KNOW.
FEELS PRETTY GOOD, RIGHT?
THE FUTURE OF OUR SPECIES IS IN YOUR HANDS.
WELL, OUR HANDS.

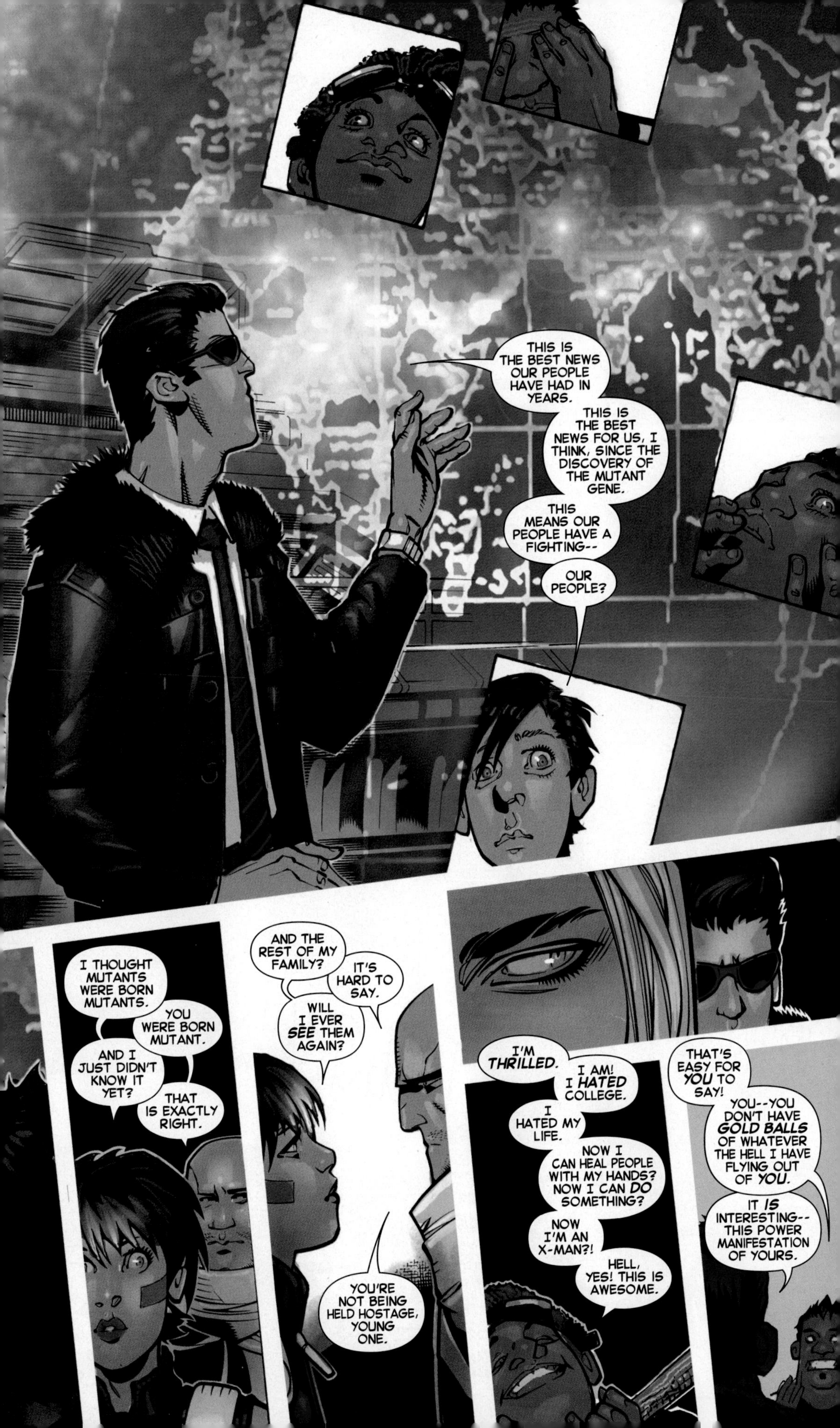
THIS IS THE BEST NEWS OUR PEOPLE HAVE HAD IN YEARS.
THIS IS THE BEST NEWS FOR US, I THINK, SINCE THE DISCOVERY OF THE MUTANT GENE.
THIS MEANS OUR PEOPLE HAVE A FIGHTING--
OUR PEOPLE?
I THOUGHT MUTANTS WERE BORN MUTANTS.
YOU WERE BORN MUTANT.
AND I JUST DIDN'T KNOW IT YET?
THAT IS EXACTLY RIGHT.
AND THE REST OF MY FAMILY?
IT'S HARD TO SAY.
WILL I EVER SEE THEM AGAIN?
YOU'RE NOT BEING HELD HOSTAGE, YOUNG ONE.
I'M THRILLED.
I AM! I HATED COLLEGE.
I HATED MY LIFE.
NOW I CAN HEAL PEOPLE WITH MY HANDS? NOW I CAN DO SOMETHING?
NOW I'M AN X-MAN?!
HELL, YES! THIS IS AWESOME.
THAT'S EASY FOR YOU TO SAY!
YOU--YOU DON'T HAVE GOLD BALLS OF WHATEVER THE HELL I HAVE FLYING OUT OF YOU.
IT IS INTERESTING-- THIS POWER MANIFESTATION OF YOURS.

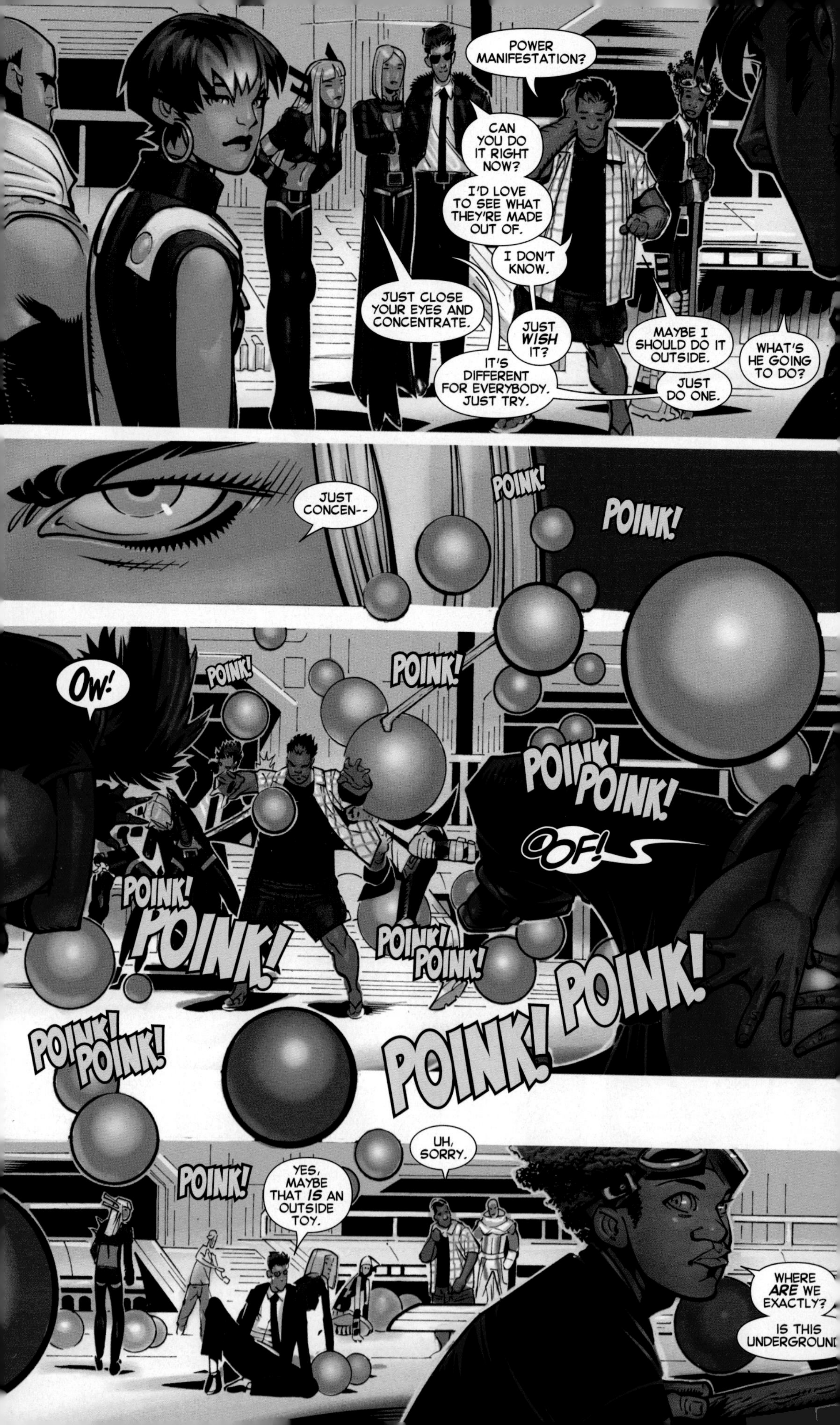
POWER MANIFESTATION?
CAN YOU DO IT RIGHT NOW?
I'D LOVE TO SEE WHAT THEY'RE MADE OUT OF.
I DON'T KNOW.
JUST CLOSE YOUR EYES AND CONCENTRATE.
JUST *WISH* IT?
IT'S DIFFERENT FOR EVERYBODY. JUST TRY.
MAYBE I SHOULD DO IT OUTSIDE.
JUST DO ONE.
WHAT'S HE GOING TO DO?
JUST CONCEN--
POINK!
POINK!
OW!
POINK!
POINK!
POINK! POINK!
OOF!
POINK! POINK!
POINK! POINK!
POINK! POINK!
POINK! POINK!
POINK!
YES, MAYBE THAT *IS* AN OUTSIDE TOY.
UH, SORRY.
WHERE *ARE* WE EXACTLY?
IS THIS UNDERGROUND

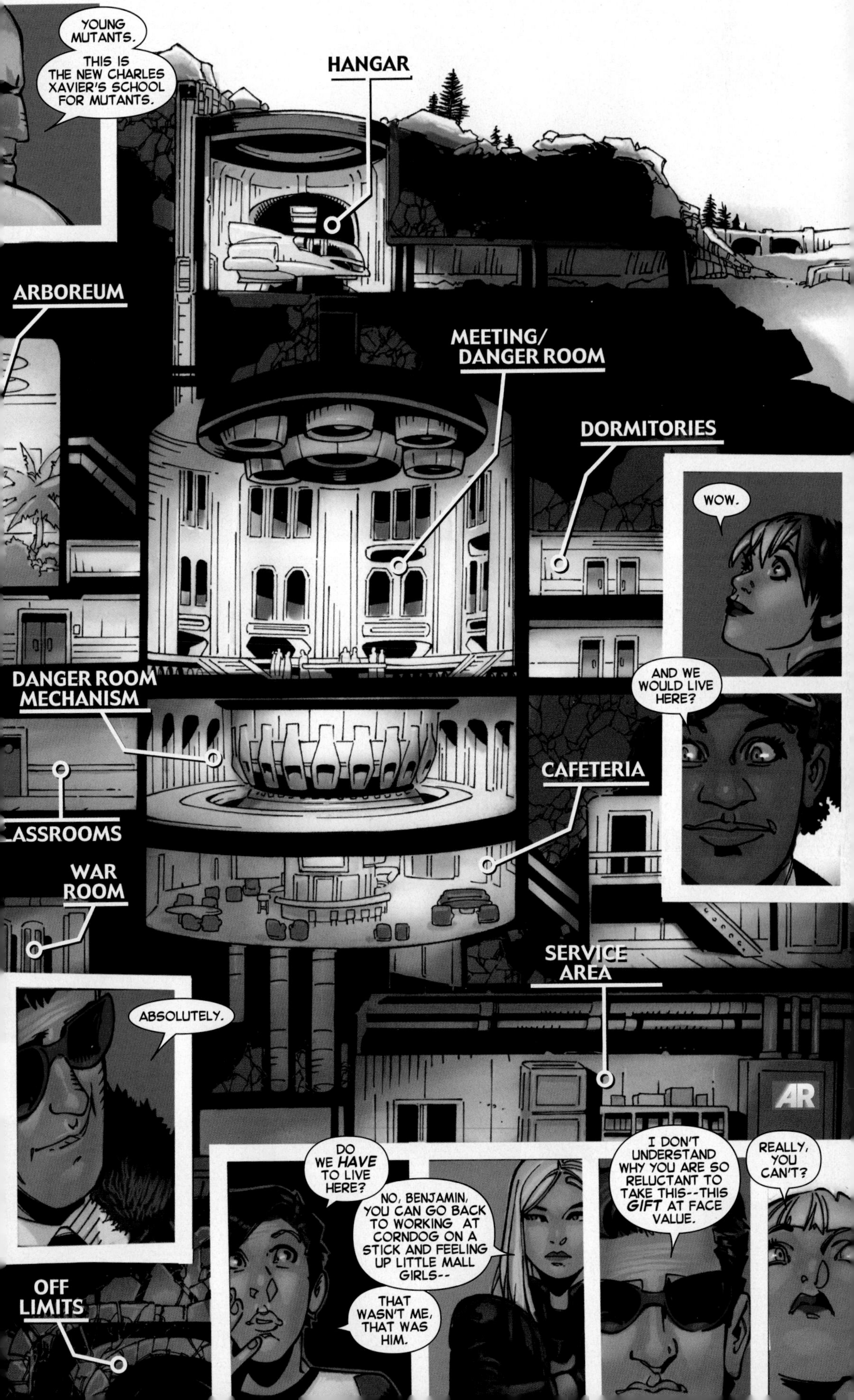

YOUNG MUTANTS.
THIS IS THE NEW CHARLES XAVIER'S SCHOOL FOR MUTANTS.
HANGAR
ARBOREUM
MEETING/ DANGER ROOM
DORMITORIES
WOW.
AND WE WOULD LIVE HERE?
DANGER ROOM MECHANISM
CLASSROOMS
CAFETERIA
WAR ROOM
SERVICE AREA
ABSOLUTELY.
DO WE *HAVE* TO LIVE HERE?
NO, BENJAMIN, YOU CAN GO BACK TO WORKING AT CORNDOG ON A STICK AND FEELING UP LITTLE MALL GIRLS--
THAT WASN'T ME, THAT WAS HIM.
I DON'T UNDERSTAND WHY YOU ARE SO RELUCTANT TO TAKE THIS--THIS *GIFT* AT FACE VALUE.
REALLY, YOU CAN'T?
OFF LIMITS

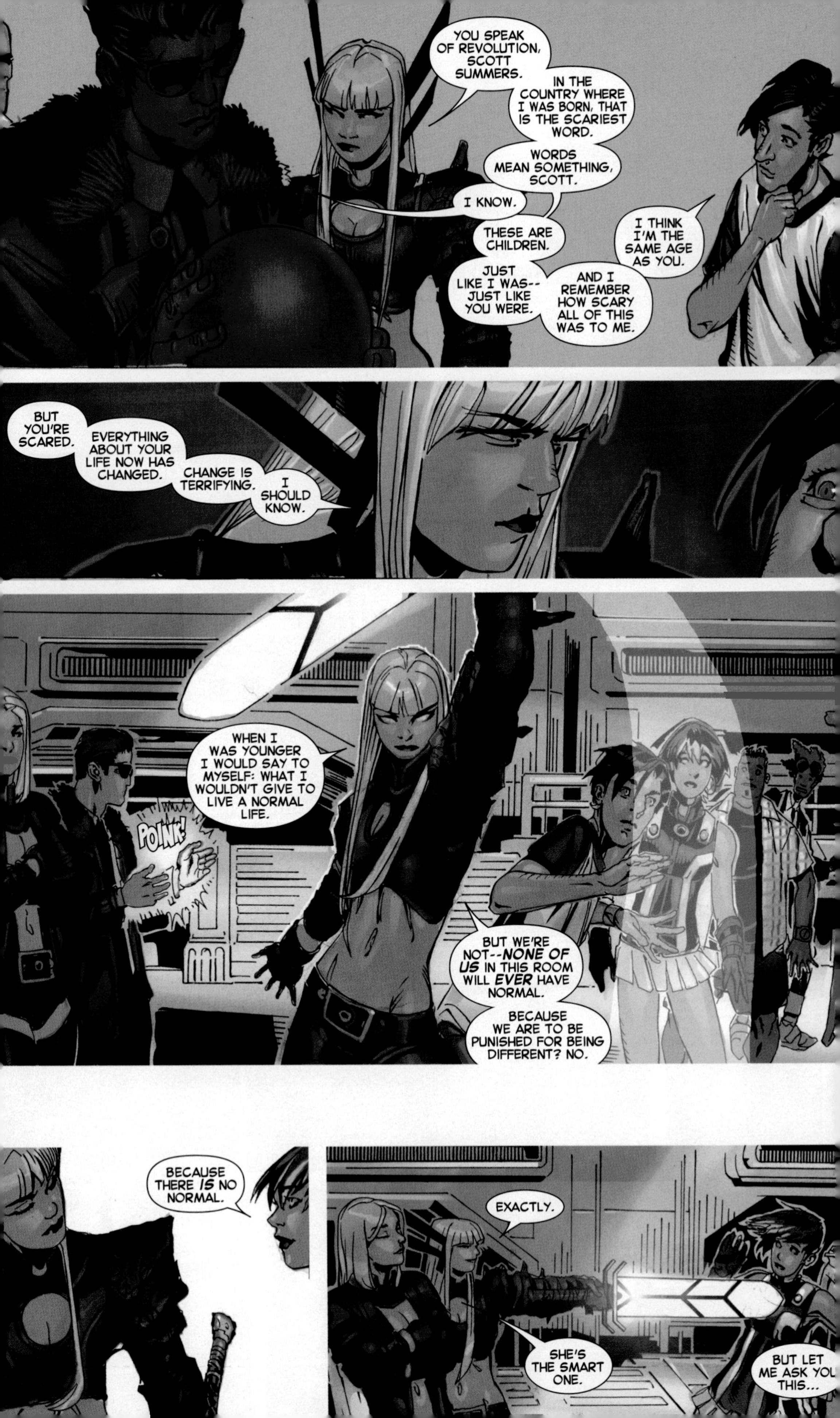
YOU SPEAK OF REVOLUTION, SCOTT SUMMERS.
IN THE COUNTRY WHERE I WAS BORN, THAT IS THE SCARIEST WORD.
WORDS MEAN SOMETHING, SCOTT.
I KNOW.
THESE ARE CHILDREN.
JUST LIKE I WAS-- JUST LIKE YOU WERE.
AND I REMEMBER HOW SCARY ALL OF THIS WAS TO ME.
I THINK I'M THE SAME AGE AS YOU.
BUT YOU'RE SCARED.
EVERYTHING ABOUT YOUR LIFE NOW HAS CHANGED.
CHANGE IS TERRIFYING.
I SHOULD KNOW.
WHEN I WAS YOUNGER I WOULD SAY TO MYSELF: WHAT I WOULDN'T GIVE TO LIVE A NORMAL LIFE.
POINK!
BUT WE'RE NOT--NONE OF US IN THIS ROOM WILL EVER HAVE NORMAL.
BECAUSE WE ARE TO BE PUNISHED FOR BEING DIFFERENT? NO.
BECAUSE THERE IS NO NORMAL.
EXACTLY.
SHE'S THE SMART ONE.
BUT LET ME ASK YOU THIS...

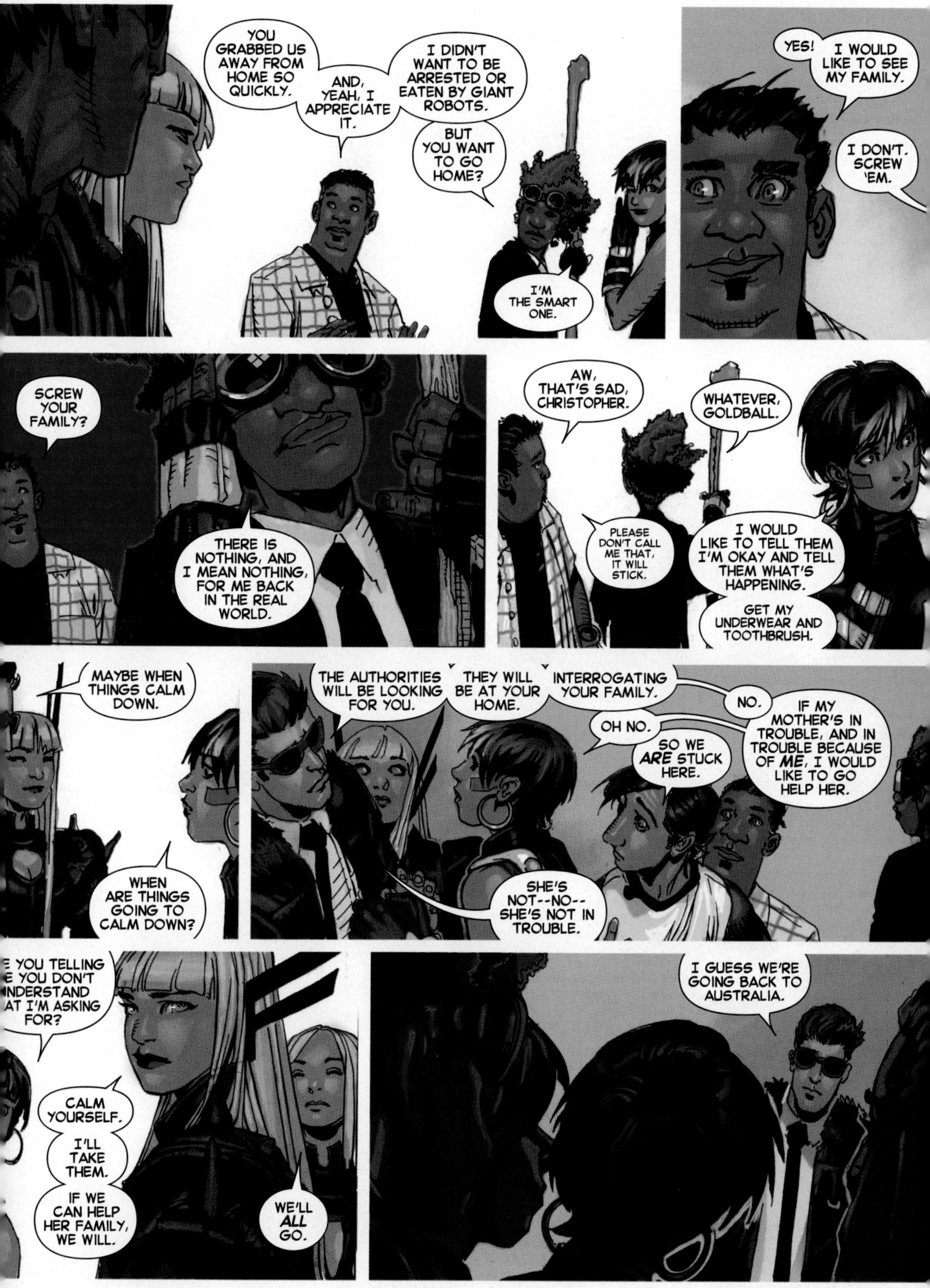
YOU GRABBED US AWAY FROM HOME SO QUICKLY.
AND, YEAH, I APPRECIATE IT.
I DIDN'T WANT TO BE ARRESTED OR EATEN BY GIANT ROBOTS.
BUT YOU WANT TO GO HOME?
I'M THE SMART ONE.
YES!
I WOULD LIKE TO SEE MY FAMILY.
I DON'T. SCREW 'EM.
SCREW YOUR FAMILY?
THERE IS NOTHING, AND I MEAN NOTHING, FOR ME BACK IN THE REAL WORLD.
AW, THAT'S SAD, CHRISTOPHER.
PLEASE DON'T CALL ME THAT, IT WILL STICK.
WHATEVER, GOLDBALL.
I WOULD LIKE TO TELL THEM I'M OKAY AND TELL THEM WHAT'S HAPPENING.
GET MY UNDERWEAR AND TOOTHBRUSH.
MAYBE WHEN THINGS CALM DOWN.
WHEN ARE THINGS GOING TO CALM DOWN?
THE AUTHORITIES WILL BE LOOKING FOR YOU.
THEY WILL BE AT YOUR HOME.
INTERROGATING YOUR FAMILY.
OH NO.
SO WE *ARE* STUCK HERE.
NO.
IF MY MOTHER'S IN TROUBLE, AND IN TROUBLE BECAUSE OF *ME*, I WOULD LIKE TO GO HELP HER.
SHE'S NOT--NO--SHE'S NOT IN TROUBLE.
E YOU TELLING E YOU DON'T NDERSTAND AT I'M ASKING FOR?
CALM YOURSELF.
I'LL TAKE THEM.
IF WE CAN HELP HER FAMILY, WE WILL.
WE'LL *ALL* GO.
I GUESS WE'RE GOING BACK TO AUSTRALIA.

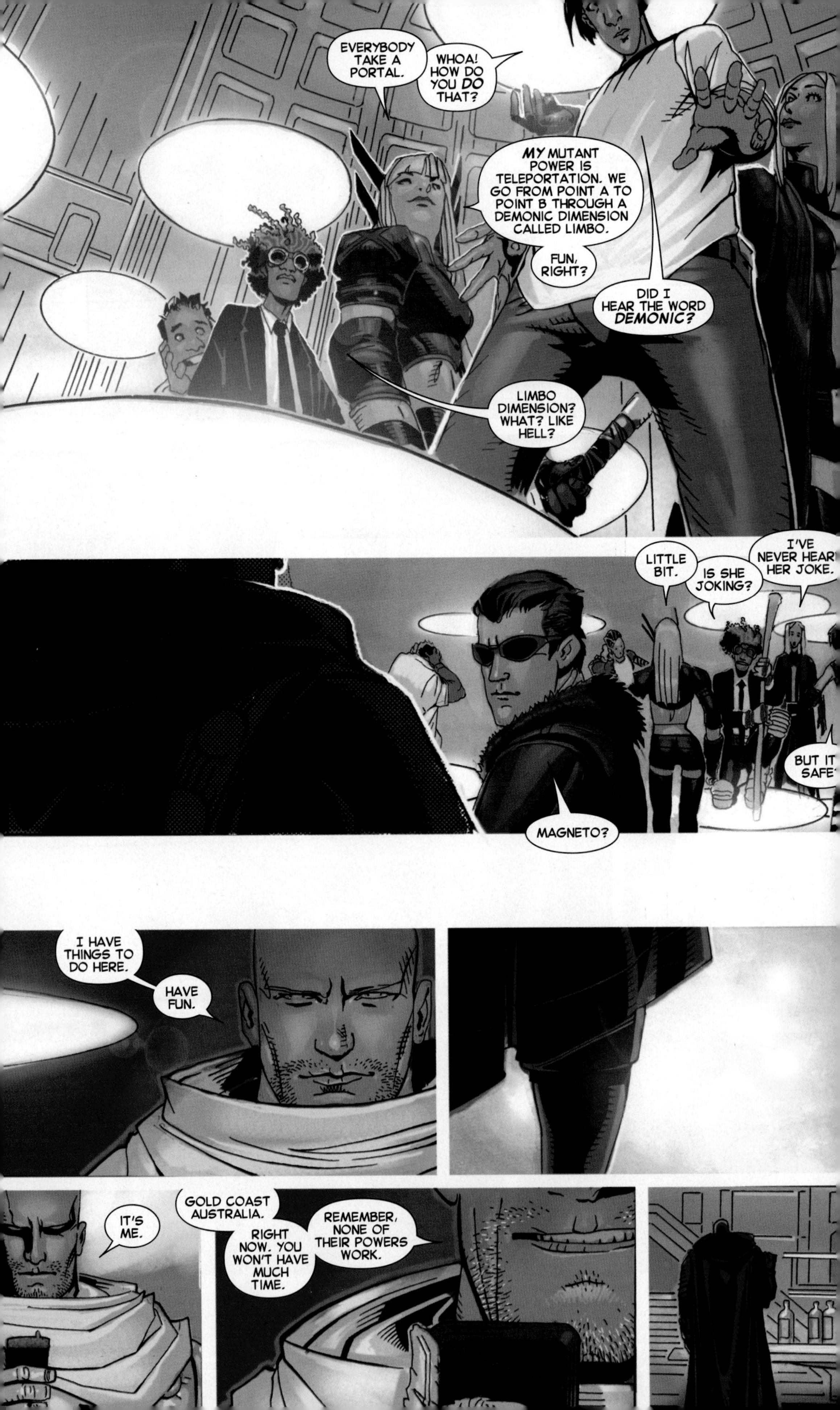

EVERYBODY TAKE A PORTAL.
WHOA! HOW DO YOU DO THAT?
MY MUTANT POWER IS TELEPORTATION. WE GO FROM POINT A TO POINT B THROUGH A DEMONIC DIMENSION CALLED LIMBO.
FUN, RIGHT?
DID I HEAR THE WORD DEMONIC?
LIMBO DIMENSION? WHAT? LIKE HELL?
LITTLE BIT.
IS SHE JOKING?
I'VE NEVER HEAR HER JOKE.
BUT IT SAFE
MAGNETO?
I HAVE THINGS TO DO HERE.
HAVE FUN.
IT'S ME.
GOLD COAST AUSTRALIA.
RIGHT NOW. YOU WON'T HAVE MUCH TIME.
REMEMBER, NONE OF THEIR POWERS WORK.

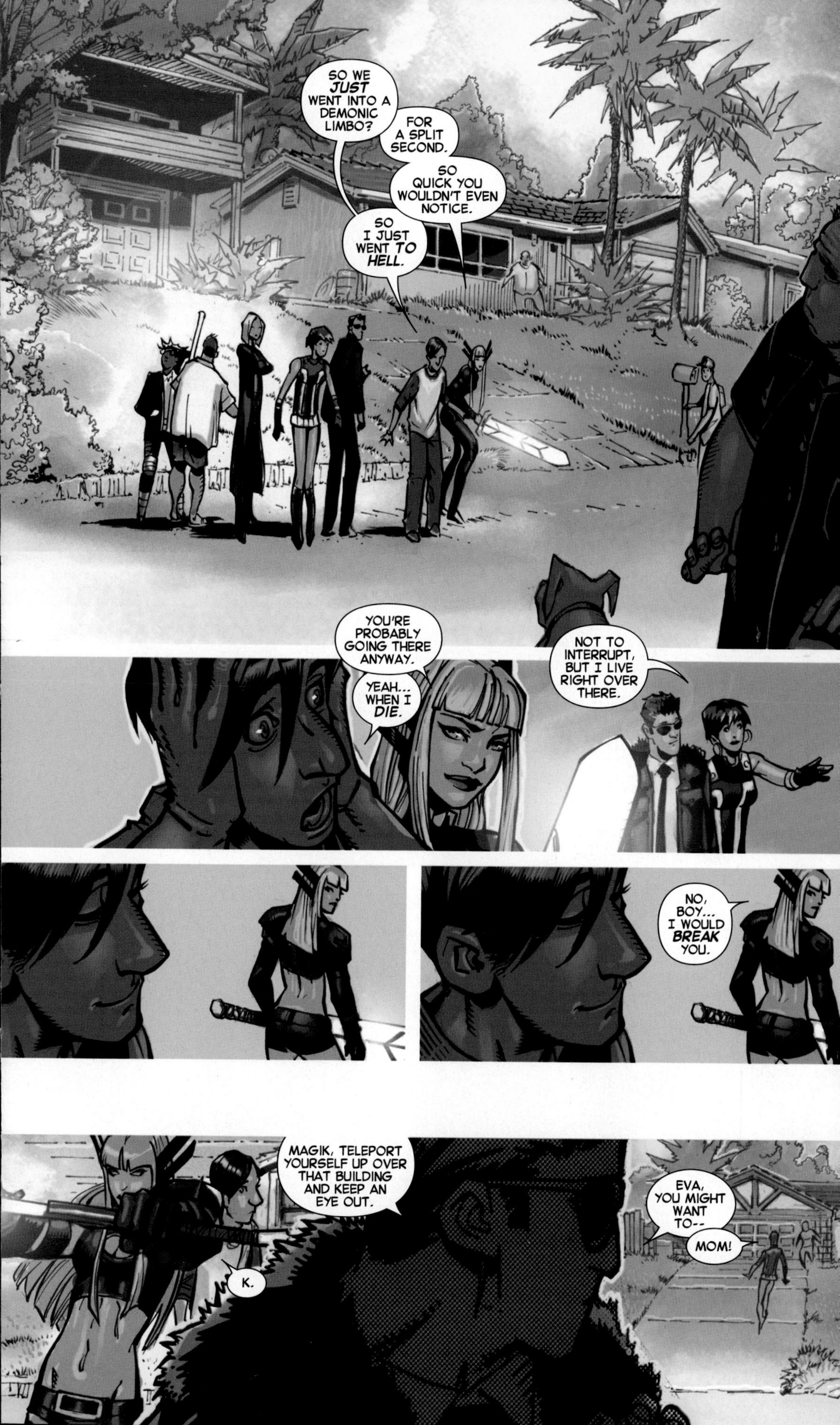
SO WE JUST WENT INTO A DEMONIC LIMBO?
FOR A SPLIT SECOND.
SO QUICK YOU WOULDN'T EVEN NOTICE.
SO I JUST WENT TO HELL.
YOU'RE PROBABLY GOING THERE ANYWAY.
YEAH... WHEN I DIE.
NOT TO INTERRUPT, BUT I LIVE RIGHT OVER THERE.
NO, BOY... I WOULD BREAK YOU.
MAGIK, TELEPORT YOURSELF UP OVER THAT BUILDING AND KEEP AN EYE OUT.
K.
EVA, YOU MIGHT WANT TO--
MOM!

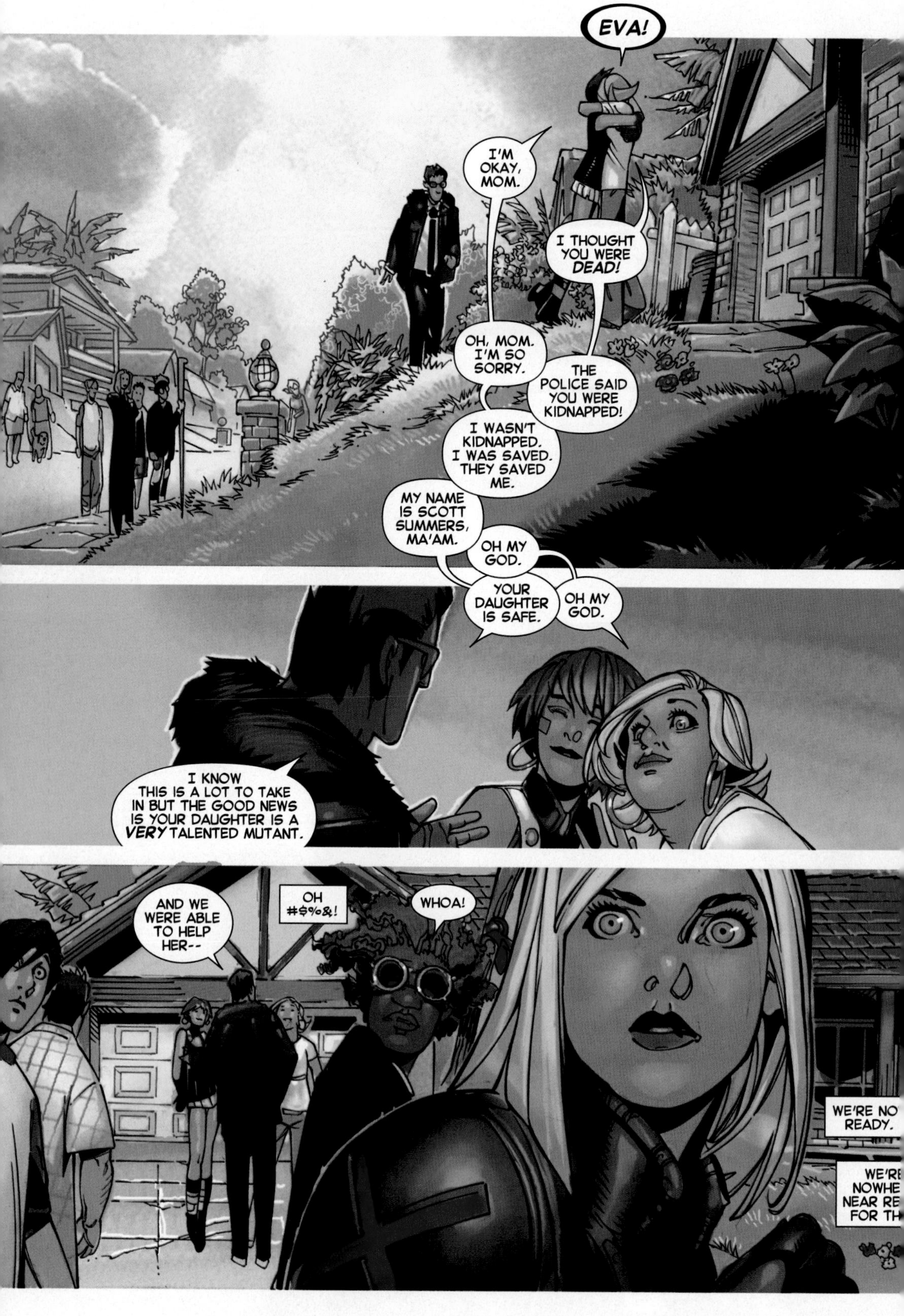
EVA!
I'M OKAY, MOM.
I THOUGHT YOU WERE DEAD!
OH, MOM. I'M SO SORRY.
THE POLICE SAID YOU WERE KIDNAPPED!
I WASN'T KIDNAPPED. I WAS SAVED. THEY SAVED ME.
MY NAME IS SCOTT SUMMERS, MA'AM.
OH MY GOD.
YOUR DAUGHTER IS SAFE.
OH MY GOD.
I KNOW THIS IS A LOT TO TAKE IN BUT THE GOOD NEWS IS YOUR DAUGHTER IS A VERY TALENTED MUTANT.
AND WE WERE ABLE TO HELP HER--
OH #$%&!
WHOA!

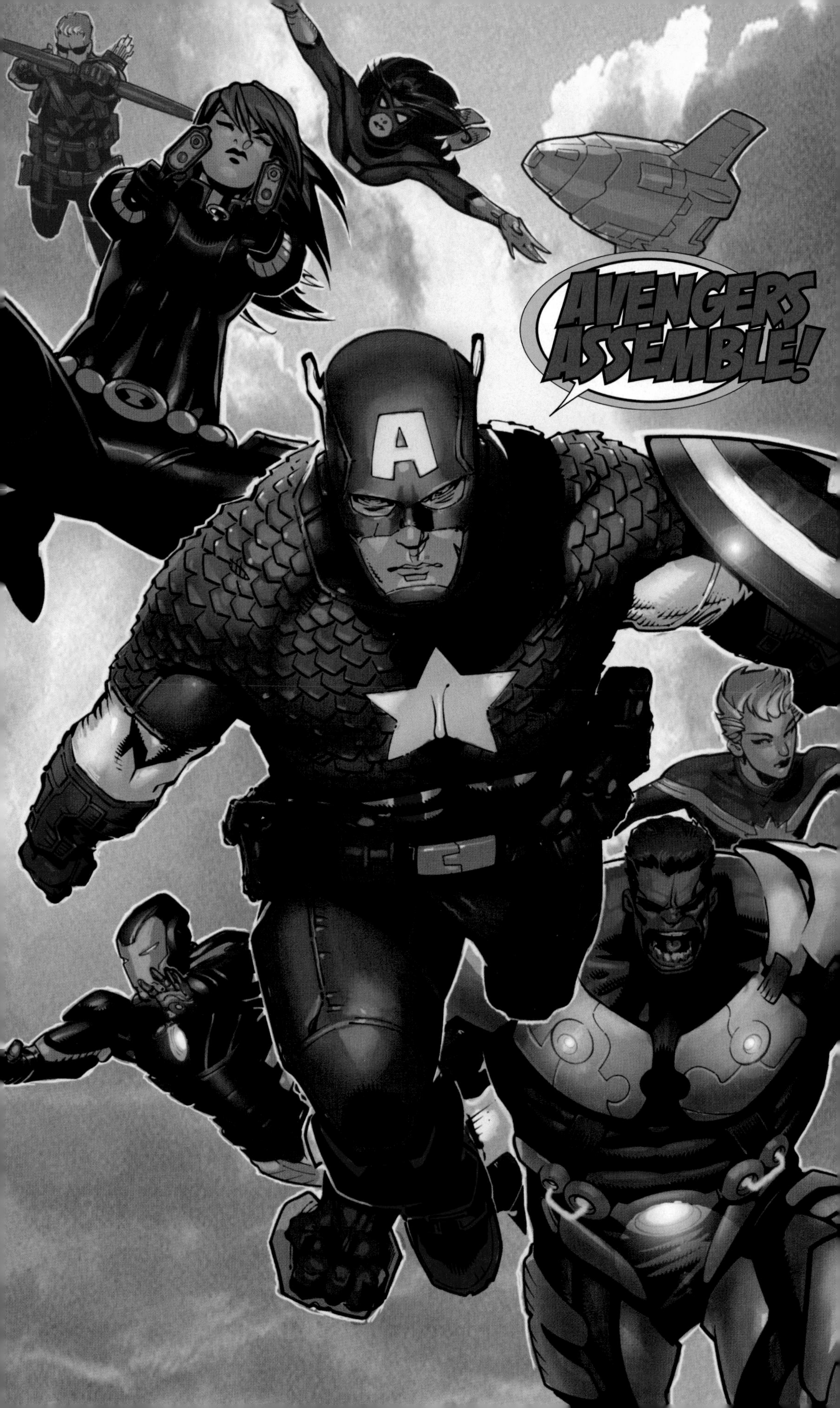
AVENGERS ASSEMBLE!

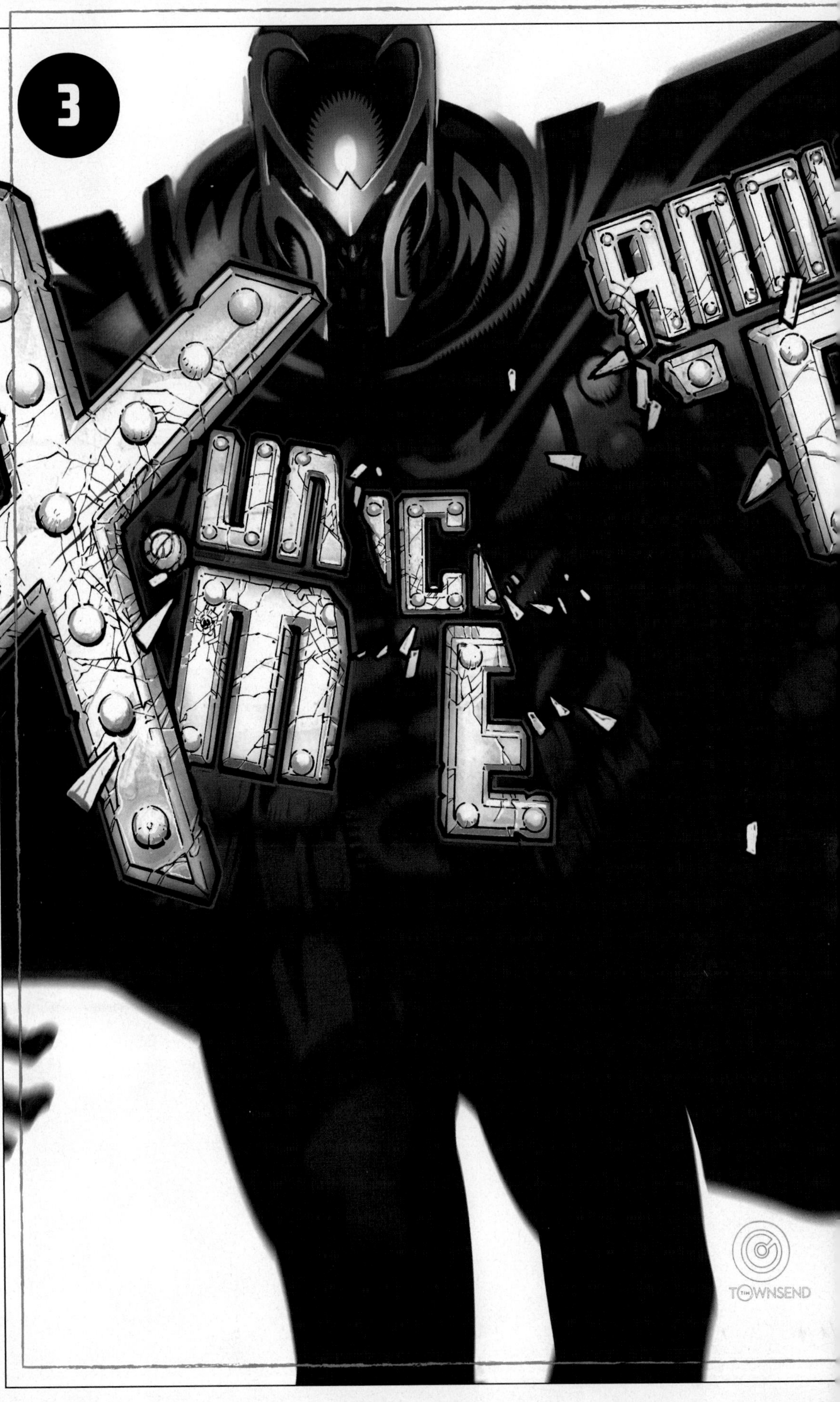
3
TOWNSEND

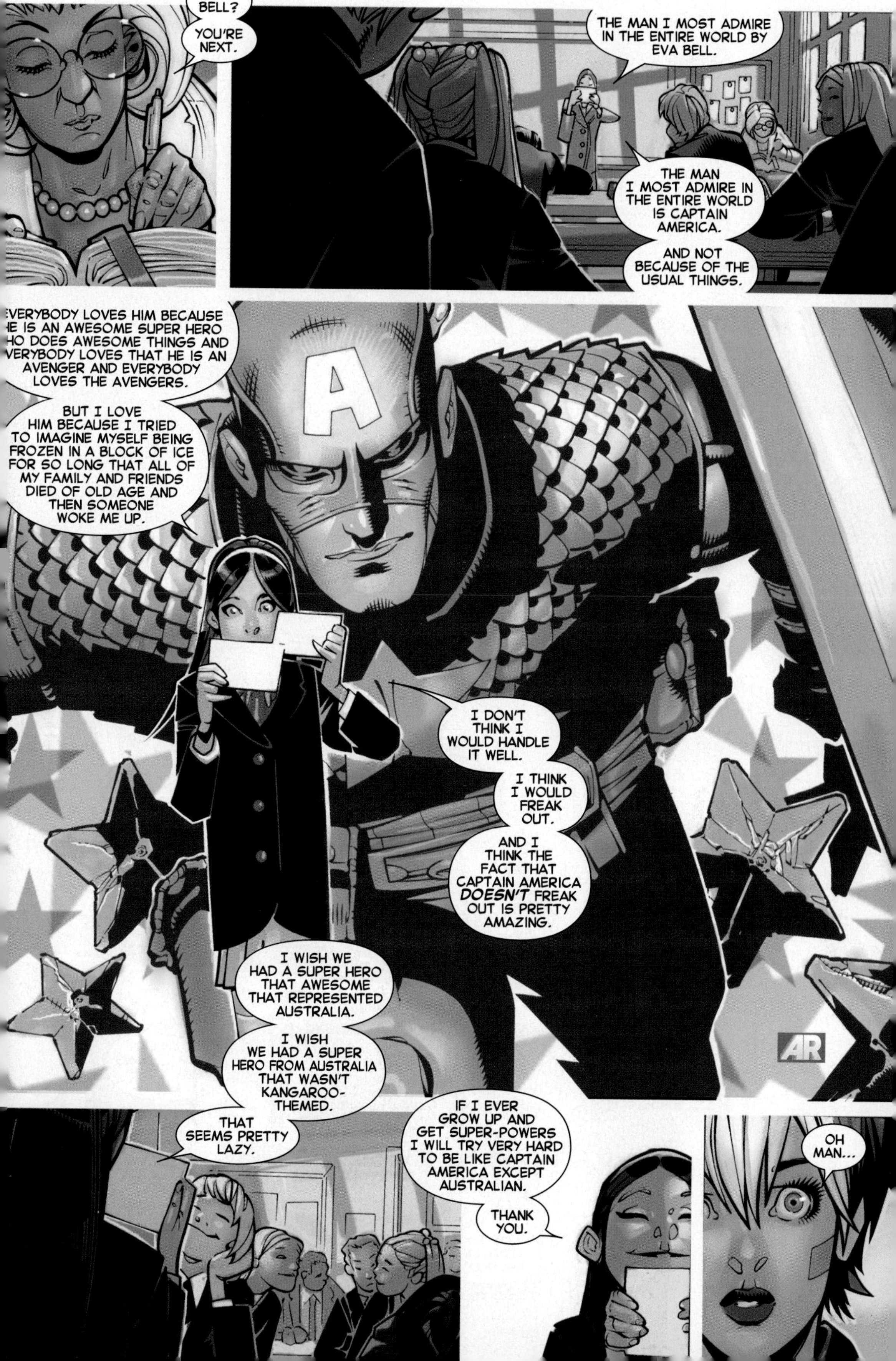
EVA BELL?
YOU'RE NEXT.
THE MAN I MOST ADMIRE IN THE ENTIRE WORLD BY EVA BELL.
THE MAN I MOST ADMIRE IN THE ENTIRE WORLD IS CAPTAIN AMERICA.
AND NOT BECAUSE OF THE USUAL THINGS.
EVERYBODY LOVES HIM BECAUSE HE IS AN AWESOME SUPER HERO WHO DOES AWESOME THINGS AND EVERYBODY LOVES THAT HE IS AN AVENGER AND EVERYBODY LOVES THE AVENGERS.
BUT I LOVE HIM BECAUSE I TRIED TO IMAGINE MYSELF BEING FROZEN IN A BLOCK OF ICE FOR SO LONG THAT ALL OF MY FAMILY AND FRIENDS DIED OF OLD AGE AND THEN SOMEONE WOKE ME UP.
I DON'T THINK I WOULD HANDLE IT WELL.
I THINK I WOULD FREAK OUT.
AND I THINK THE FACT THAT CAPTAIN AMERICA *DOESN'T* FREAK OUT IS PRETTY AMAZING.
I WISH WE HAD A SUPER HERO THAT AWESOME THAT REPRESENTED AUSTRALIA.
I WISH WE HAD A SUPER HERO FROM AUSTRALIA THAT WASN'T KANGAROO-THEMED.
THAT SEEMS PRETTY LAZY.
IF I EVER GROW UP AND GET SUPER-POWERS I WILL TRY VERY HARD TO BE LIKE CAPTAIN AMERICA EXCEPT AUSTRALIAN.
THANK YOU.
OH MAN...

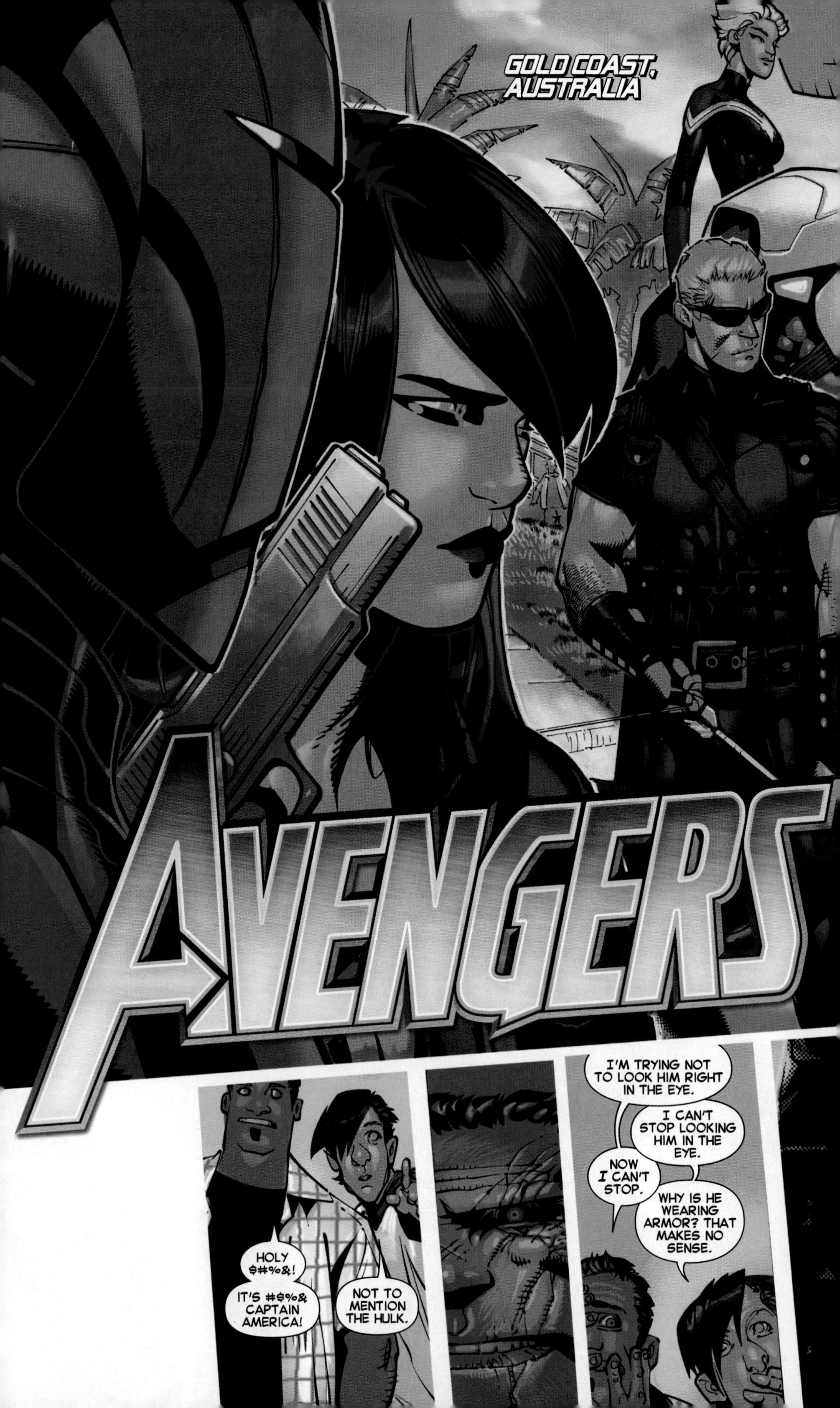
GOLD COAST, AUSTRALIA
AVENGERS
HOLY $#%&!
IT'S #$%& CAPTAIN AMERICA!
NOT TO MENTION THE HULK.
I'M TRYING NOT TO LOOK HIM RIGHT IN THE EYE.
I CAN'T STOP LOOKING HIM IN THE EYE.
NOW I CAN'T STOP.
WHY IS HE WEARING ARMOR? THAT MAKES NO SENSE.

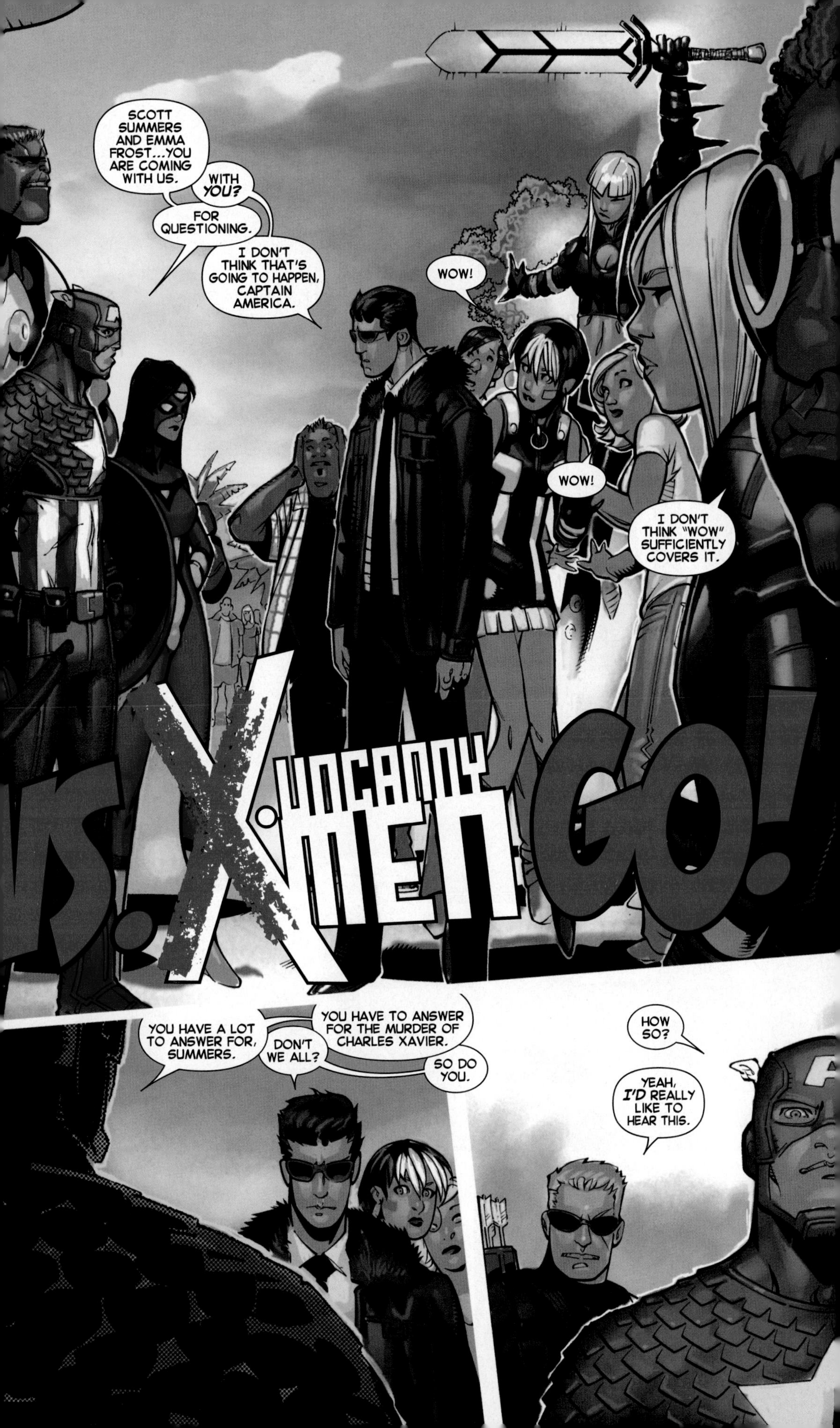
SCOTT SUMMERS AND EMMA FROST...YOU ARE COMING WITH US.
WITH YOU?
FOR QUESTIONING.
I DON'T THINK THAT'S GOING TO HAPPEN, CAPTAIN AMERICA.
WOW!
WOW!
I DON'T THINK "WOW" SUFFICIENTLY COVERS IT.
UNCANNY X-MEN
YOU HAVE A LOT TO ANSWER FOR, SUMMERS.
DON'T WE ALL?
YOU HAVE TO ANSWER FOR THE MURDER OF CHARLES XAVIER.
SO DO YOU.
HOW SO?
YEAH, I'D REALLY LIKE TO HEAR THIS.

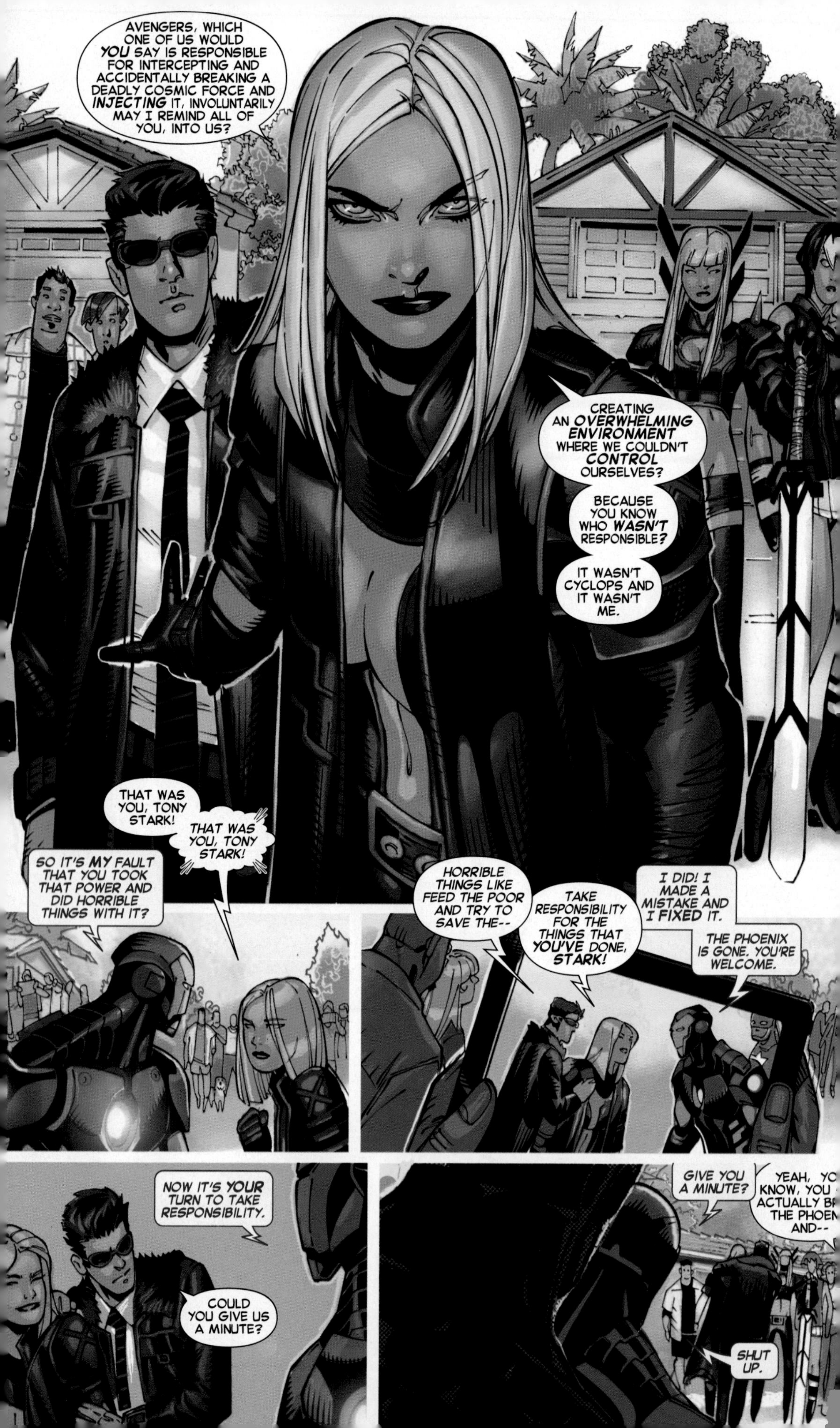

AVENGERS, WHICH ONE OF US WOULD YOU SAY IS RESPONSIBLE FOR INTERCEPTING AND ACCIDENTALLY BREAKING A DEADLY COSMIC FORCE AND INJECTING IT, INVOLUNTARILY MAY I REMIND ALL OF YOU, INTO US?
CREATING AN OVERWHELMING ENVIRONMENT WHERE WE COULDN'T CONTROL OURSELVES?
BECAUSE YOU KNOW WHO WASN'T RESPONSIBLE?
IT WASN'T CYCLOPS AND IT WASN'T ME.
THAT WAS YOU, TONY STARK!
THAT WAS YOU, TONY STARK!
SO IT'S MY FAULT THAT YOU TOOK THAT POWER AND DID HORRIBLE THINGS WITH IT?
HORRIBLE THINGS LIKE FEED THE POOR AND TRY TO SAVE THE--
TAKE RESPONSIBILITY FOR THE THINGS THAT YOU'VE DONE, STARK!
I DID! I MADE A MISTAKE AND I FIXED IT.
THE PHOENIX IS GONE. YOU'RE WELCOME.
NOW IT'S YOUR TURN TO TAKE RESPONSIBILITY.
COULD YOU GIVE US A MINUTE?
GIVE YOU A MINUTE?
SHUT UP.

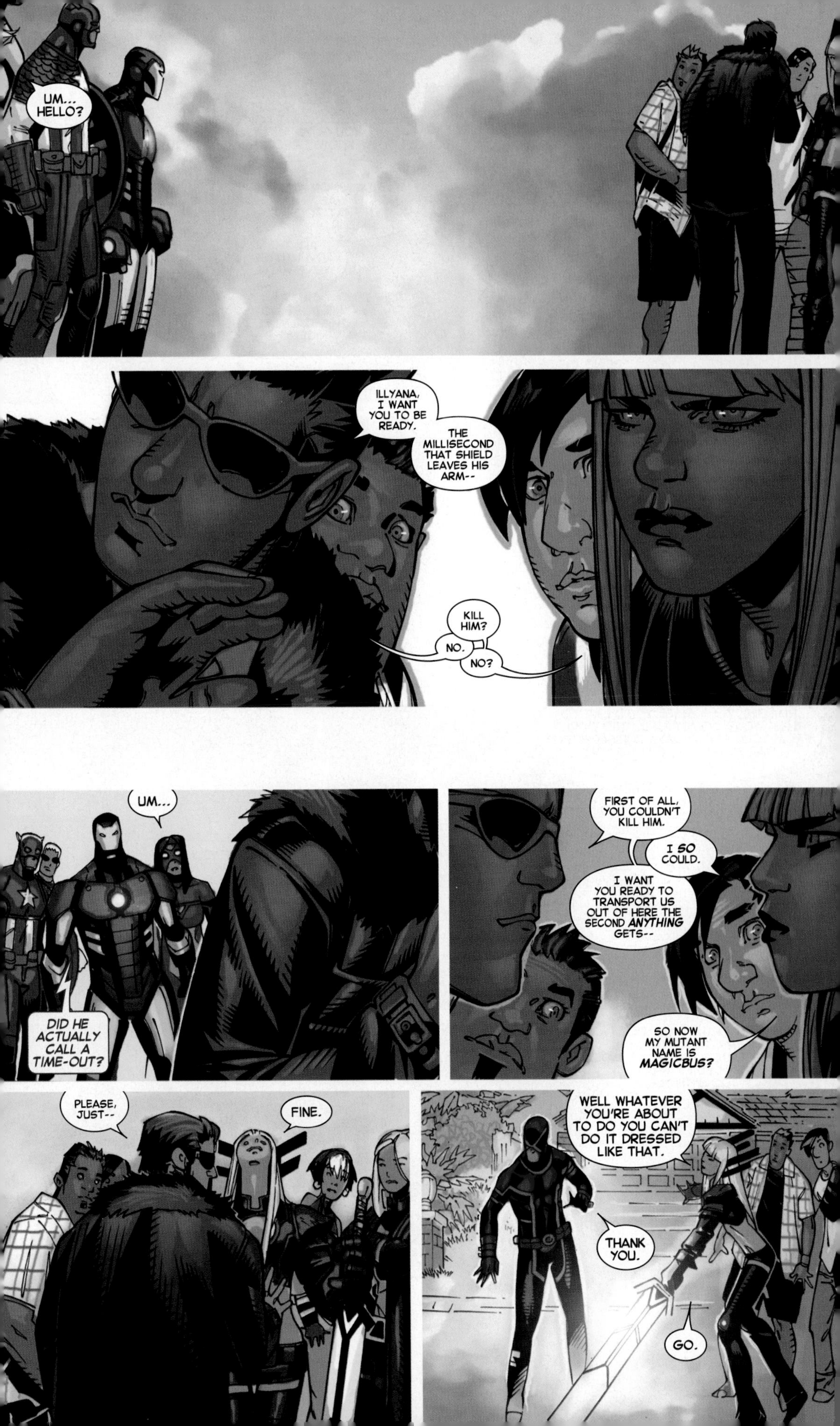
UM... HELLO?
ILLYANA, I WANT YOU TO BE READY.
THE MILLISECOND THAT SHIELD LEAVES HIS ARM--
KILL HIM?
NO.
NO?
UM...
DID HE ACTUALLY CALL A TIME-OUT?
FIRST OF ALL, YOU COULDN'T KILL HIM.
I *SO* COULD.
I WANT YOU READY TO TRANSPORT US OUT OF HERE THE SECOND *ANYTHING* GETS--
SO NOW MY MUTANT NAME IS *MAGICBUS?*
PLEASE, JUST--
FINE.
WELL WHATEVER YOU'RE ABOUT TO DO YOU CAN'T DO IT DRESSED LIKE THAT.
THANK YOU.
GO.

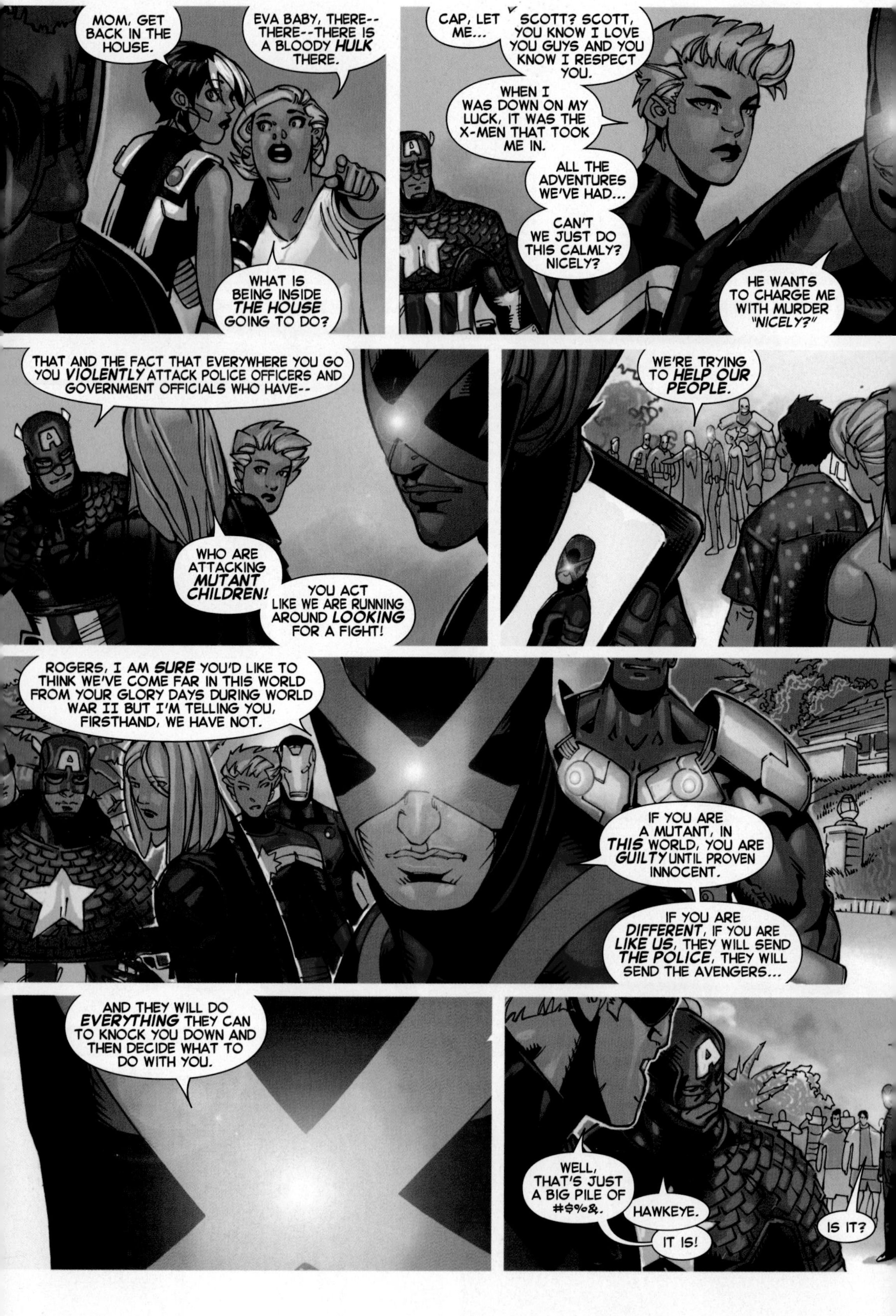
MOM, GET BACK IN THE HOUSE.
EVA BABY, THERE--THERE--THERE IS A BLOODY HULK THERE.
WHAT IS BEING INSIDE THE HOUSE GOING TO DO?
CAP, LET ME...
SCOTT? SCOTT, YOU KNOW I LOVE YOU GUYS AND YOU KNOW I RESPECT YOU.
WHEN I WAS DOWN ON MY LUCK, IT WAS THE X-MEN THAT TOOK ME IN.
ALL THE ADVENTURES WE'VE HAD...
CAN'T WE JUST DO THIS CALMLY? NICELY?
HE WANTS TO CHARGE ME WITH MURDER "NICELY?"
THAT AND THE FACT THAT EVERYWHERE YOU GO YOU VIOLENTLY ATTACK POLICE OFFICERS AND GOVERNMENT OFFICIALS WHO HAVE--
WHO ARE ATTACKING MUTANT CHILDREN!
YOU ACT LIKE WE ARE RUNNING AROUND LOOKING FOR A FIGHT!
WE'RE TRYING TO HELP OUR PEOPLE.
ROGERS, I AM SURE YOU'D LIKE TO THINK WE'VE COME FAR IN THIS WORLD FROM YOUR GLORY DAYS DURING WORLD WAR II BUT I'M TELLING YOU, FIRSTHAND, WE HAVE NOT.
IF YOU ARE A MUTANT, IN THIS WORLD, YOU ARE GUILTY UNTIL PROVEN INNOCENT.
IF YOU ARE DIFFERENT, IF YOU ARE LIKE US, THEY WILL SEND THE POLICE, THEY WILL SEND THE AVENGERS...
AND THEY WILL DO EVERYTHING THEY CAN TO KNOCK YOU DOWN AND THEN DECIDE WHAT TO DO WITH YOU.
WELL, THAT'S JUST A BIG PILE OF #$%&.
HAWKEYE.
IT IS!
IS IT?

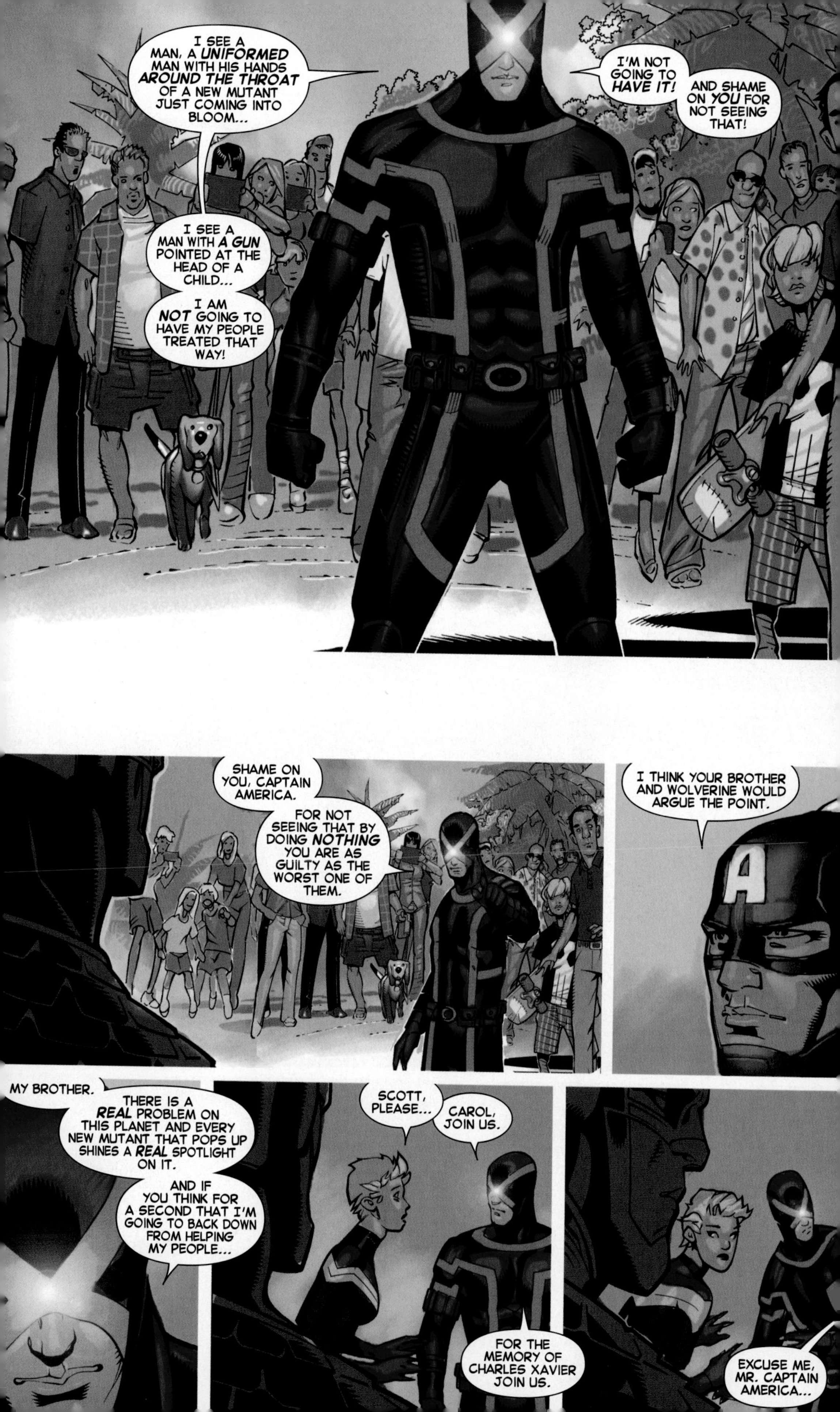

I SEE A MAN, A UNIFORMED MAN WITH HIS HANDS AROUND THE THROAT OF A NEW MUTANT JUST COMING INTO BLOOM...
I SEE A MAN WITH A GUN POINTED AT THE HEAD OF A CHILD...
I AM NOT GOING TO HAVE MY PEOPLE TREATED THAT WAY!
I'M NOT GOING TO HAVE IT!
AND SHAME ON YOU FOR NOT SEEING THAT!
SHAME ON YOU, CAPTAIN AMERICA.
FOR NOT SEEING THAT BY DOING NOTHING YOU ARE AS GUILTY AS THE WORST ONE OF THEM.
I THINK YOUR BROTHER AND WOLVERINE WOULD ARGUE THE POINT.
MY BROTHER.
THERE IS A REAL PROBLEM ON THIS PLANET AND EVERY NEW MUTANT THAT POPS UP SHINES A REAL SPOTLIGHT ON IT.
AND IF YOU THINK FOR A SECOND THAT I'M GOING TO BACK DOWN FROM HELPING MY PEOPLE...
SCOTT, PLEASE...
CAROL, JOIN US.
FOR THE MEMORY OF CHARLES XAVIER JOIN US.
EXCUSE ME, MR. CAPTAIN AMERICA...

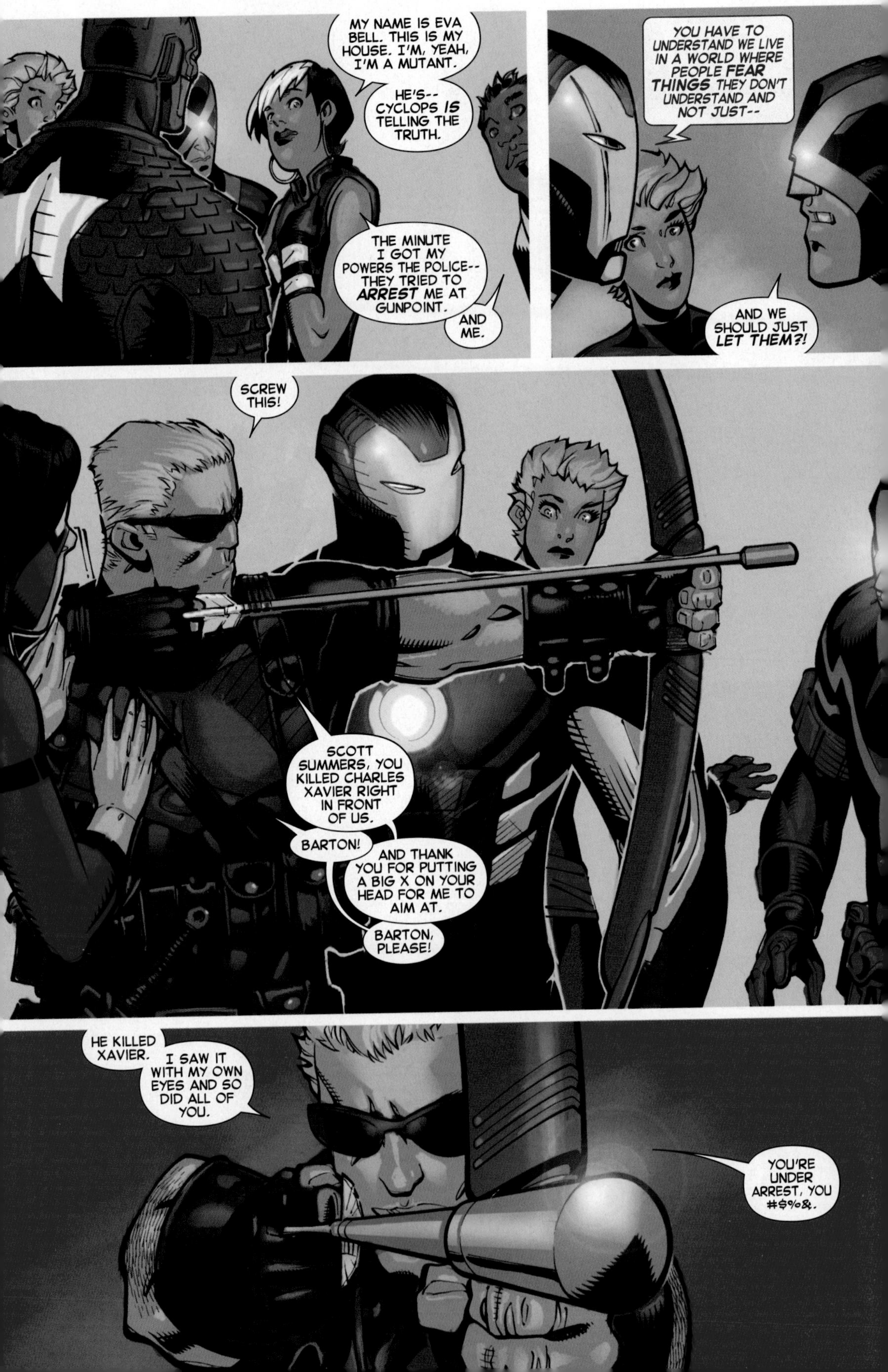
MY NAME IS EVA BELL. THIS IS MY HOUSE. I'M, YEAH, I'M A MUTANT.
HE'S-- CYCLOPS IS TELLING THE TRUTH.
THE MINUTE I GOT MY POWERS THE POLICE-- THEY TRIED TO ARREST ME AT GUNPOINT.
AND ME.
YOU HAVE TO UNDERSTAND WE LIVE IN A WORLD WHERE PEOPLE FEAR THINGS THEY DON'T UNDERSTAND AND NOT JUST--
AND WE SHOULD JUST LET THEM?!
SCREW THIS!
SCOTT SUMMERS, YOU KILLED CHARLES XAVIER RIGHT IN FRONT OF US.
BARTON!
AND THANK YOU FOR PUTTING A BIG X ON YOUR HEAD FOR ME TO AIM AT.
BARTON, PLEASE!
HE KILLED XAVIER.
I SAW IT WITH MY OWN EYES AND SO DID ALL OF YOU.
YOU'RE UNDER ARREST, YOU #$%&.

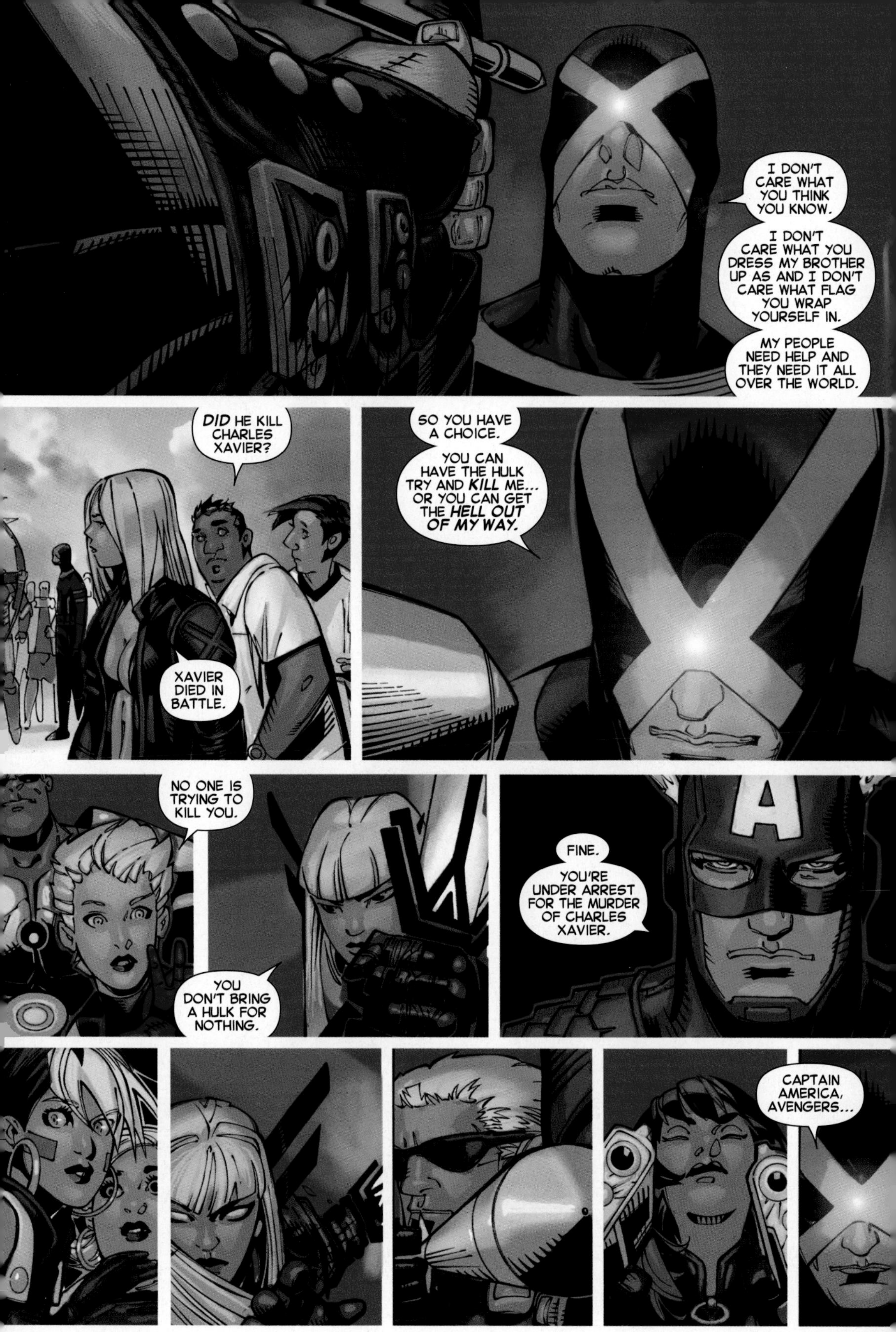
I DON'T CARE WHAT YOU THINK YOU KNOW.
I DON'T CARE WHAT YOU DRESS MY BROTHER UP AS AND I DON'T CARE WHAT FLAG YOU WRAP YOURSELF IN.
MY PEOPLE NEED HELP AND THEY NEED IT ALL OVER THE WORLD.
DID HE KILL CHARLES XAVIER?
XAVIER DIED IN BATTLE.
SO YOU HAVE A CHOICE.
YOU CAN HAVE THE HULK TRY AND KILL ME... OR YOU CAN GET THE HELL OUT OF MY WAY.
NO ONE IS TRYING TO KILL YOU.
YOU DON'T BRING A HULK FOR NOTHING.
FINE.
YOU'RE UNDER ARREST FOR THE MURDER OF CHARLES XAVIER.
CAPTAIN AMERICA, AVENGERS...

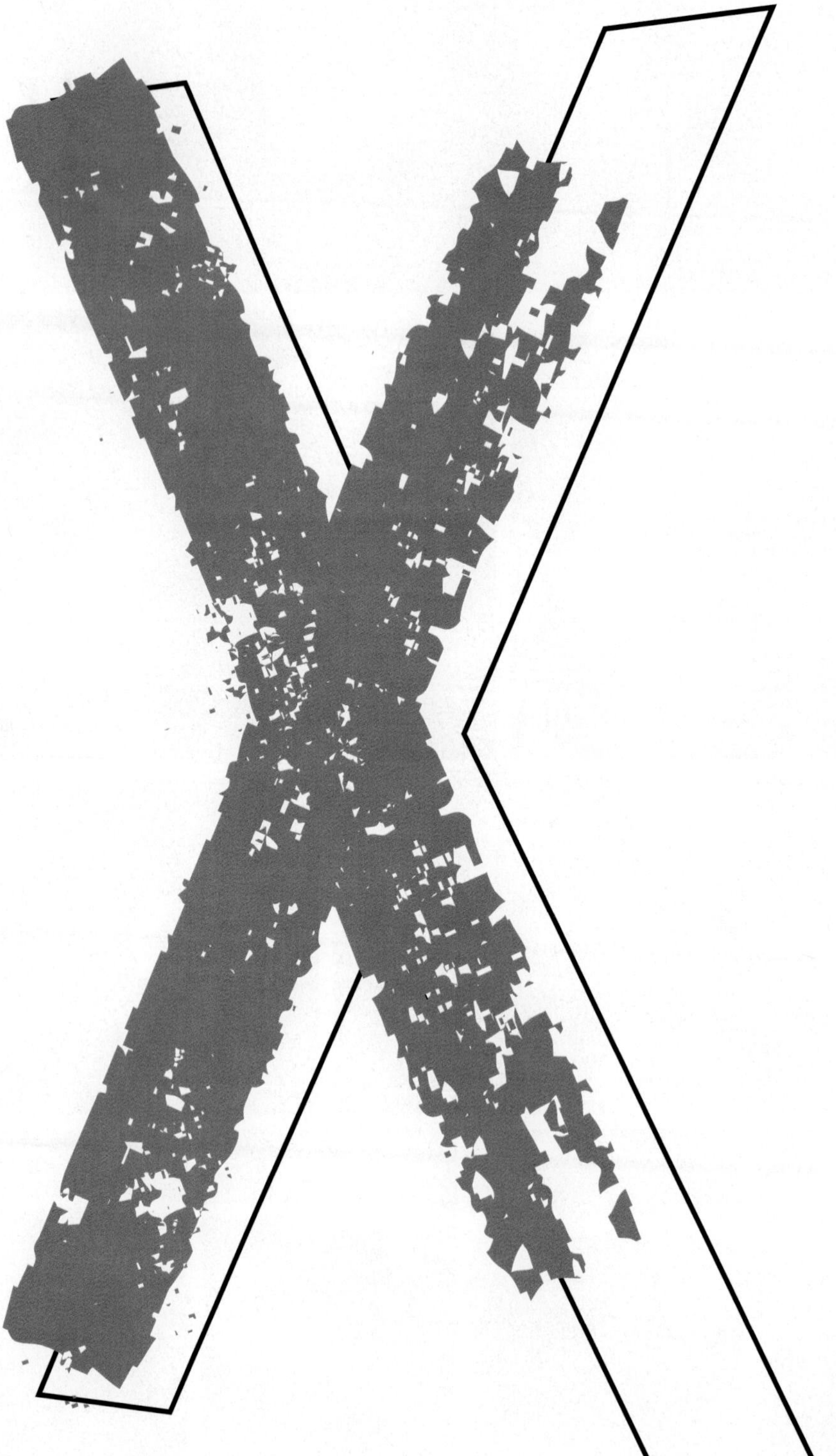

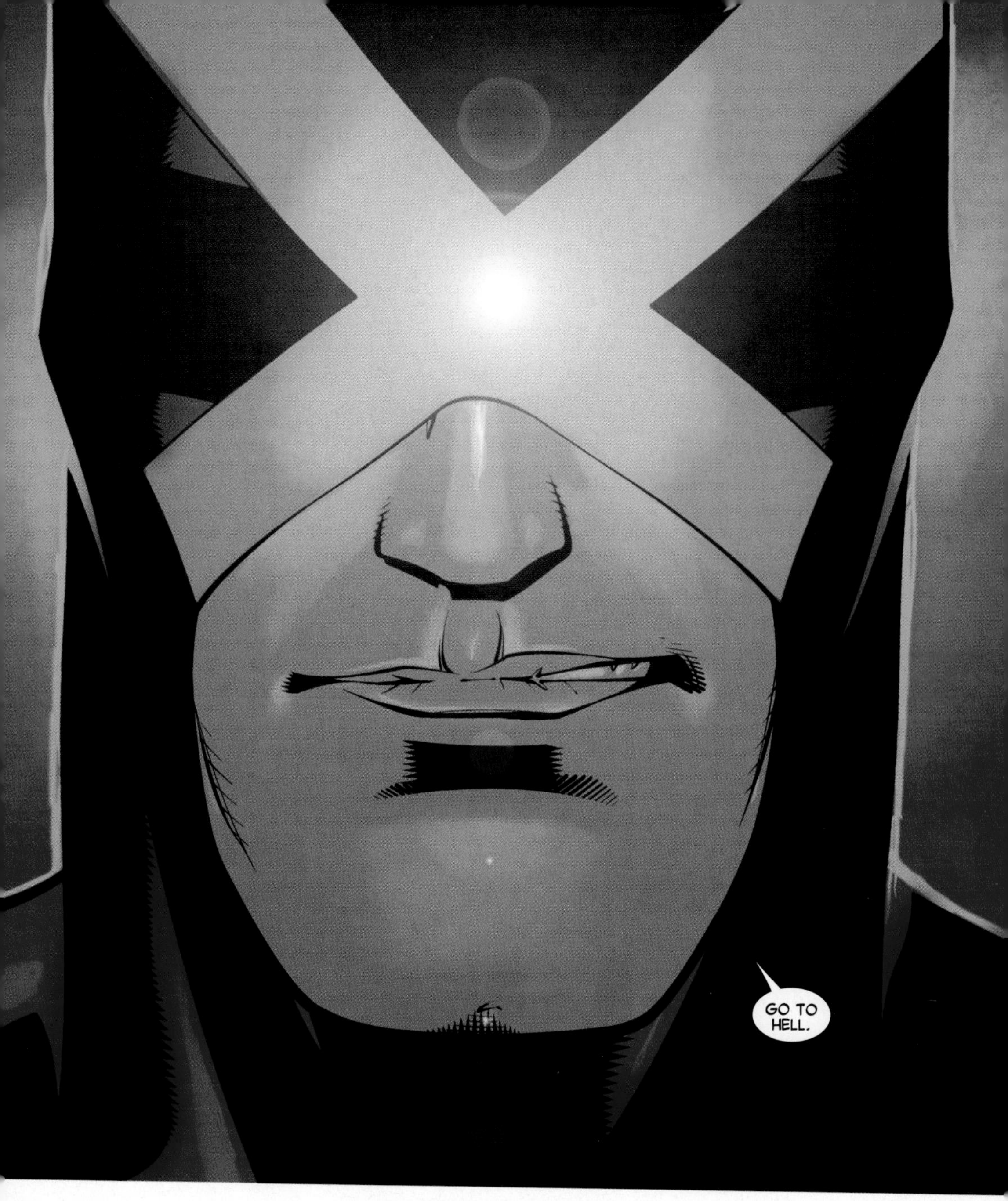
GO TO HELL.

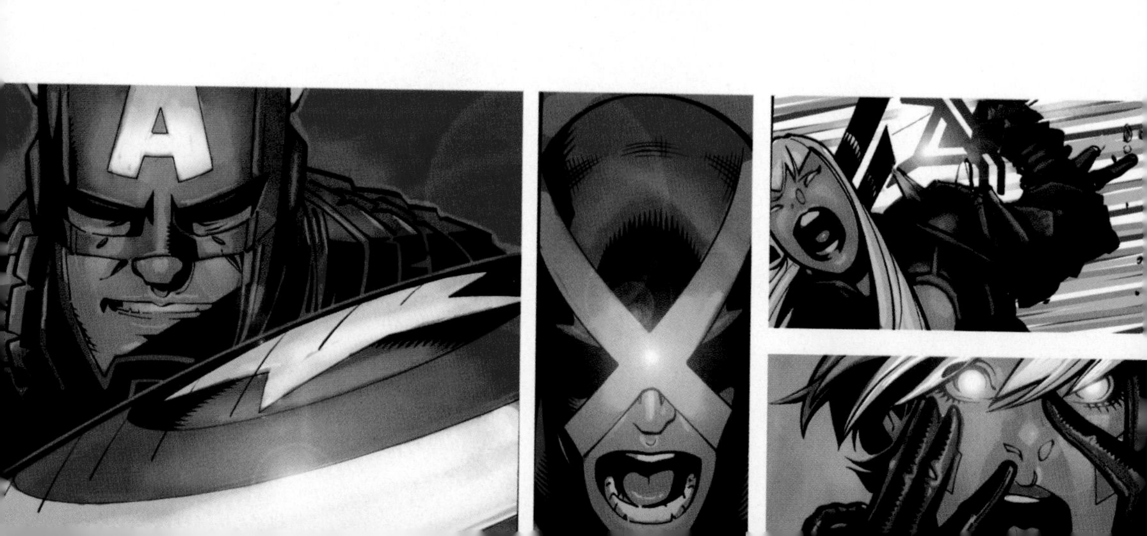

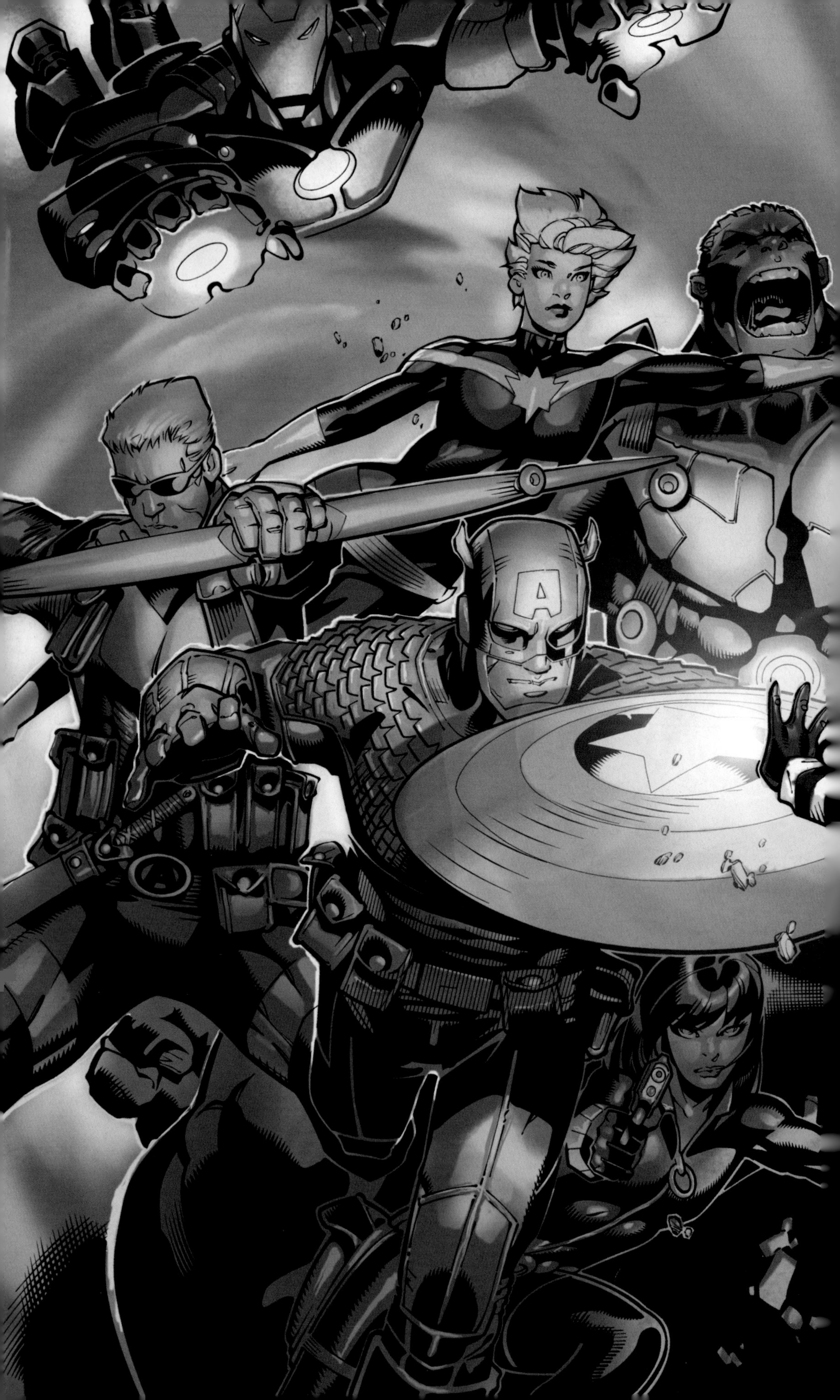

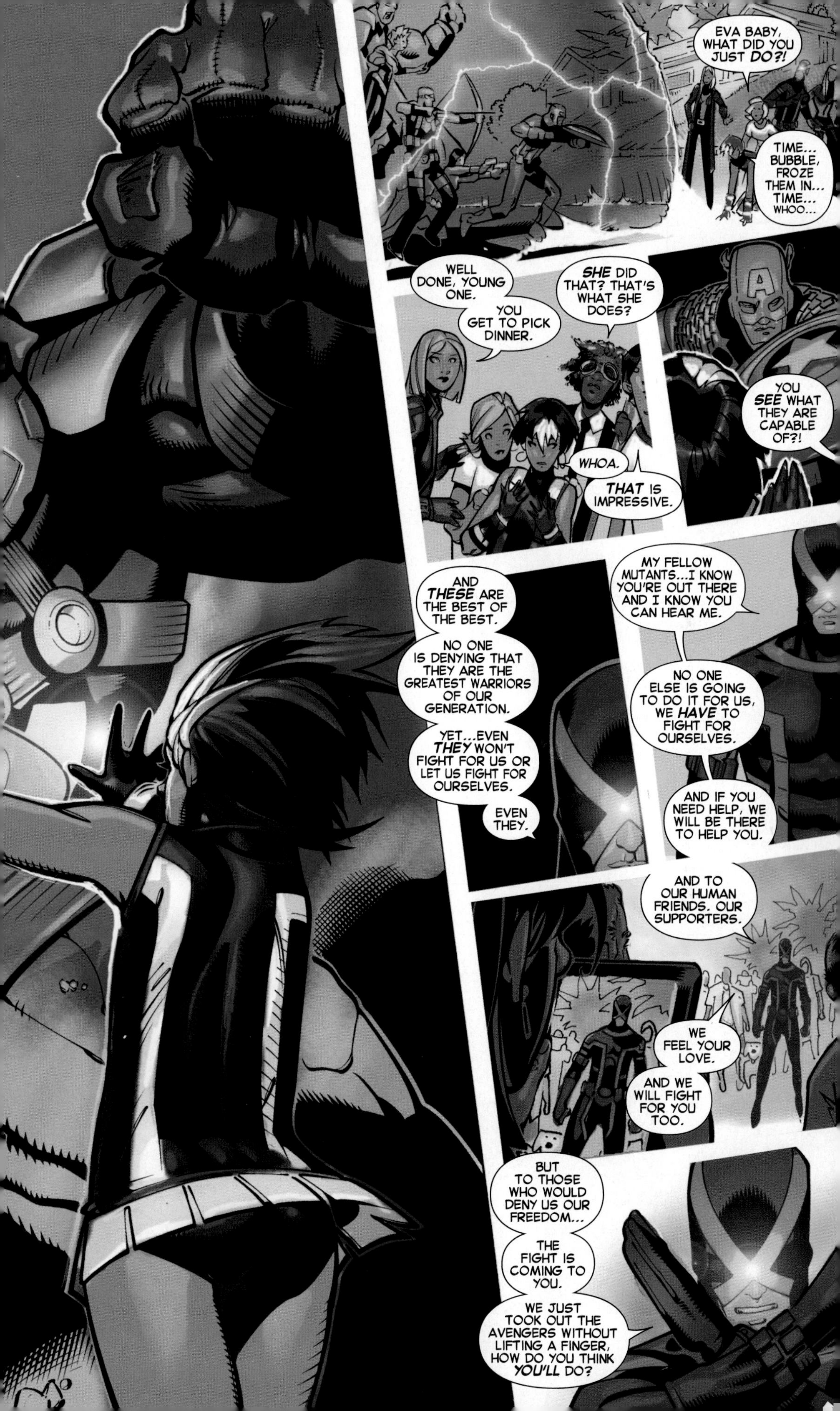
EVA BABY, WHAT DID YOU JUST DO?!
TIME... BUBBLE, FROZE THEM IN... TIME... WHOO...
WELL DONE, YOUNG ONE.
YOU GET TO PICK DINNER.
SHE DID THAT? THAT'S WHAT SHE DOES?
WHOA.
THAT IS IMPRESSIVE.
YOU SEE WHAT THEY ARE CAPABLE OF?!
AND THESE ARE THE BEST OF THE BEST.
NO ONE IS DENYING THAT THEY ARE THE GREATEST WARRIORS OF OUR GENERATION.
YET...EVEN THEY WON'T FIGHT FOR US OR LET US FIGHT FOR OURSELVES.
EVEN THEY.
MY FELLOW MUTANTS...I KNOW YOU'RE OUT THERE AND I KNOW YOU CAN HEAR ME.
NO ONE ELSE IS GOING TO DO IT FOR US, WE HAVE TO FIGHT FOR OURSELVES.
AND IF YOU NEED HELP, WE WILL BE THERE TO HELP YOU.
AND TO OUR HUMAN FRIENDS. OUR SUPPORTERS.
WE FEEL YOUR LOVE.
AND WE WILL FIGHT FOR YOU TOO.
BUT TO THOSE WHO WOULD DENY US OUR FREEDOM...
THE FIGHT IS COMING TO YOU.
WE JUST TOOK OUT THE AVENGERS WITHOUT LIFTING A FINGER, HOW DO YOU THINK YOU'LL DO?

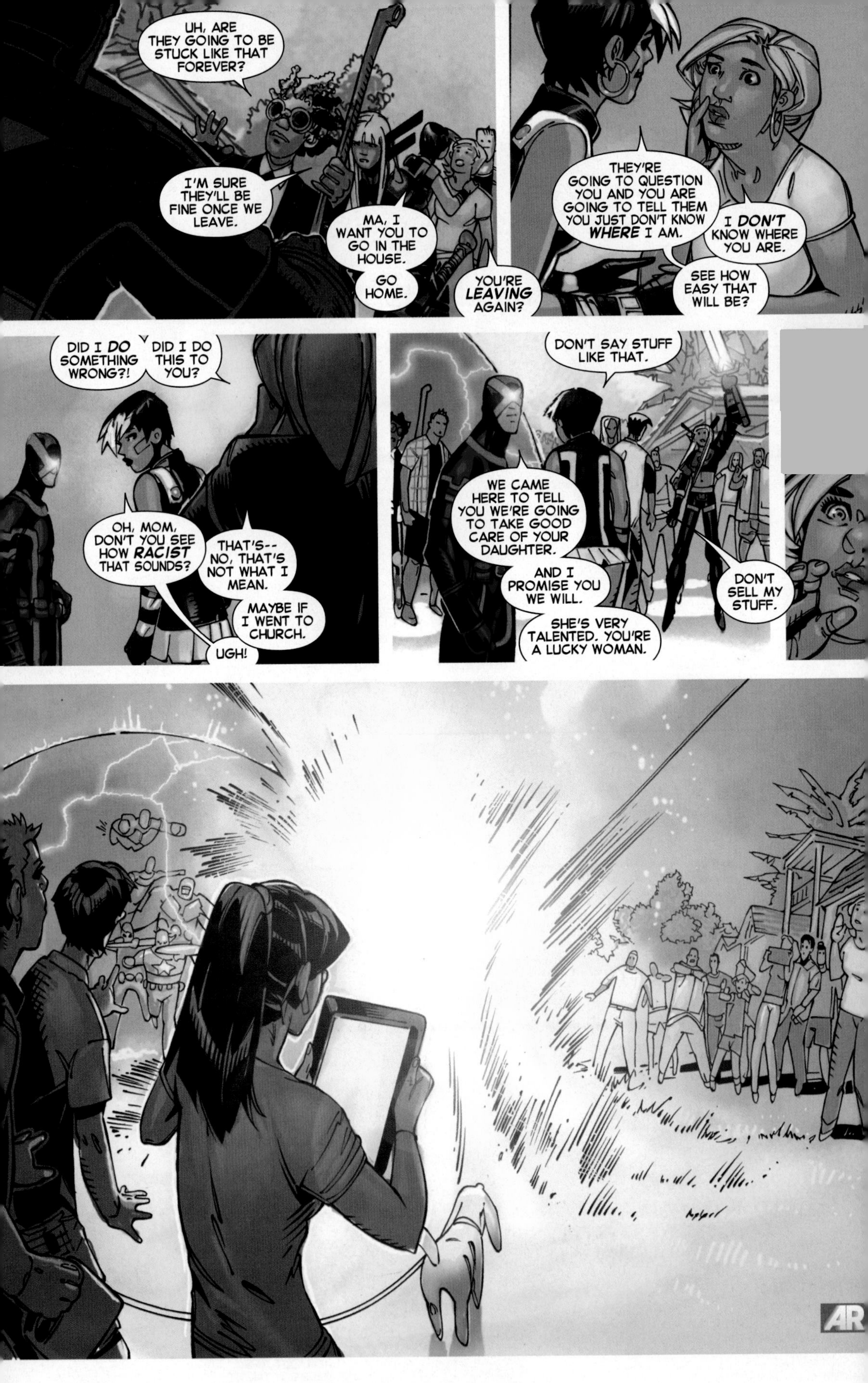
UH, ARE THEY GOING TO BE STUCK LIKE THAT FOREVER?
I'M SURE THEY'LL BE FINE ONCE WE LEAVE.
MA, I WANT YOU TO GO IN THE HOUSE.
GO HOME.
YOU'RE *LEAVING* AGAIN?
THEY'RE GOING TO QUESTION YOU AND YOU ARE GOING TO TELL THEM YOU JUST DON'T KNOW *WHERE* I AM.
I *DON'T* KNOW WHERE YOU ARE.
SEE HOW EASY THAT WILL BE?
DID I *DO* SOMETHING WRONG?!
DID I DO THIS TO YOU?
OH, MOM, DON'T YOU SEE HOW *RACIST* THAT SOUNDS?
THAT'S-- NO, THAT'S NOT WHAT I MEAN.
MAYBE IF I WENT TO CHURCH.
UGH!
DON'T SAY STUFF LIKE THAT.
WE CAME HERE TO TELL YOU WE'RE GOING TO TAKE GOOD CARE OF YOUR DAUGHTER.
AND I PROMISE YOU WE WILL.
SHE'S VERY TALENTED. YOU'RE A LUCKY WOMAN.
DON'T SELL MY STUFF.
AR

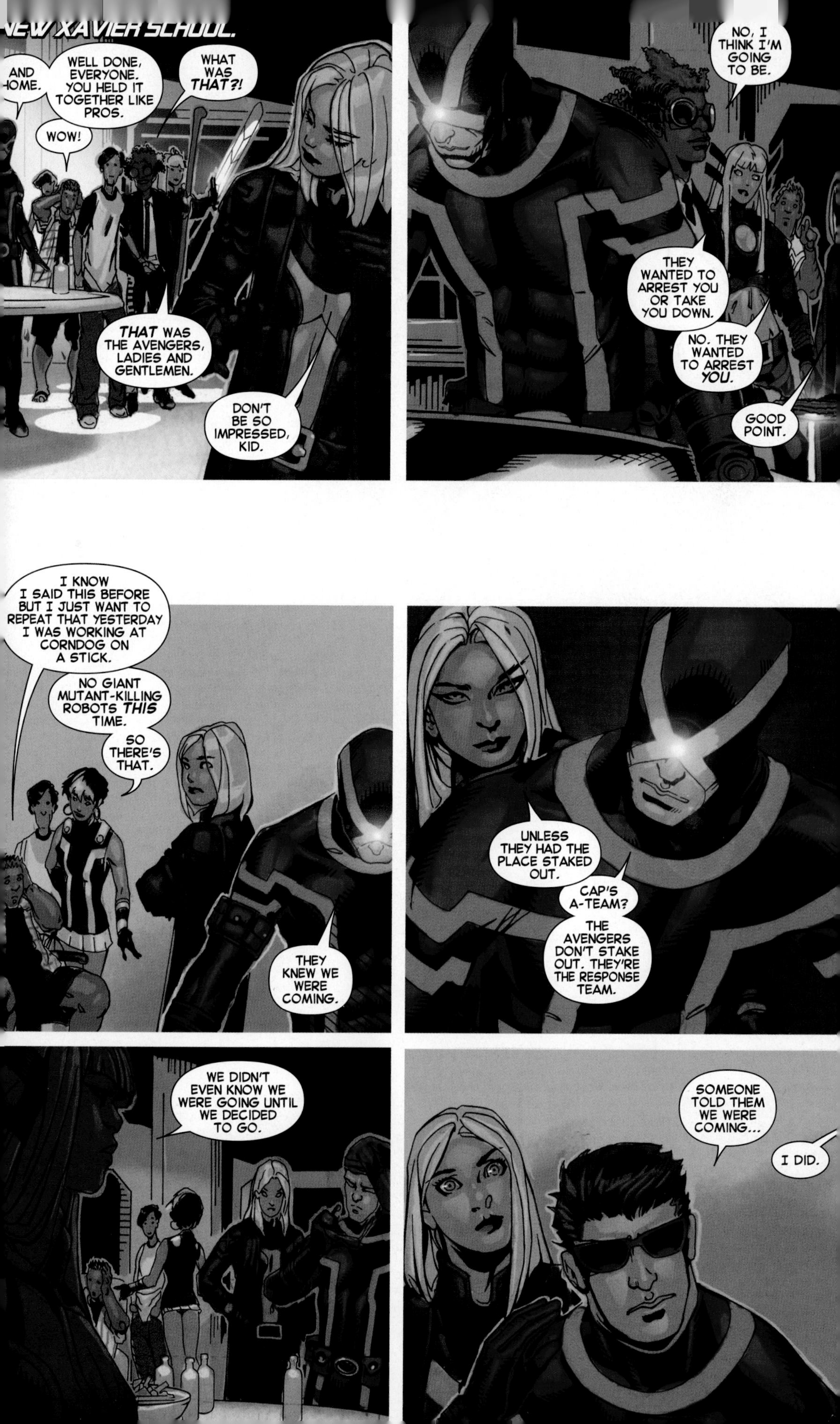

NEW XAVIER SCHOOL.
AND HOME.
WELL DONE, EVERYONE. YOU HELD IT TOGETHER LIKE PROS.
WOW!
WHAT WAS THAT?!
THAT WAS THE AVENGERS, LADIES AND GENTLEMEN.
DON'T BE SO IMPRESSED, KID.
NO, I THINK I'M GOING TO BE.
THEY WANTED TO ARREST YOU OR TAKE YOU DOWN.
NO. THEY WANTED TO ARREST YOU.
GOOD POINT.
I KNOW I SAID THIS BEFORE BUT I JUST WANT TO REPEAT THAT YESTERDAY I WAS WORKING AT CORNDOG ON A STICK.
NO GIANT MUTANT-KILLING ROBOTS THIS TIME.
SO THERE'S THAT.
THEY KNEW WE WERE COMING.
UNLESS THEY HAD THE PLACE STAKED OUT.
CAP'S A-TEAM?
THE AVENGERS DON'T STAKE OUT. THEY'RE THE RESPONSE TEAM.
WE DIDN'T EVEN KNOW WE WERE GOING UNTIL WE DECIDED TO GO.
SOMEONE TOLD THEM WE WERE COMING...
I DID.

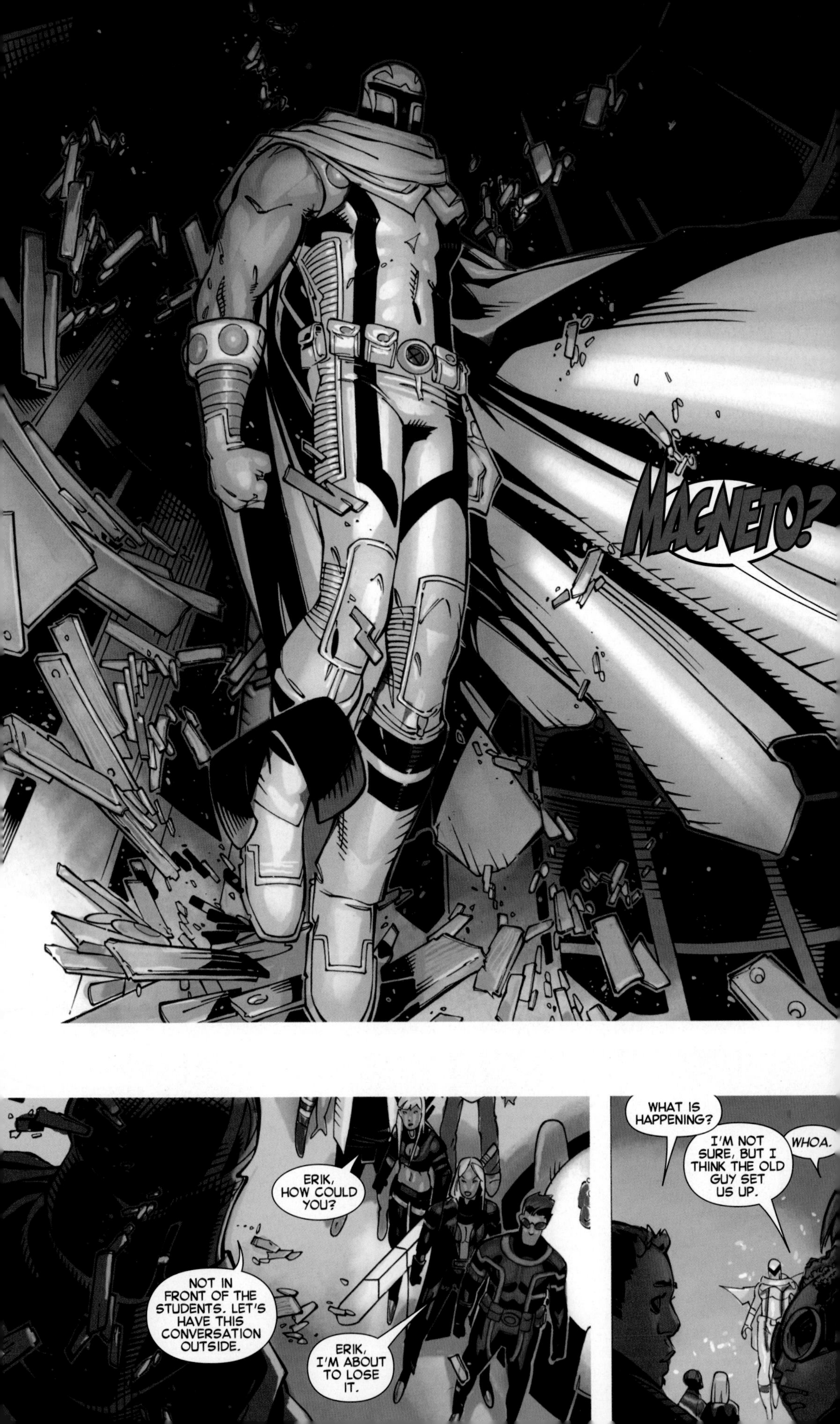
MAGNETO?
ERIK, HOW COULD YOU?
...
NOT IN FRONT OF THE STUDENTS. LET'S HAVE THIS CONVERSATION OUTSIDE.
ERIK, I'M ABOUT TO LOSE IT.
WHAT IS HAPPENING?
I'M NOT SURE, BUT I THINK THE OLD GUY SET US UP.
WHOA.

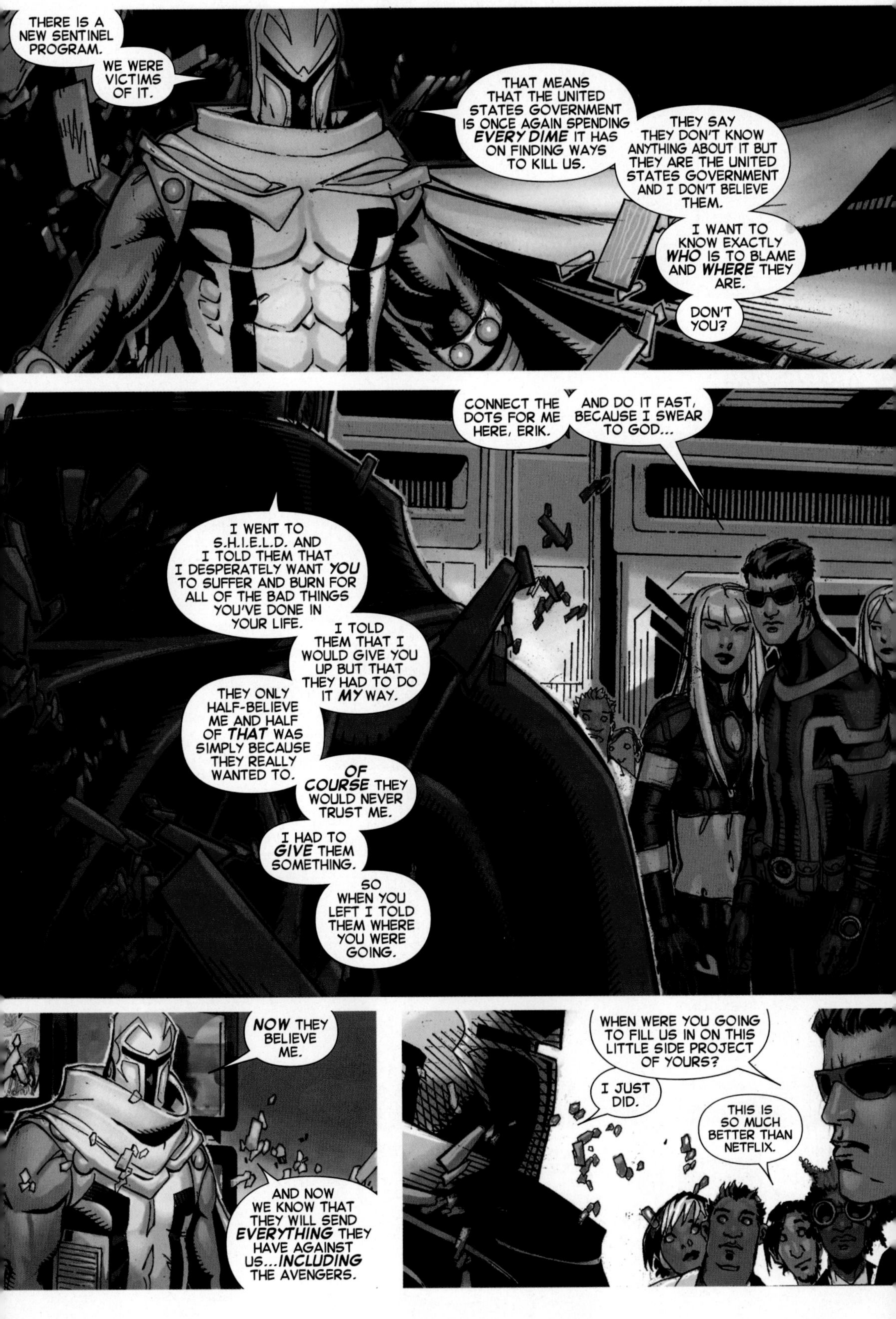

THERE IS A NEW SENTINEL PROGRAM.
WE WERE VICTIMS OF IT.
THAT MEANS THAT THE UNITED STATES GOVERNMENT IS ONCE AGAIN SPENDING EVERY DIME IT HAS ON FINDING WAYS TO KILL US.
THEY SAY THEY DON'T KNOW ANYTHING ABOUT IT BUT THEY ARE THE UNITED STATES GOVERNMENT AND I DON'T BELIEVE THEM.
I WANT TO KNOW EXACTLY WHO IS TO BLAME AND WHERE THEY ARE.
DON'T YOU?
CONNECT THE DOTS FOR ME HERE, ERIK.
AND DO IT FAST, BECAUSE I SWEAR TO GOD...
I WENT TO S.H.I.E.L.D. AND I TOLD THEM THAT I DESPERATELY WANT YOU TO SUFFER AND BURN FOR ALL OF THE BAD THINGS YOU'VE DONE IN YOUR LIFE.
I TOLD THEM THAT I WOULD GIVE YOU UP BUT THAT THEY HAD TO DO IT MY WAY.
THEY ONLY HALF-BELIEVE ME AND HALF OF THAT WAS SIMPLY BECAUSE THEY REALLY WANTED TO.
OF COURSE THEY WOULD NEVER TRUST ME.
I HAD TO GIVE THEM SOMETHING.
SO WHEN YOU LEFT I TOLD THEM WHERE YOU WERE GOING.
NOW THEY BELIEVE ME.
AND NOW WE KNOW THAT THEY WILL SEND EVERYTHING THEY HAVE AGAINST US...INCLUDING THE AVENGERS.
WHEN WERE YOU GOING TO FILL US IN ON THIS LITTLE SIDE PROJECT OF YOURS?
I JUST DID.
THIS IS SO MUCH BETTER THAN NETFLIX.

THIS IS UNACCEPTABLE, ERIK.

I THINK IT'S BEST THAT YOU LEAVE.

NO... IT'S-- IT'S PRETTY MUCH BRILLIANT.

IF I TOLD YOU BEFORE NOW, YOU WOULD'VE BLOWN MY COVER.

IF THEY HAD A PSYCHIC WITH THEM... I NEEDED YOU TO BE YOU.

NOW THEY KNOW THEY CAN TRUST ME.

NOW, WHILE THEY ARE TRYING TO GET YOU FROM ME I WILL GET THINGS FROM THEM.

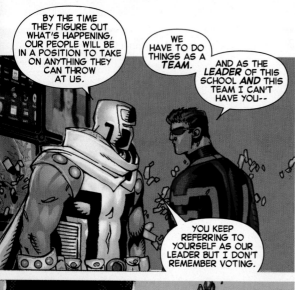

BY THE TIME THEY FIGURE OUT WHAT'S HAPPENING, OUR PEOPLE WILL BE IN A POSITION TO TAKE ON ANYTHING THEY CAN THROW AT US.

WE HAVE TO DO THINGS AS A TEAM.

AND AS THE LEADER OF THIS SCHOOL AND THIS TEAM I CAN'T HAVE YOU--

YOU KEEP REFERRING TO YOURSELF AS OUR LEADER BUT I DON'T REMEMBER VOTING.

I THINK YOU'RE ONLY TELLING US THIS NOW BECAUSE A CHILD COULD FIGURE OUT IT WAS YOU WHO SOLD US OUT.

THE HOMO SAPIENS ARE LOOKING TO DESTROY US.

IF OUR POWERS ARE BROKEN THEN WE HAVE TO BE TWICE AS SMART.

WE HAVE TO DO THINGS THEY DON'T EXPECT.

WE HAVE TO SURPRISE EVEN OURSELVES.

I THINK, ALL THINGS CONSIDERED, THIS WENT VERY WELL.

YOUNG LADY, YOU ARE A POWERFUL MUTANT.

I HAVE NO IDEA HOW I DID THAT.

IT'S TIME TO START YOUR TRAINING.

OH NO... MY MOM'S ON TELEVISION.

MY DAUGHTER IS A GOOD GIRL.

AND--AND-- AND THIS SCOTT SUMMERS MADE SOME GOOD POINTS.

THE AVENGERS AND ALL THAT--THEY SEEM AWFULLY THREATENED.

METOWN MUTANT DRA

I WISH YOU COULD STILL READ MINDS.

YOU SAY THAT NOW, BUT COME VALENTINE'S DAY...

WHAT DO I DO HERE? WHAT DO I DO WITH HIM?

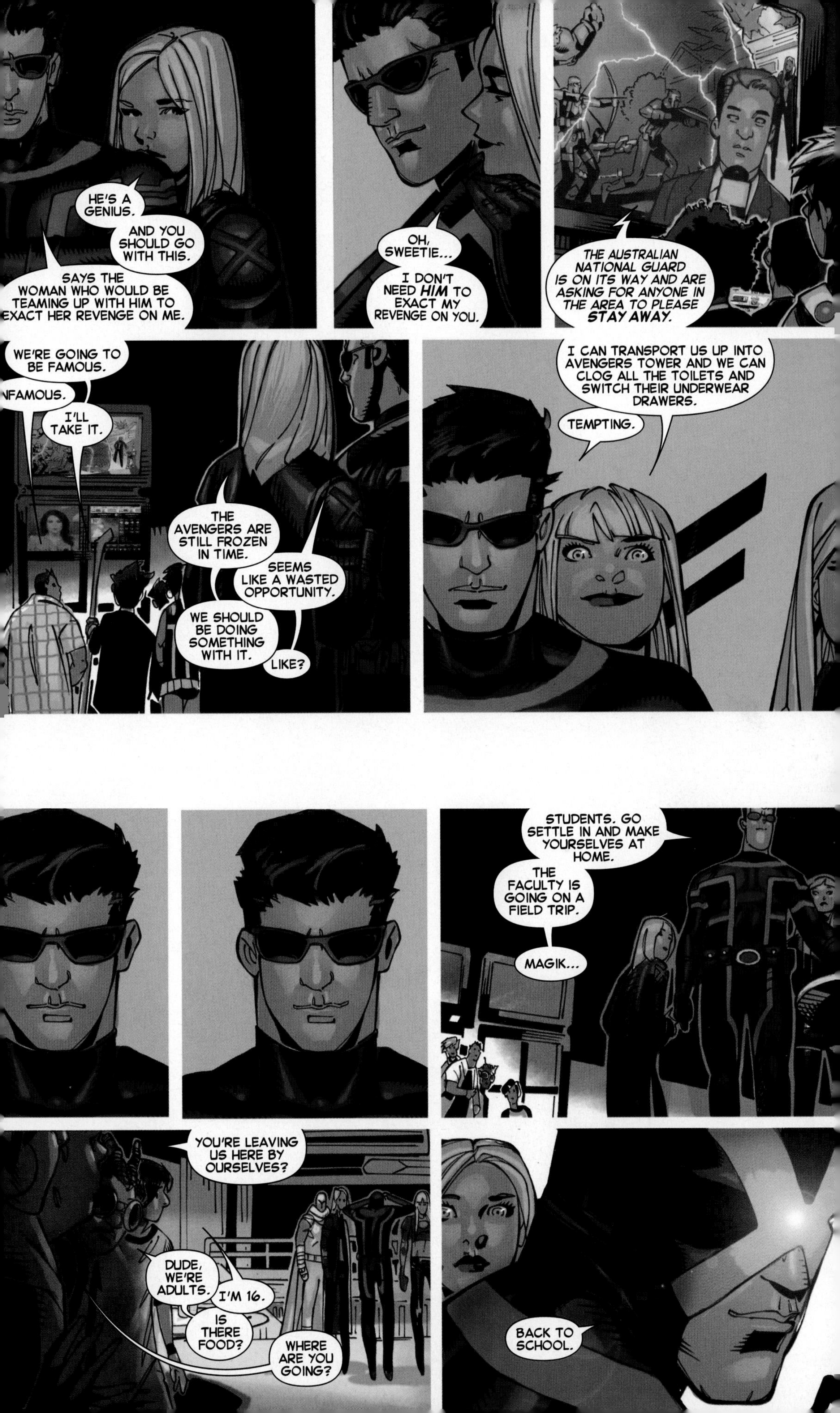
HE'S A GENIUS.
AND YOU SHOULD GO WITH THIS.
SAYS THE WOMAN WHO WOULD BE TEAMING UP WITH HIM TO EXACT HER REVENGE ON ME.
OH, SWEETIE...
I DON'T NEED HIM TO EXACT MY REVENGE ON YOU.
THE AUSTRALIAN NATIONAL GUARD IS ON ITS WAY AND ARE ASKING FOR ANYONE IN THE AREA TO PLEASE STAY AWAY.
WE'RE GOING TO BE FAMOUS.
NFAMOUS.
I'LL TAKE IT.
THE AVENGERS ARE STILL FROZEN IN TIME.
SEEMS LIKE A WASTED OPPORTUNITY.
WE SHOULD BE DOING SOMETHING WITH IT.
LIKE?
I CAN TRANSPORT US UP INTO AVENGERS TOWER AND WE CAN CLOG ALL THE TOILETS AND SWITCH THEIR UNDERWEAR DRAWERS.
TEMPTING.
STUDENTS. GO SETTLE IN AND MAKE YOURSELVES AT HOME.
THE FACULTY IS GOING ON A FIELD TRIP.
MAGIK...
YOU'RE LEAVING US HERE BY OURSELVES?
DUDE, WE'RE ADULTS.
I'M 16.
IS THERE FOOD?
WHERE ARE YOU GOING?
BACK TO SCHOOL.

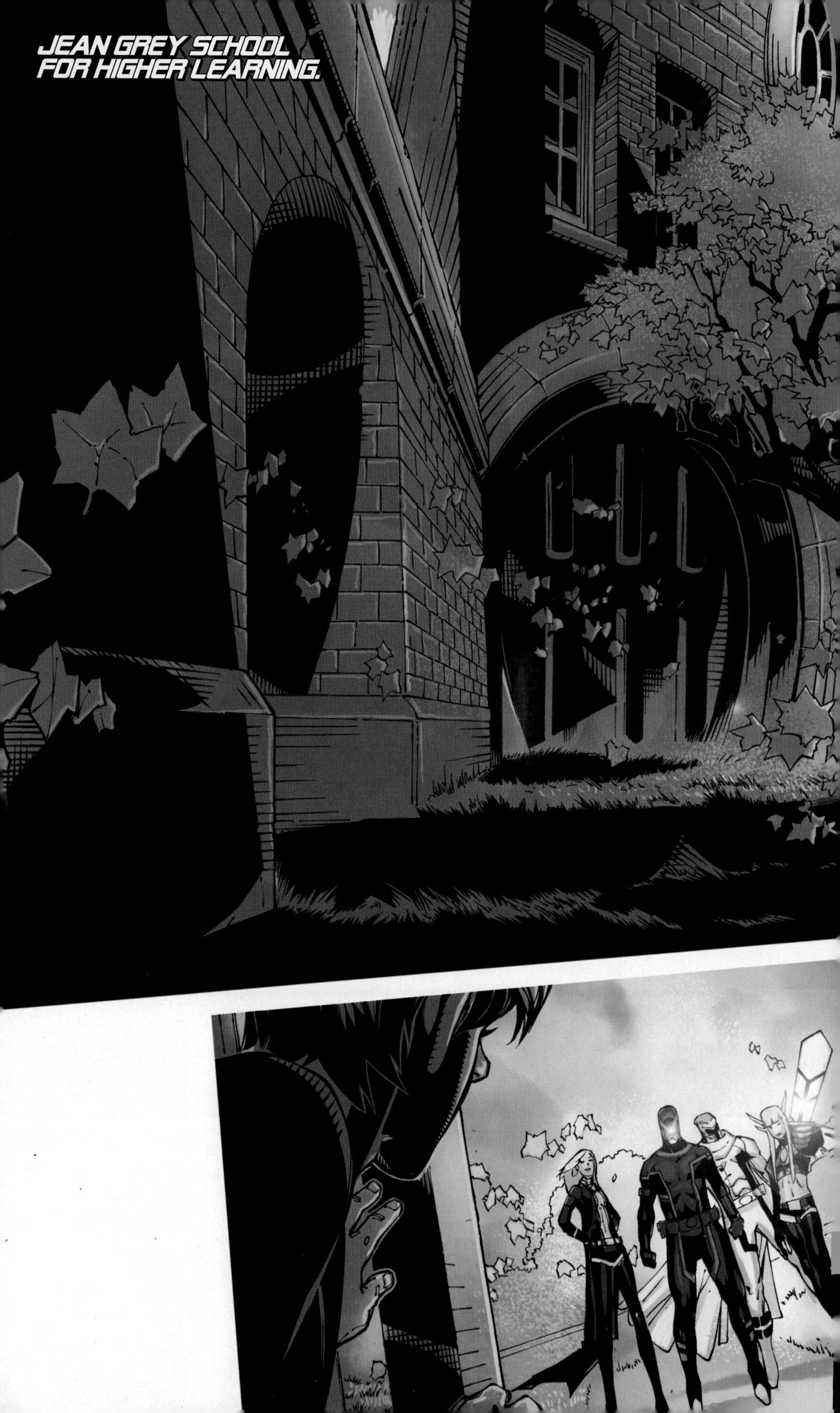
JEAN GREY SCHOOL FOR HIGHER LEARNING.

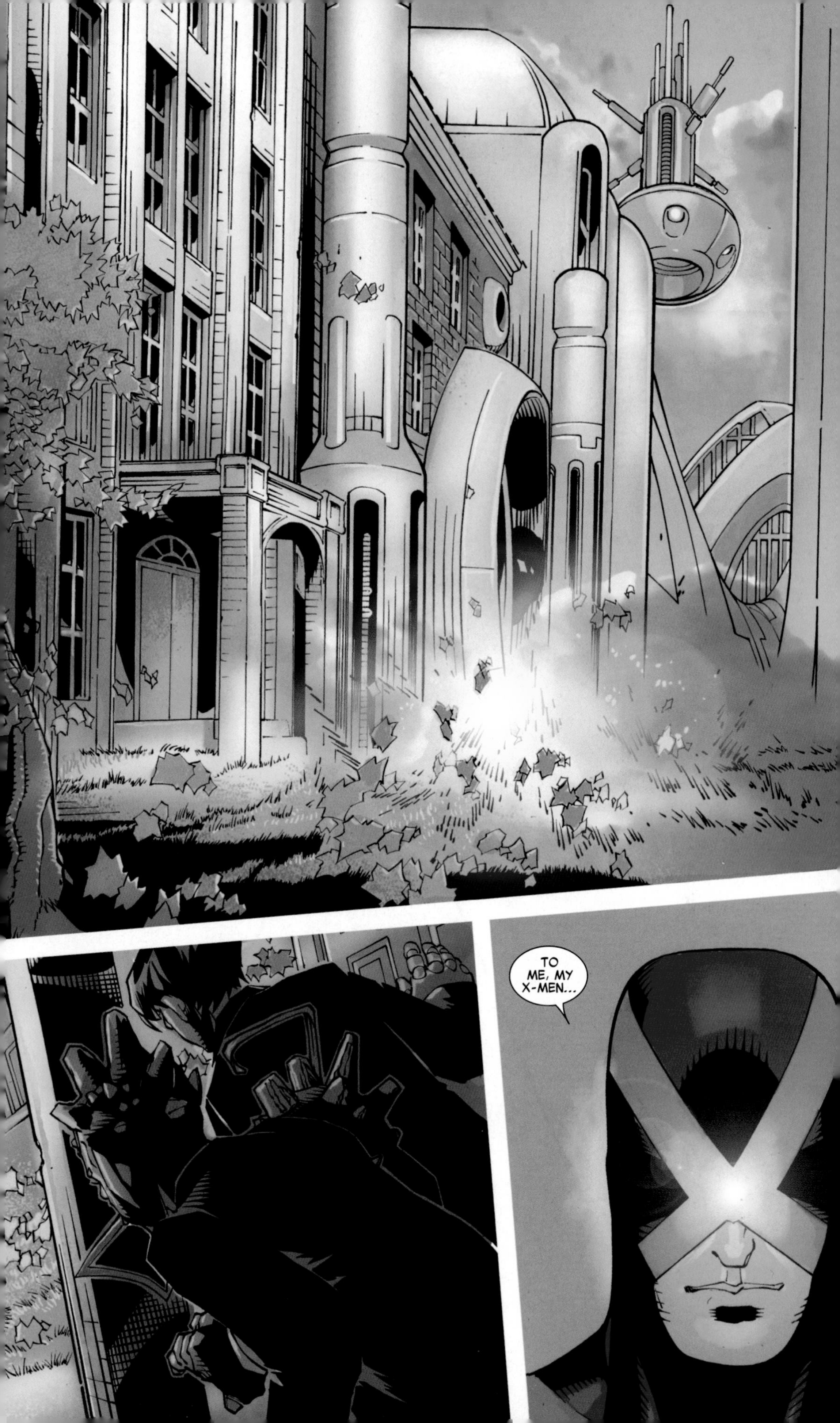
TO ME, MY X-MEN...

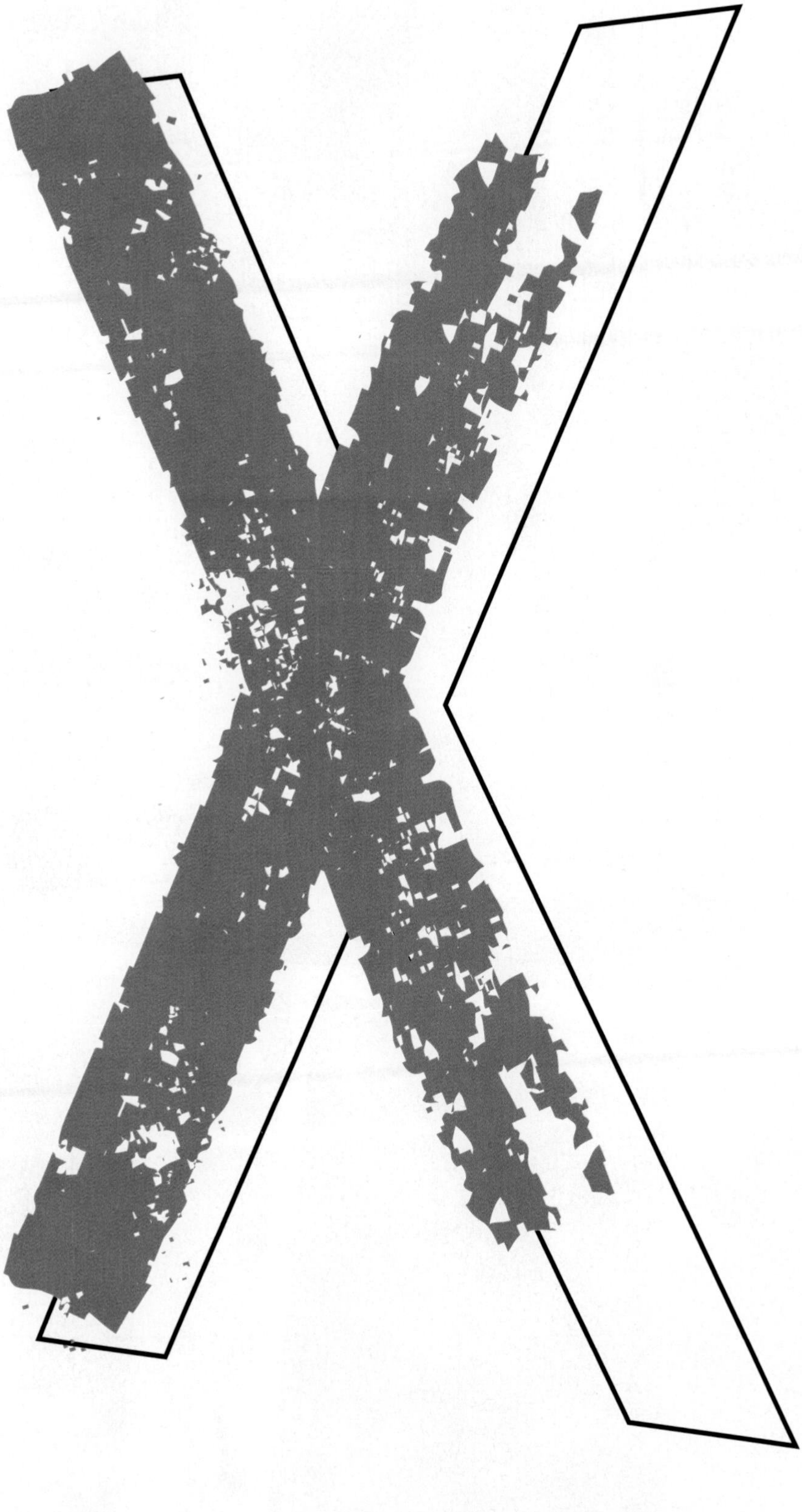

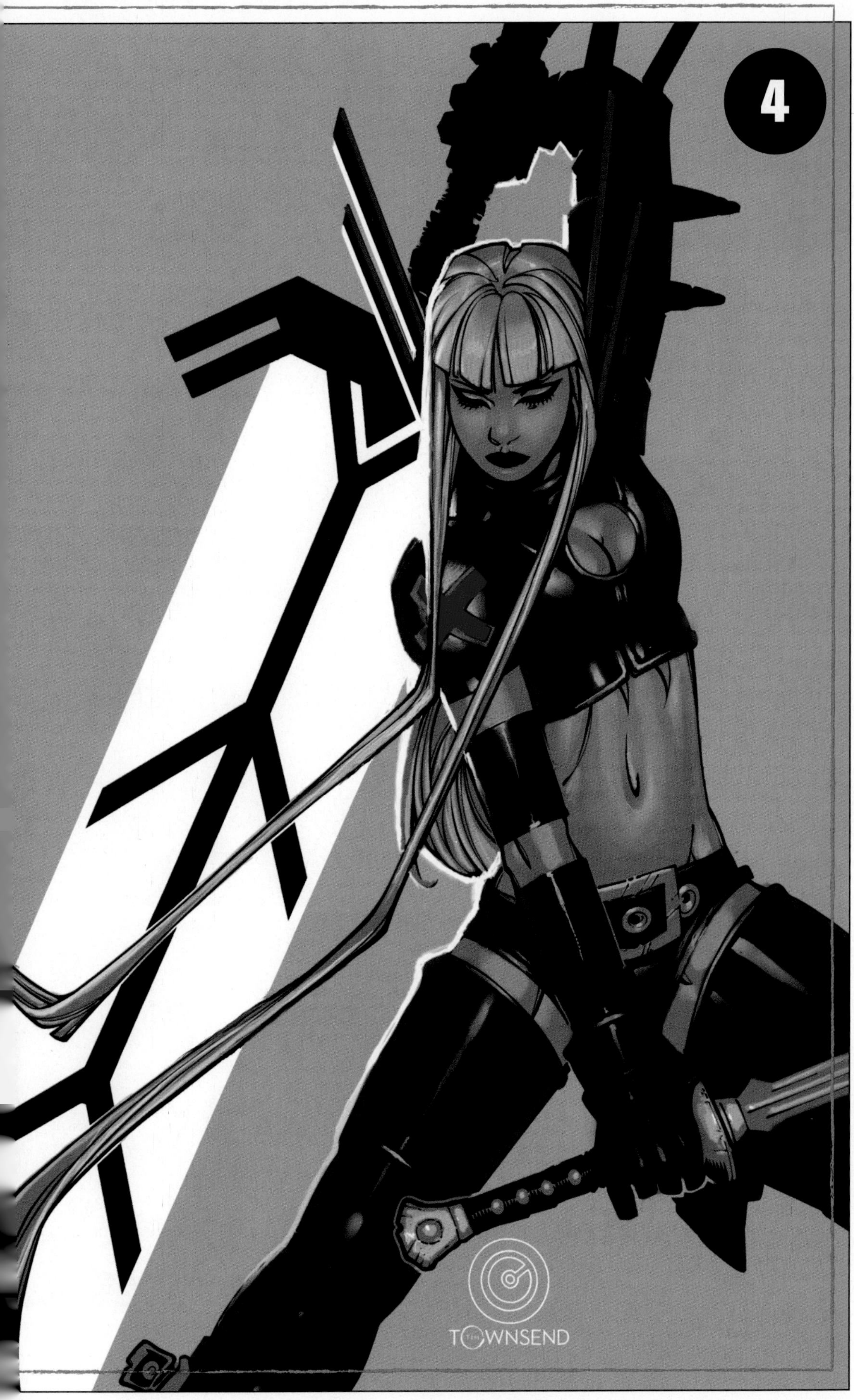
4
TOWNSEND

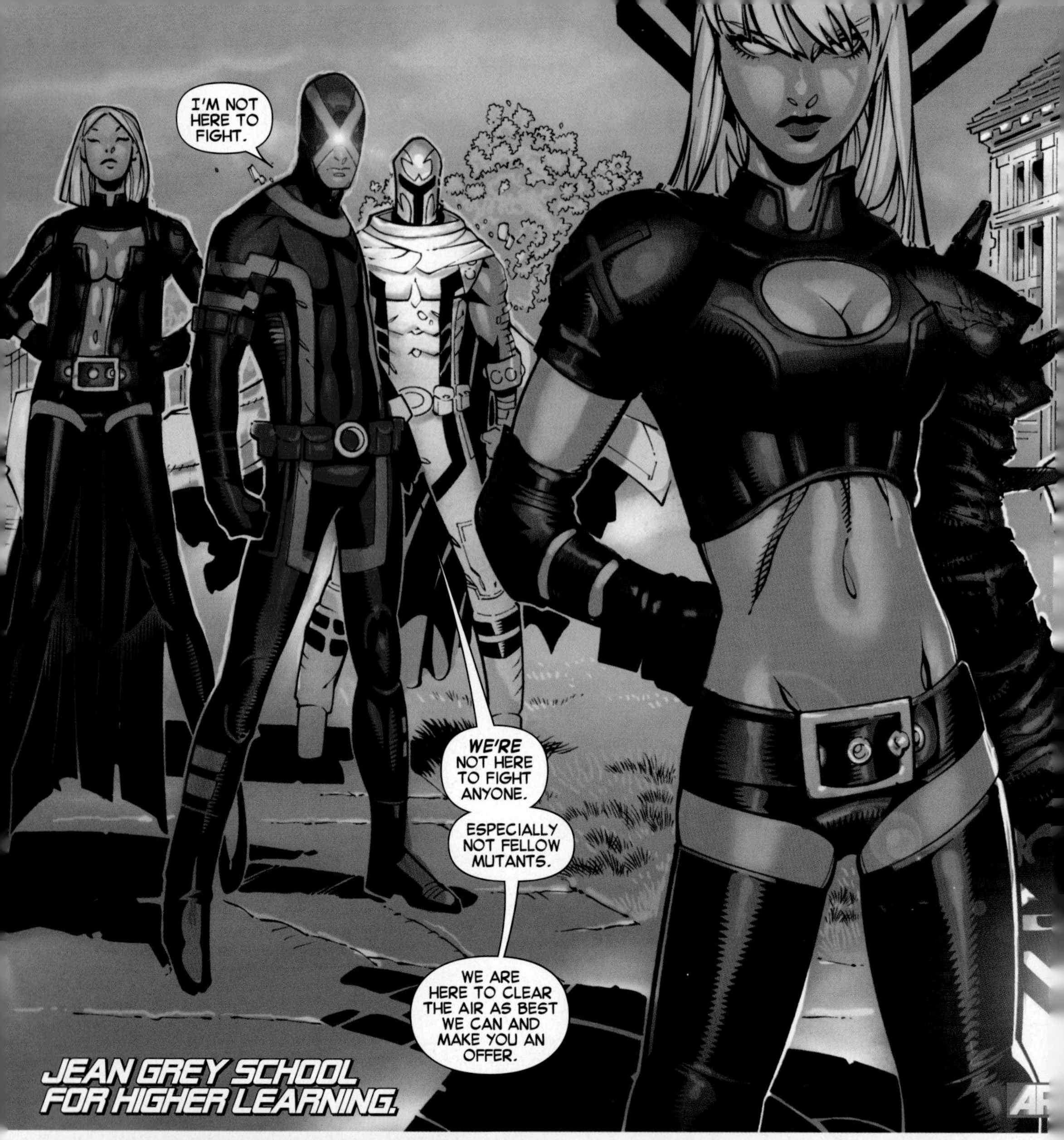
I'M NOT HERE TO FIGHT.
WE'RE NOT HERE TO FIGHT ANYONE.
ESPECIALLY NOT FELLOW MUTANTS.
WE ARE HERE TO CLEAR THE AIR AS BEST WE CAN AND MAKE YOU AN OFFER.
JEAN GREY SCHOOL FOR HIGHER LEARNING.

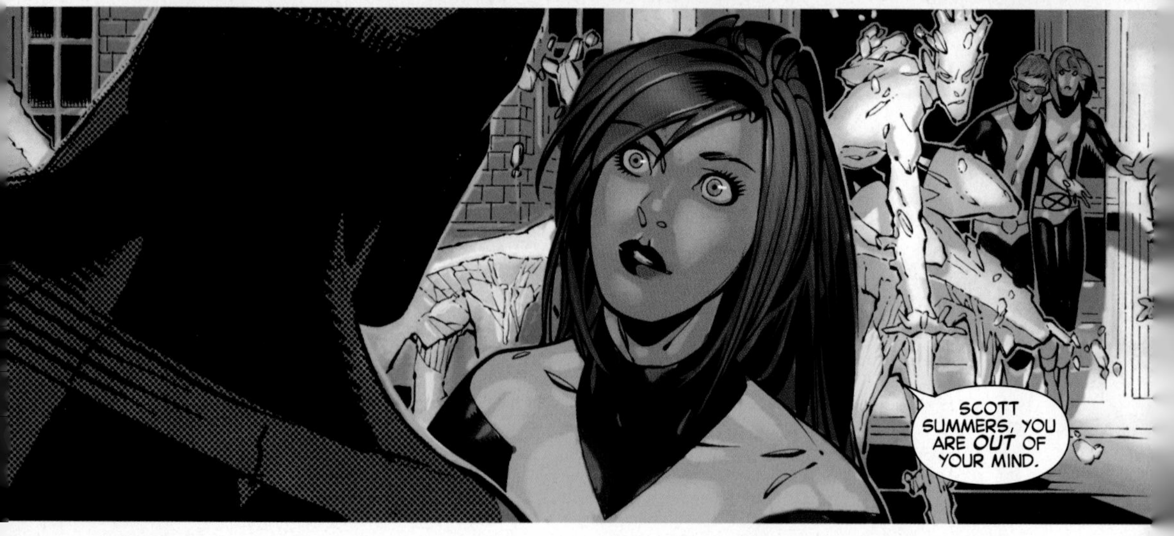
SCOTT SUMMERS, YOU ARE OUT OF YOUR MIND.

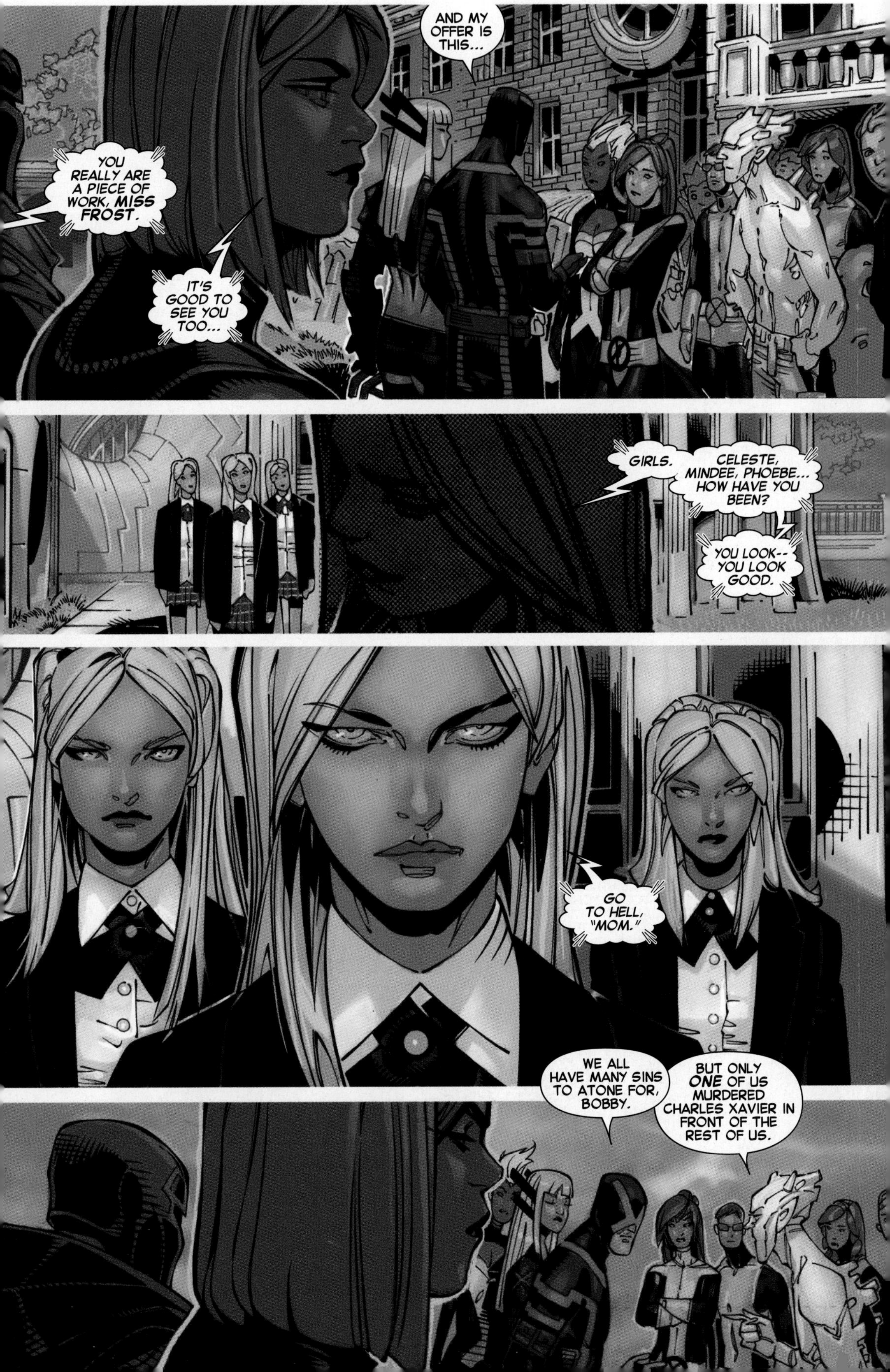
AND MY OFFER IS THIS...
YOU REALLY ARE A PIECE OF WORK, MISS FROST.
IT'S GOOD TO SEE YOU TOO...
GIRLS.
CELESTE, MINDEE, PHOEBE... HOW HAVE YOU BEEN?
YOU LOOK-- YOU LOOK GOOD.
GO TO HELL, "MOM."
WE ALL HAVE MANY SINS TO ATONE FOR, BOBBY.
BUT ONLY ONE OF US MURDERED CHARLES XAVIER IN FRONT OF THE REST OF US.

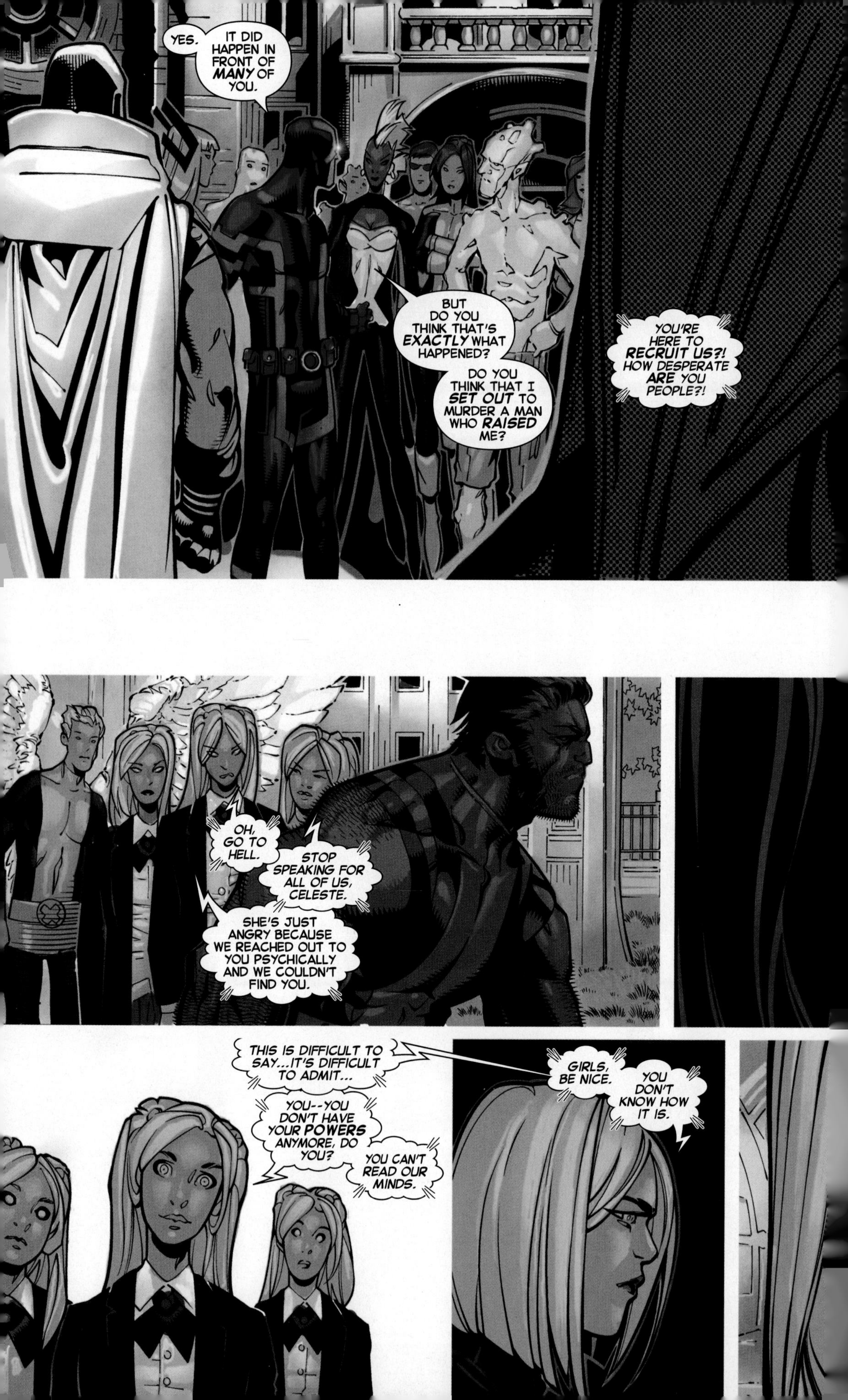
YES.
IT DID HAPPEN IN FRONT OF MANY OF YOU.
BUT DO YOU THINK THAT'S EXACTLY WHAT HAPPENED?
DO YOU THINK THAT I SET OUT TO MURDER A MAN WHO RAISED ME?
YOU'RE HERE TO RECRUIT US?! HOW DESPERATE ARE YOU PEOPLE?!
OH, GO TO HELL.
STOP SPEAKING FOR ALL OF US, CELESTE.
SHE'S JUST ANGRY BECAUSE WE REACHED OUT TO YOU PSYCHICALLY AND WE COULDN'T FIND YOU.
THIS IS DIFFICULT TO SAY...IT'S DIFFICULT TO ADMIT...
YOU--YOU DON'T HAVE YOUR POWERS ANYMORE, DO YOU?
YOU CAN'T READ OUR MINDS.
GIRLS, BE NICE.
YOU DON'T KNOW HOW IT IS.

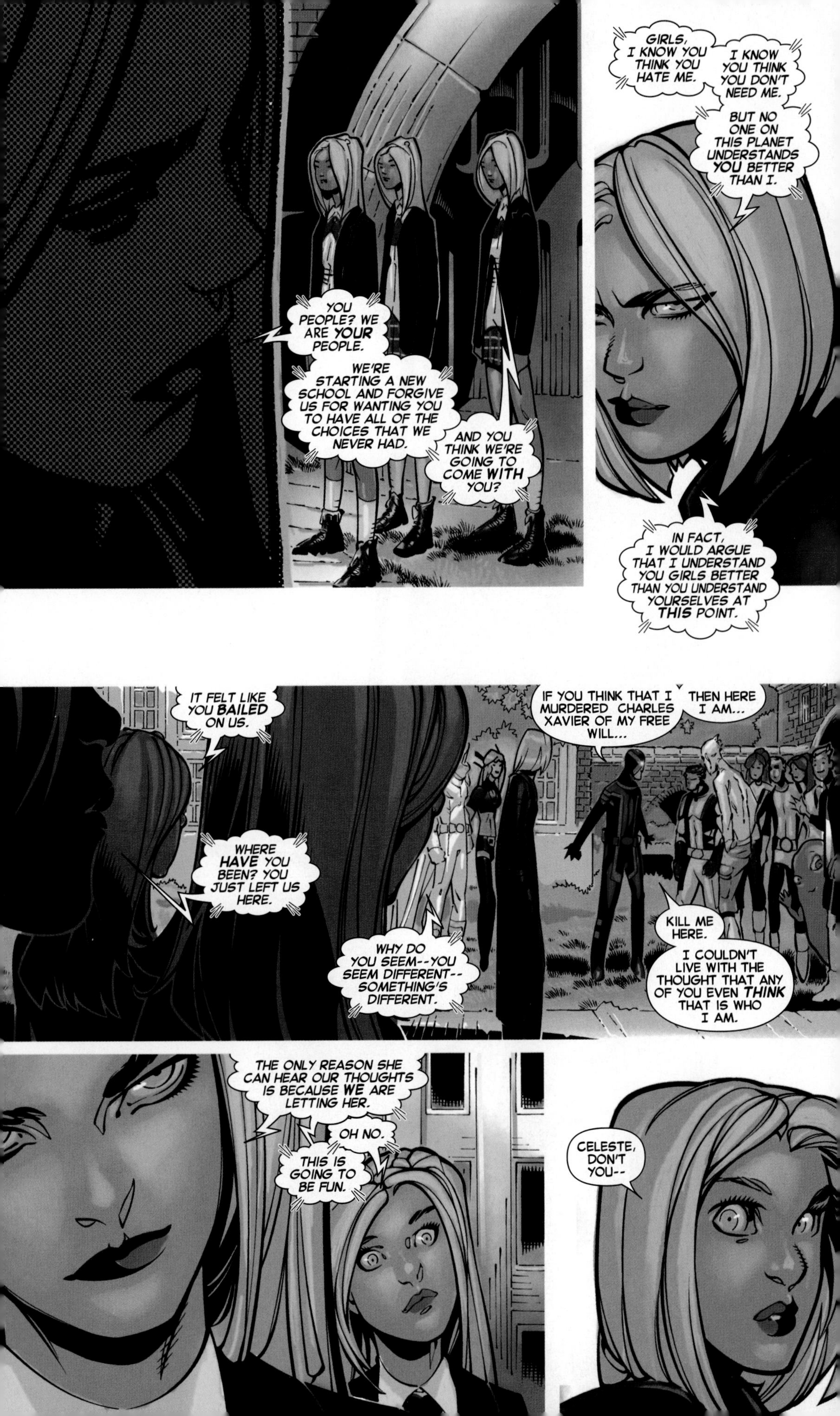
YOU PEOPLE? WE ARE YOUR PEOPLE.
WE'RE STARTING A NEW SCHOOL AND FORGIVE US FOR WANTING YOU TO HAVE ALL OF THE CHOICES THAT WE NEVER HAD.
AND YOU THINK WE'RE GOING TO COME WITH YOU?
GIRLS, I KNOW YOU THINK YOU HATE ME.
I KNOW YOU THINK YOU DON'T NEED ME.
BUT NO ONE ON THIS PLANET UNDERSTANDS YOU BETTER THAN I.
IN FACT, I WOULD ARGUE THAT I UNDERSTAND YOU GIRLS BETTER THAN YOU UNDERSTAND YOURSELVES AT THIS POINT.
IT FELT LIKE YOU BAILED ON US.
WHERE HAVE YOU BEEN? YOU JUST LEFT US HERE.
WHY DO YOU SEEM--YOU SEEM DIFFERENT--SOMETHING'S DIFFERENT.
IF YOU THINK THAT I MURDERED CHARLES XAVIER OF MY FREE WILL...
THEN HERE I AM...
KILL ME HERE.
I COULDN'T LIVE WITH THE THOUGHT THAT ANY OF YOU EVEN THINK THAT IS WHO I AM.
THE ONLY REASON SHE CAN HEAR OUR THOUGHTS IS BECAUSE WE ARE LETTING HER.
OH NO.
THIS IS GOING TO BE FUN.
CELESTE, DON'T YOU--

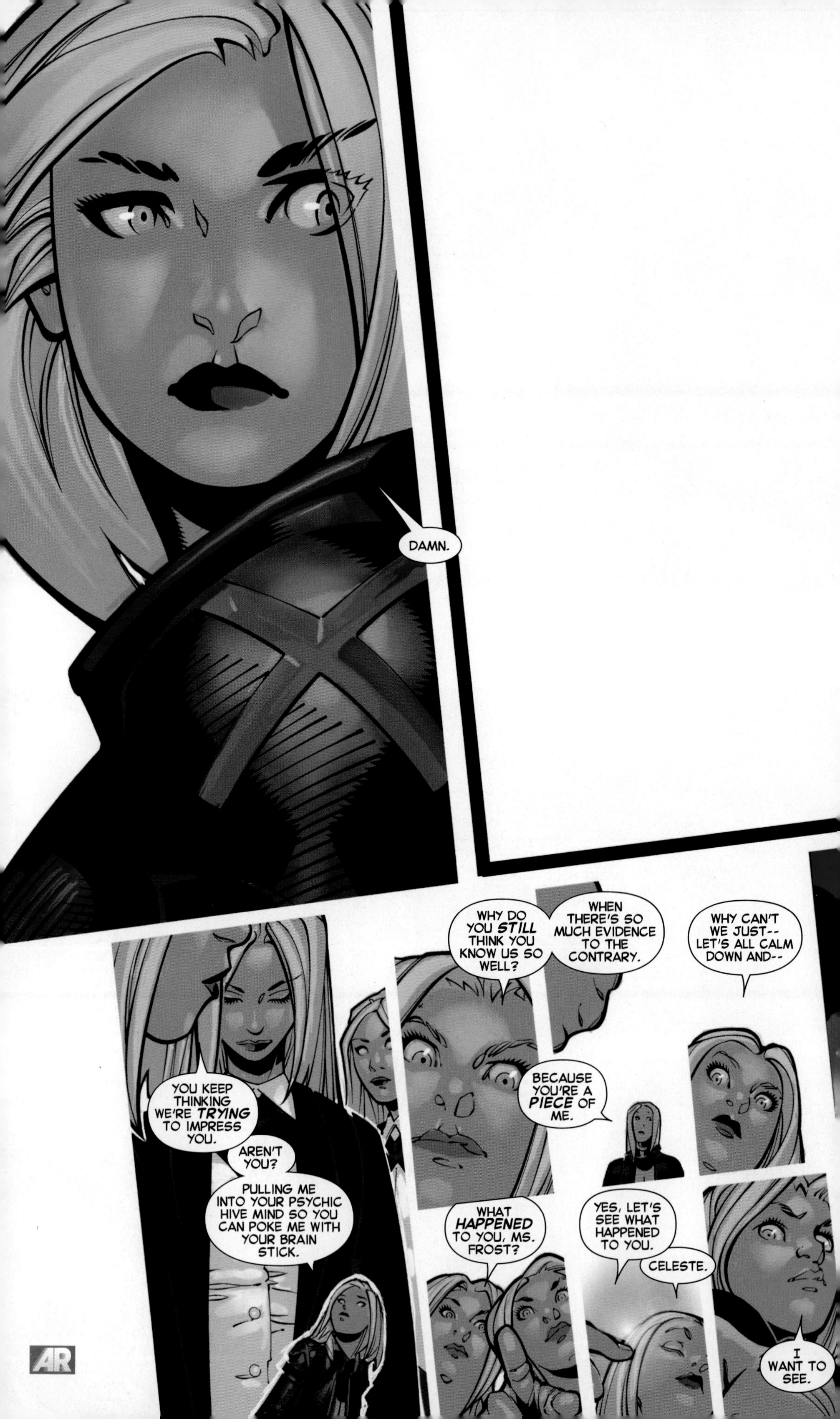
DAMN.
YOU KEEP THINKING WE'RE TRYING TO IMPRESS YOU.
AREN'T YOU?
PULLING ME INTO YOUR PSYCHIC HIVE MIND SO YOU CAN POKE ME WITH YOUR BRAIN STICK.
WHY DO YOU STILL THINK YOU KNOW US SO WELL?
WHEN THERE'S SO MUCH EVIDENCE TO THE CONTRARY.
BECAUSE YOU'RE A PIECE OF ME.
WHY CAN'T WE JUST-- LET'S ALL CALM DOWN AND--
WHAT HAPPENED TO YOU, MS. FROST?
YES, LET'S SEE WHAT HAPPENED TO YOU.
CELESTE.
I WANT TO SEE.

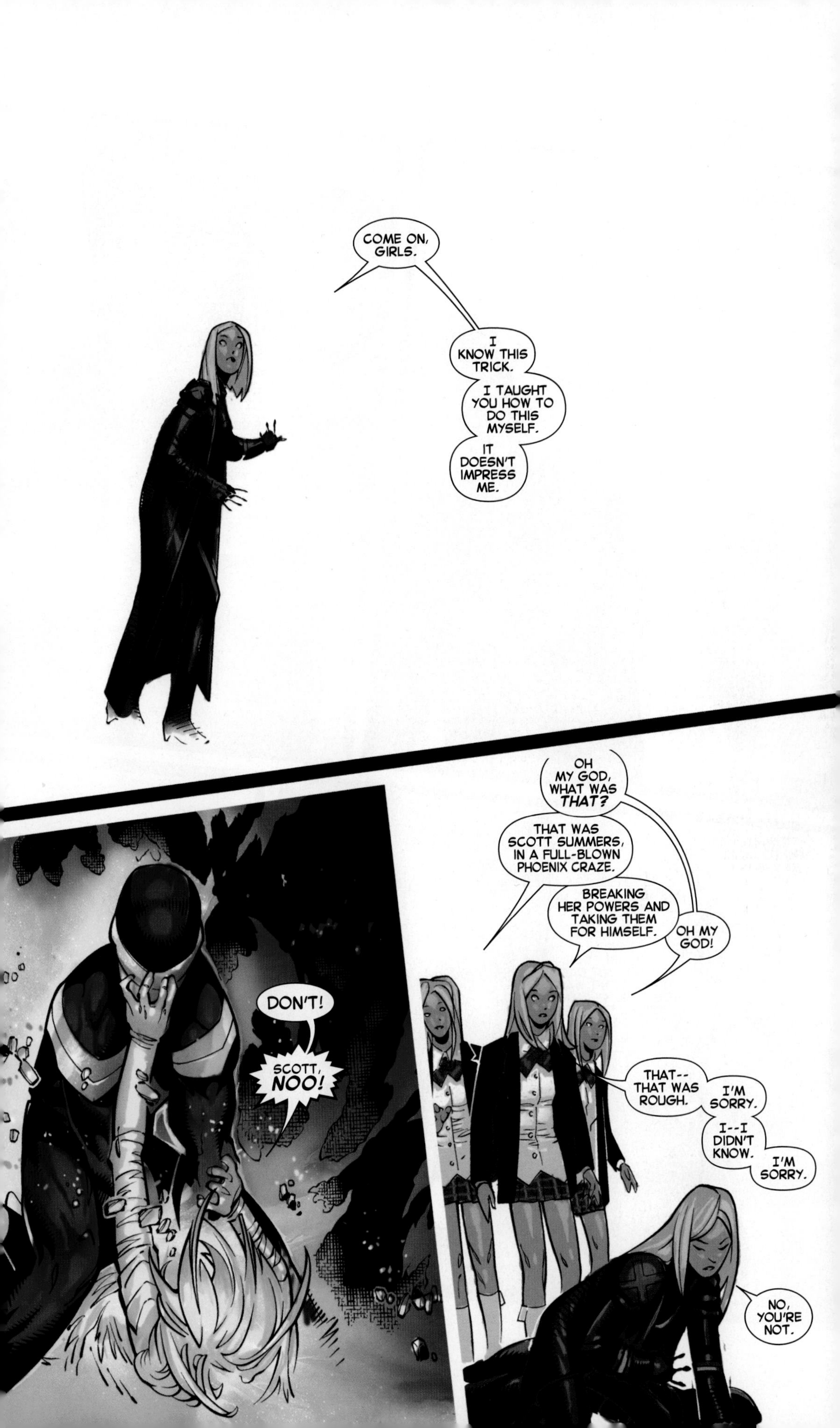
COME ON, GIRLS.
I KNOW THIS TRICK.
I TAUGHT YOU HOW TO DO THIS MYSELF.
IT DOESN'T IMPRESS ME.
DON'T!
SCOTT, NOO!
OH MY GOD, WHAT WAS THAT?
THAT WAS SCOTT SUMMERS, IN A FULL-BLOWN PHOENIX CRAZE.
BREAKING HER POWERS AND TAKING THEM FOR HIMSELF.
OH MY GOD!
THAT-- THAT WAS ROUGH.
I'M SORRY.
I--I DIDN'T KNOW.
I'M SORRY.
NO, YOU'RE NOT.

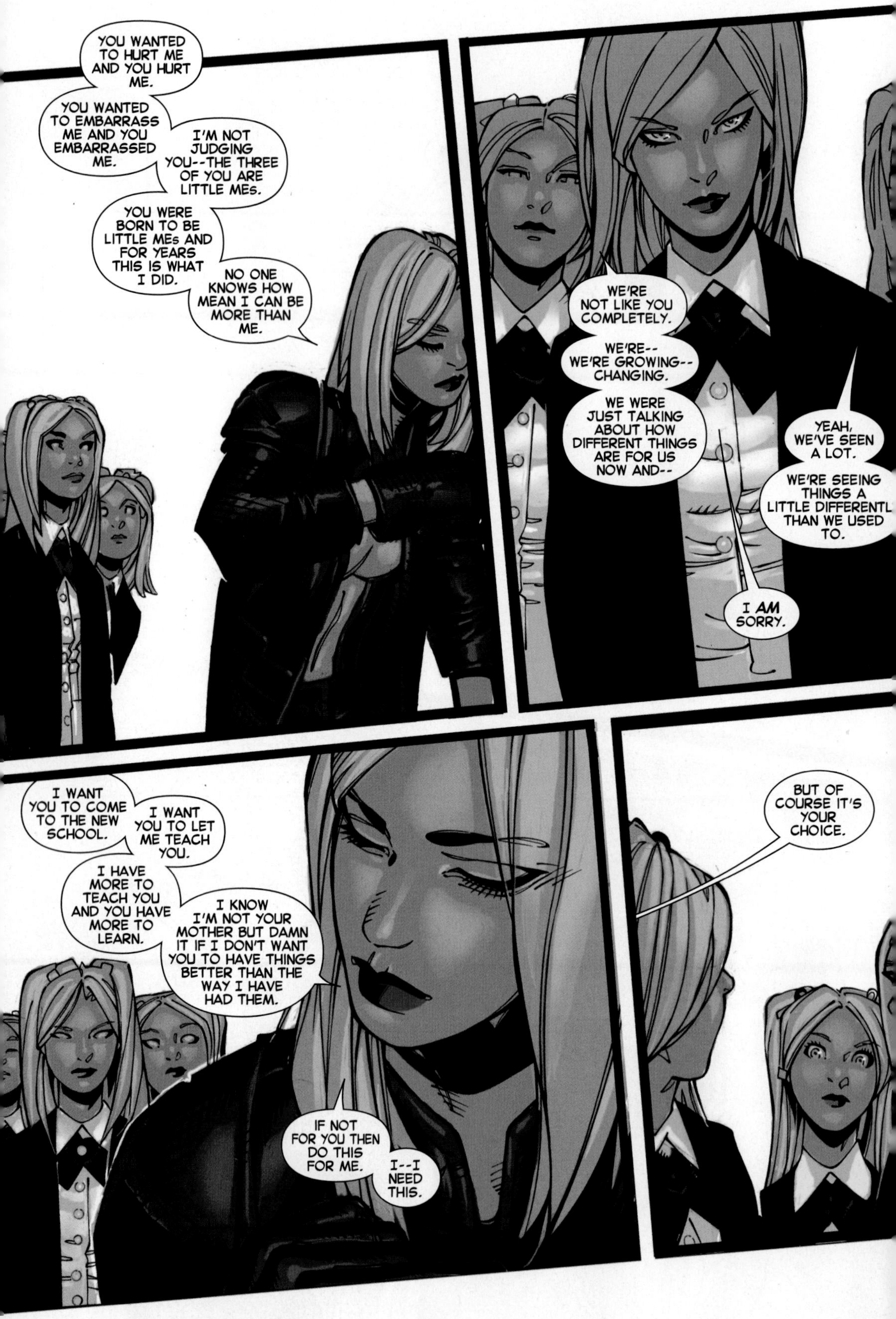
YOU WANTED TO HURT ME AND YOU HURT ME.
YOU WANTED TO EMBARRASS ME AND YOU EMBARRASSED ME.
I'M NOT JUDGING YOU--THE THREE OF YOU ARE LITTLE MEs.
YOU WERE BORN TO BE LITTLE MEs AND FOR YEARS THIS IS WHAT I DID.
NO ONE KNOWS HOW MEAN I CAN BE MORE THAN ME.
WE'RE NOT LIKE YOU COMPLETELY.
WE'RE-- WE'RE GROWING-- CHANGING.
WE WERE JUST TALKING ABOUT HOW DIFFERENT THINGS ARE FOR US NOW AND--
YEAH, WE'VE SEEN A LOT.
WE'RE SEEING THINGS A LITTLE DIFFERENTLY THAN WE USED TO.
I AM SORRY.
I WANT YOU TO COME TO THE NEW SCHOOL.
I WANT YOU TO LET ME TEACH YOU.
I HAVE MORE TO TEACH YOU AND YOU HAVE MORE TO LEARN.
I KNOW I'M NOT YOUR MOTHER BUT DAMN IT IF I DON'T WANT YOU TO HAVE THINGS BETTER THAN THE WAY I HAVE HAD THEM.
IF NOT FOR YOU THEN DO THIS FOR ME.
I--I NEED THIS.
BUT OF COURSE IT'S YOUR CHOICE.

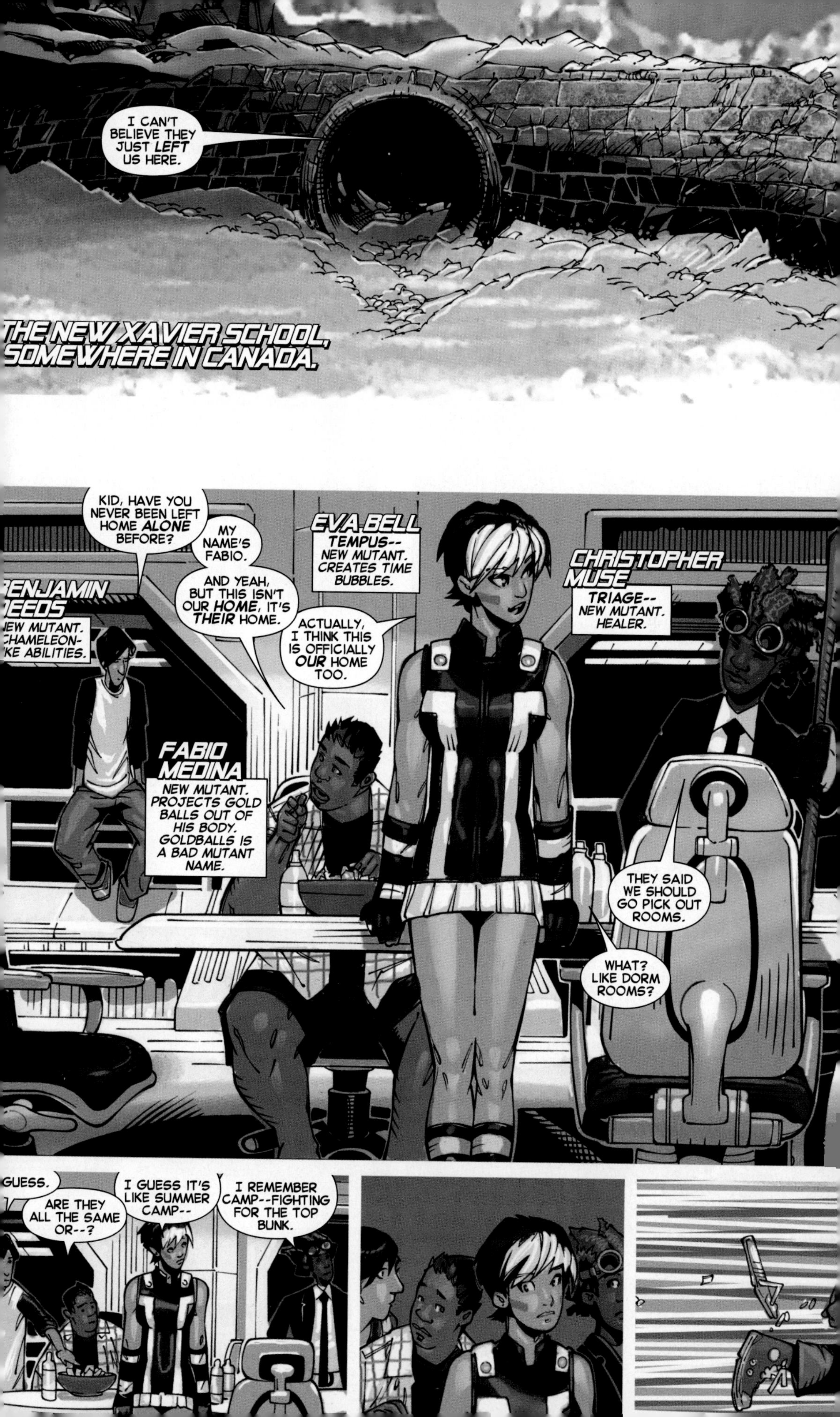
I CAN'T BELIEVE THEY JUST LEFT US HERE.
THE NEW XAVIER SCHOOL, SOMEWHERE IN CANADA.
KID, HAVE YOU NEVER BEEN LEFT HOME ALONE BEFORE?
MY NAME'S FABIO.
AND YEAH, BUT THIS ISN'T OUR HOME, IT'S THEIR HOME.
EVA BELL
TEMPUS-- NEW MUTANT. CREATES TIME BUBBLES.
ACTUALLY, I THINK THIS IS OFFICIALLY OUR HOME TOO.
CHRISTOPHER MUSE
TRIAGE-- NEW MUTANT. HEALER.
ENJAMIN EEDS
EW MUTANT. CHAMELEON- KE ABILITIES.
FABIO MEDINA
NEW MUTANT. PROJECTS GOLD BALLS OUT OF HIS BODY. GOLDBALLS IS A BAD MUTANT NAME.
THEY SAID WE SHOULD GO PICK OUT ROOMS.
WHAT? LIKE DORM ROOMS?
GUESS.
ARE THEY ALL THE SAME OR--?
I GUESS IT'S LIKE SUMMER CAMP--
I REMEMBER CAMP--FIGHTING FOR THE TOP BUNK.

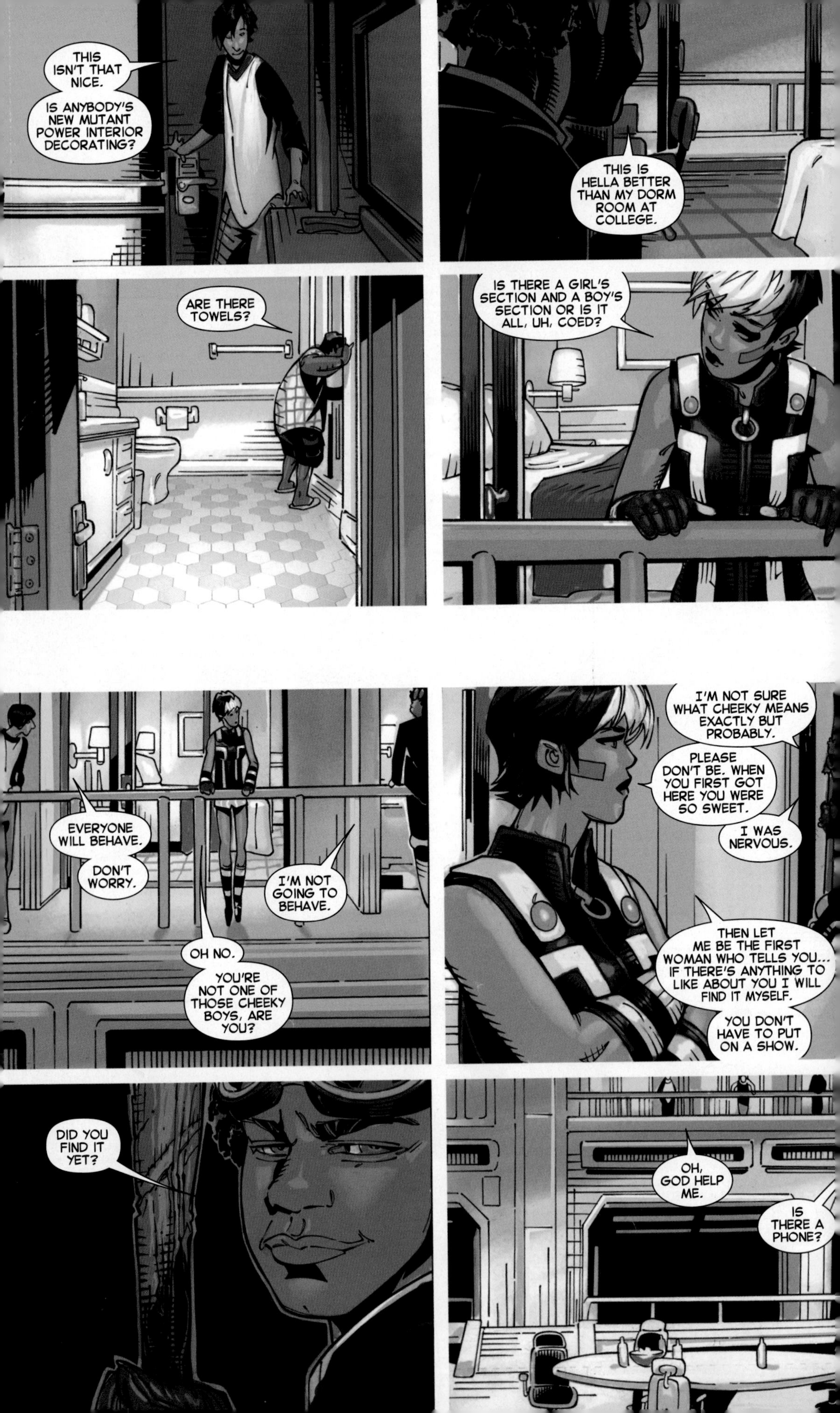

THIS ISN'T THAT NICE.
IS ANYBODY'S NEW MUTANT POWER INTERIOR DECORATING?
THIS IS HELLA BETTER THAN MY DORM ROOM AT COLLEGE.
ARE THERE TOWELS?
IS THERE A GIRL'S SECTION AND A BOY'S SECTION OR IS IT ALL, UH, COED?
EVERYONE WILL BEHAVE.
DON'T WORRY.
I'M NOT GOING TO BEHAVE.
OH NO.
YOU'RE NOT ONE OF THOSE CHEEKY BOYS, ARE YOU?
I'M NOT SURE WHAT CHEEKY MEANS EXACTLY BUT PROBABLY.
PLEASE DON'T BE. WHEN YOU FIRST GOT HERE YOU WERE SO SWEET.
I WAS NERVOUS.
THEN LET ME BE THE FIRST WOMAN WHO TELLS YOU... IF THERE'S ANYTHING TO LIKE ABOUT YOU I WILL FIND IT MYSELF.
YOU DON'T HAVE TO PUT ON A SHOW.
DID YOU FIND IT YET?
OH, GOD HELP ME.
IS THERE A PHONE?

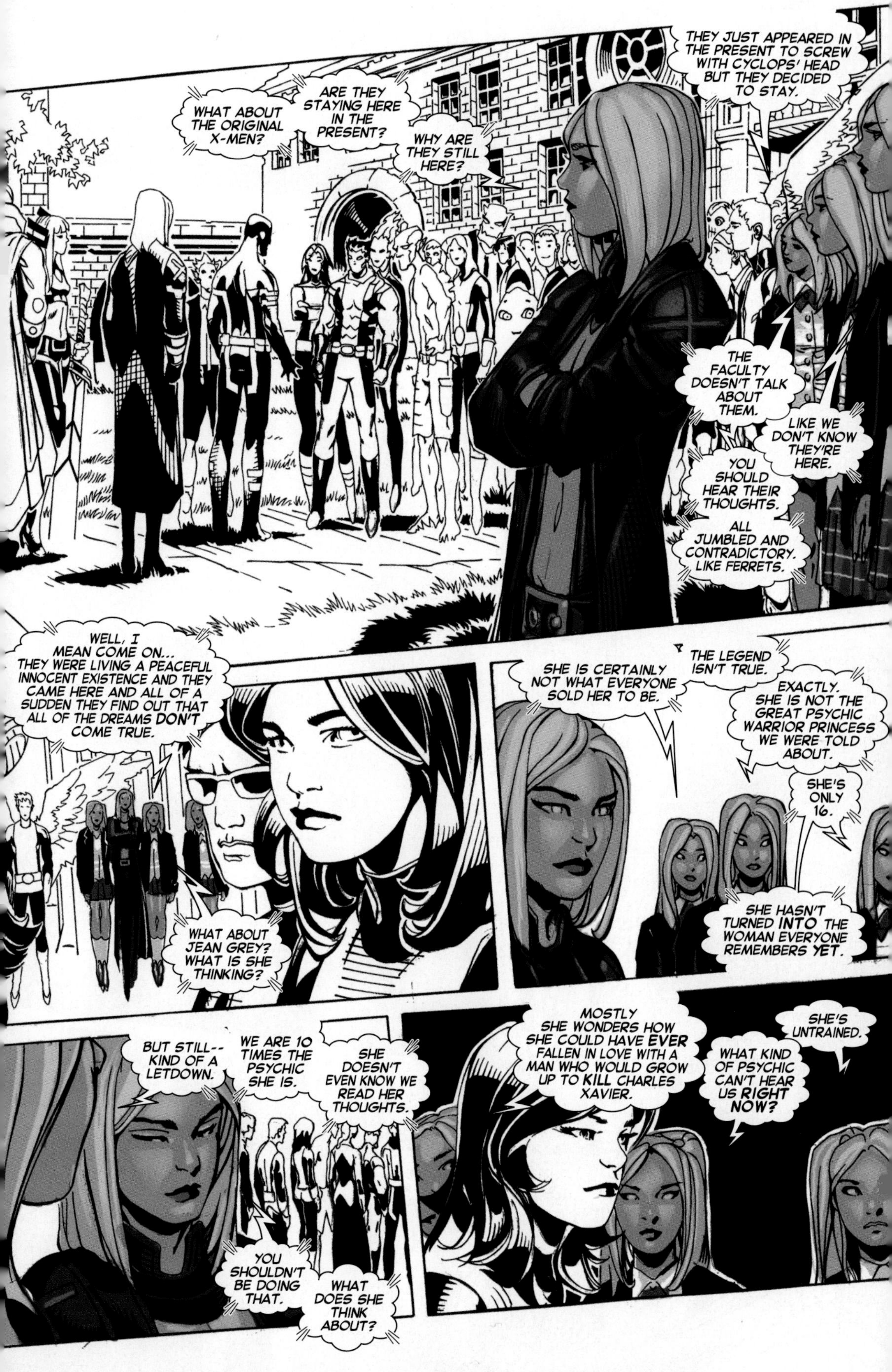

WHAT ABOUT THE ORIGINAL X-MEN?
ARE THEY STAYING HERE IN THE PRESENT?
WHY ARE THEY STILL HERE?
THEY JUST APPEARED IN THE PRESENT TO SCREW WITH CYCLOPS' HEAD BUT THEY DECIDED TO STAY.
THE FACULTY DOESN'T TALK ABOUT THEM.
LIKE WE DON'T KNOW THEY'RE HERE.
YOU SHOULD HEAR THEIR THOUGHTS.
ALL JUMBLED AND CONTRADICTORY. LIKE FERRETS.
WELL, I MEAN COME ON... THEY WERE LIVING A PEACEFUL INNOCENT EXISTENCE AND THEY CAME HERE AND ALL OF A SUDDEN THEY FIND OUT THAT ALL OF THE DREAMS DON'T COME TRUE.
WHAT ABOUT JEAN GREY? WHAT IS SHE THINKING?
SHE IS CERTAINLY NOT WHAT EVERYONE SOLD HER TO BE.
THE LEGEND ISN'T TRUE.
EXACTLY. SHE IS NOT THE GREAT PSYCHIC WARRIOR PRINCESS WE WERE TOLD ABOUT.
SHE'S ONLY 16.
SHE HASN'T TURNED INTO THE WOMAN EVERYONE REMEMBERS YET.
BUT STILL-- KIND OF A LETDOWN.
WE ARE 10 TIMES THE PSYCHIC SHE IS.
SHE DOESN'T EVEN KNOW WE READ HER THOUGHTS.
YOU SHOULDN'T BE DOING THAT.
WHAT DOES SHE THINK ABOUT?
MOSTLY SHE WONDERS HOW SHE COULD HAVE EVER FALLEN IN LOVE WITH A MAN WHO WOULD GROW UP TO KILL CHARLES XAVIER.
SHE'S UNTRAINED.
WHAT KIND OF PSYCHIC CAN'T HEAR US RIGHT NOW?

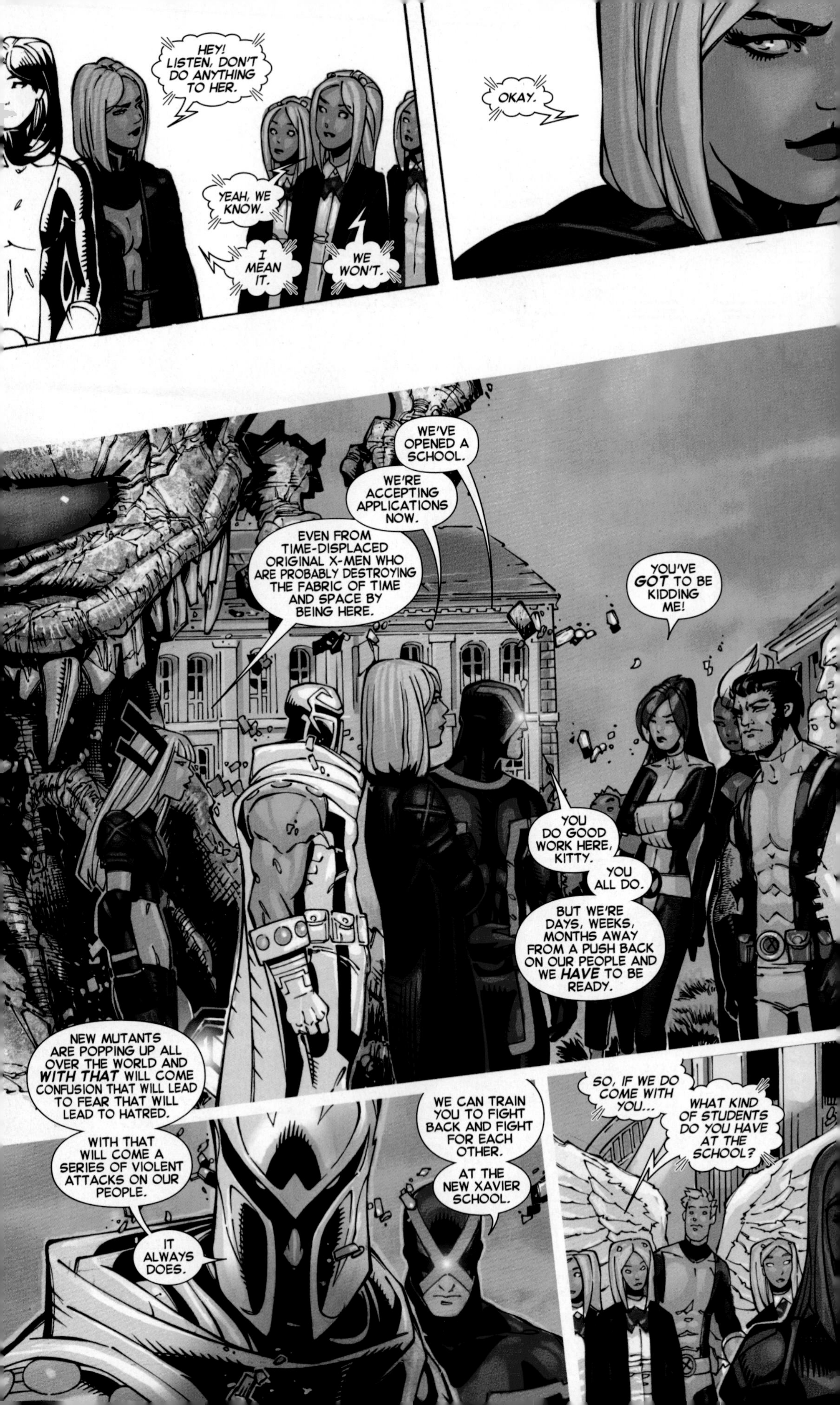
HEY! LISTEN, DON'T DO ANYTHING TO HER.
YEAH, WE KNOW.
I MEAN IT.
WE WON'T.
OKAY.
WE'VE OPENED A SCHOOL.
WE'RE ACCEPTING APPLICATIONS NOW.
EVEN FROM TIME-DISPLACED ORIGINAL X-MEN WHO ARE PROBABLY DESTROYING THE FABRIC OF TIME AND SPACE BY BEING HERE.
YOU'VE GOT TO BE KIDDING ME!
YOU DO GOOD WORK HERE, KITTY.
YOU ALL DO.
BUT WE'RE DAYS, WEEKS, MONTHS AWAY FROM A PUSH BACK ON OUR PEOPLE AND WE HAVE TO BE READY.
NEW MUTANTS ARE POPPING UP ALL OVER THE WORLD AND WITH THAT WILL COME CONFUSION THAT WILL LEAD TO FEAR THAT WILL LEAD TO HATRED.
WITH THAT WILL COME A SERIES OF VIOLENT ATTACKS ON OUR PEOPLE.
IT ALWAYS DOES.
WE CAN TRAIN YOU TO FIGHT BACK AND FIGHT FOR EACH OTHER.
AT THE NEW XAVIER SCHOOL.
SO, IF WE DO COME WITH YOU...
WHAT KIND OF STUDENTS DO YOU HAVE AT THE SCHOOL?

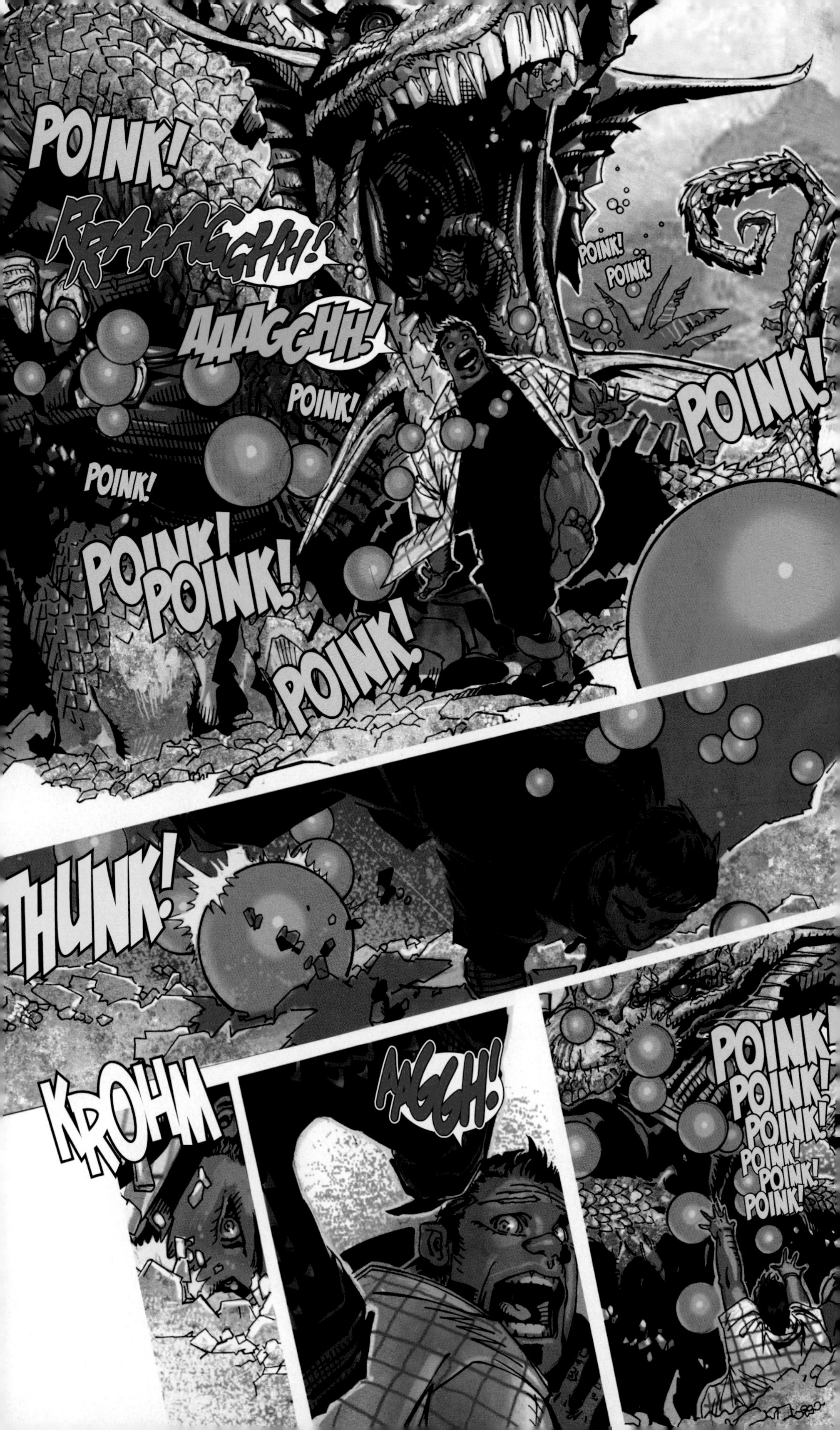
POINK!
RRAAAGGHH!
AAAGGHH!
POINK!
POINK!
POINK!
POINK!
POINK!
POINK!
POINK!
POINK!
THUNK!
KROHM
AAGGH!
POINK!
POINK!
POINK!
POINK!
POINK!
POINK!

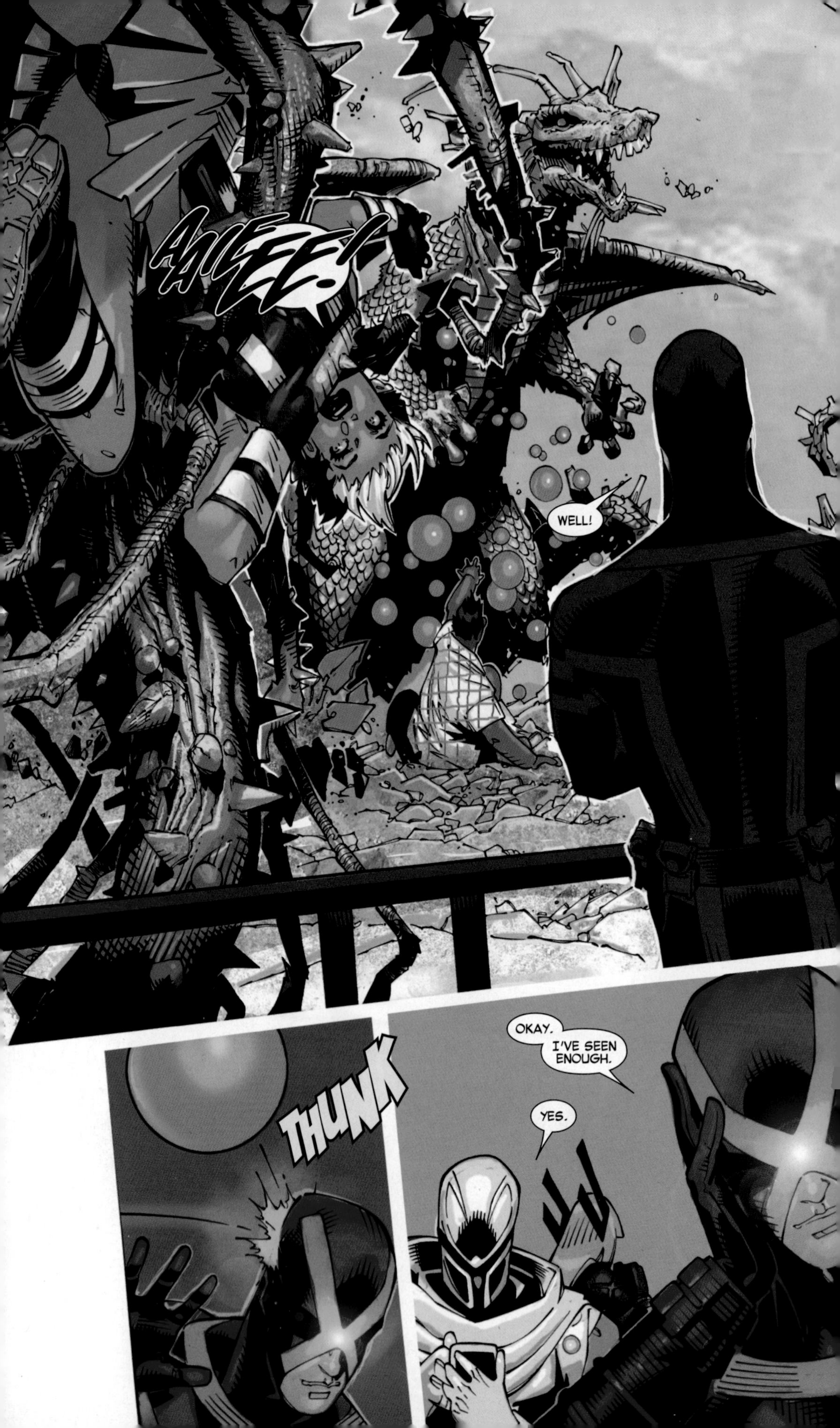
AAIEEE!
WELL!
THUNK
OKAY.
I'VE SEEN ENOUGH.
YES.

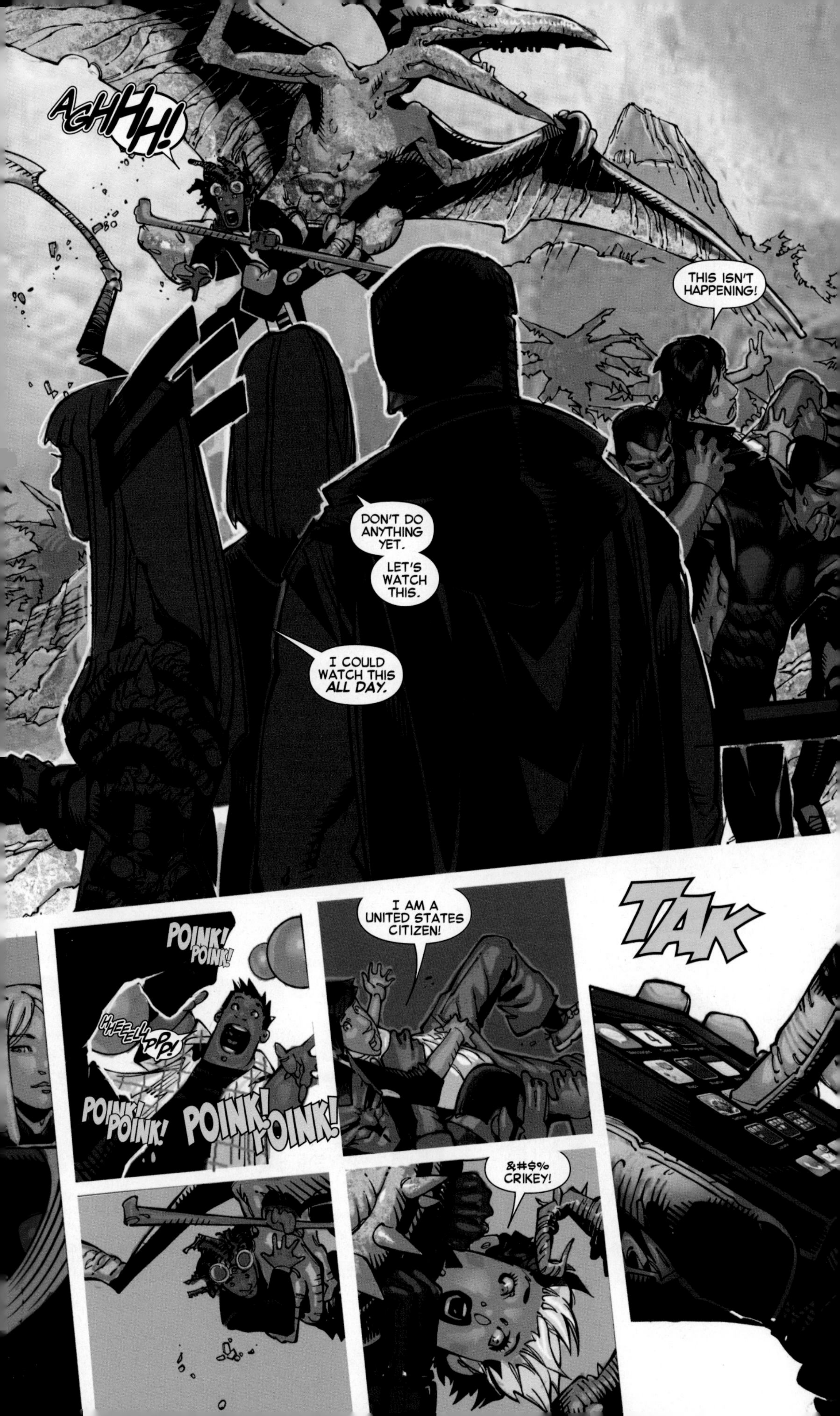
AGHHH!
THIS ISN'T HAPPENING!
DON'T DO ANYTHING YET.
LET'S WATCH THIS.
I COULD WATCH THIS ALL DAY.
POINK! POINK!
HHEEELLPPP!
POINK! POINK!
POINK! POINK!
I AM A UNITED STATES CITIZEN!
TAK
&#$% CRIKEY!

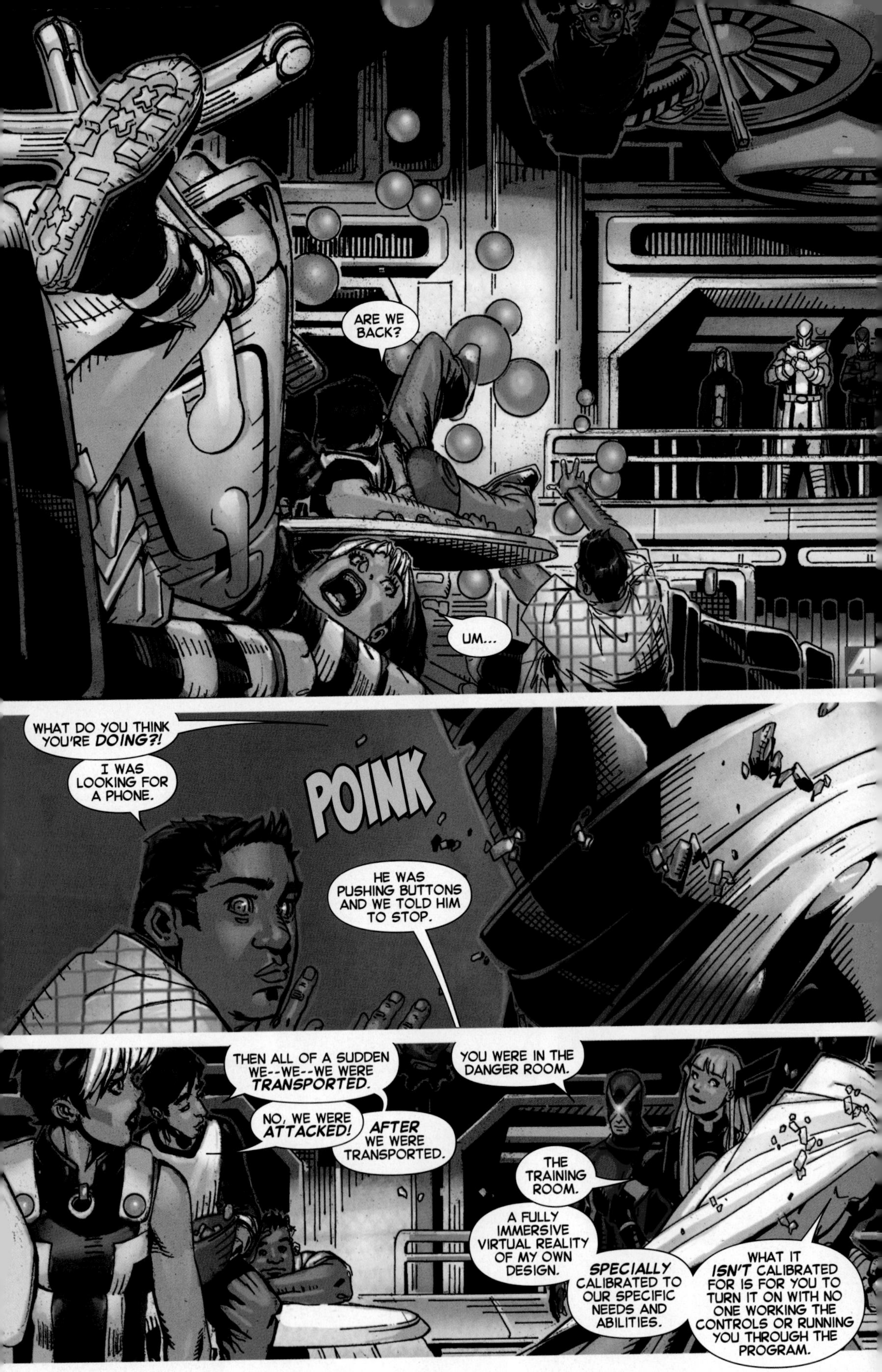
ARE WE BACK?
UM...
WHAT DO YOU THINK YOU'RE *DOING?!*
I WAS LOOKING FOR A PHONE.
POINK
HE WAS PUSHING BUTTONS AND WE TOLD HIM TO STOP.
THEN ALL OF A SUDDEN WE--WE--WE WERE *TRANSPORTED.*
NO, WE WERE *ATTACKED!*
AFTER WE WERE TRANSPORTED.
YOU WERE IN THE DANGER ROOM.
THE TRAINING ROOM.
A FULLY IMMERSIVE VIRTUAL REALITY OF MY OWN DESIGN.
SPECIALLY CALIBRATED TO OUR SPECIFIC NEEDS AND ABILITIES.
WHAT IT *ISN'T* CALIBRATED FOR IS FOR YOU TO TURN IT ON WITH NO ONE WORKING THE CONTROLS OR RUNNING YOU THROUGH THE PROGRAM.

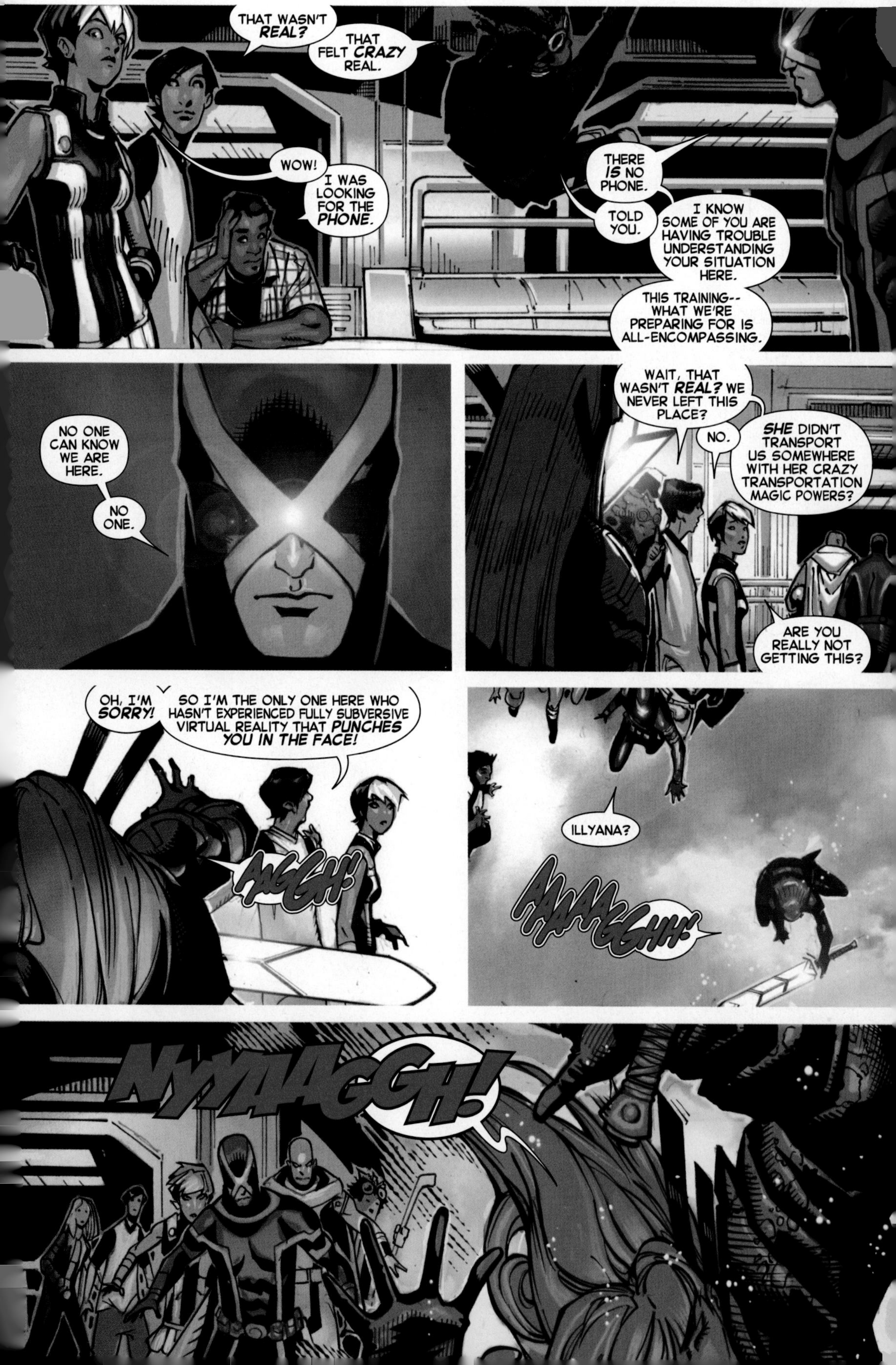
THAT WASN'T REAL?
THAT FELT CRAZY REAL.
WOW! I WAS LOOKING FOR THE PHONE.
THERE IS NO PHONE.
TOLD YOU.
I KNOW SOME OF YOU ARE HAVING TROUBLE UNDERSTANDING YOUR SITUATION HERE.
THIS TRAINING-- WHAT WE'RE PREPARING FOR IS ALL-ENCOMPASSING.
NO ONE CAN KNOW WE ARE HERE.
NO ONE.
WAIT, THAT WASN'T REAL? WE NEVER LEFT THIS PLACE?
NO.
SHE DIDN'T TRANSPORT US SOMEWHERE WITH HER CRAZY TRANSPORTATION MAGIC POWERS?
ARE YOU REALLY NOT GETTING THIS?
OH, I'M SORRY!
SO I'M THE ONLY ONE HERE WHO HASN'T EXPERIENCED FULLY SUBVERSIVE VIRTUAL REALITY THAT PUNCHES YOU IN THE FACE!
AAGGH!
ILLYANA?
AAAAAGGHH!
NYYAAGGH!

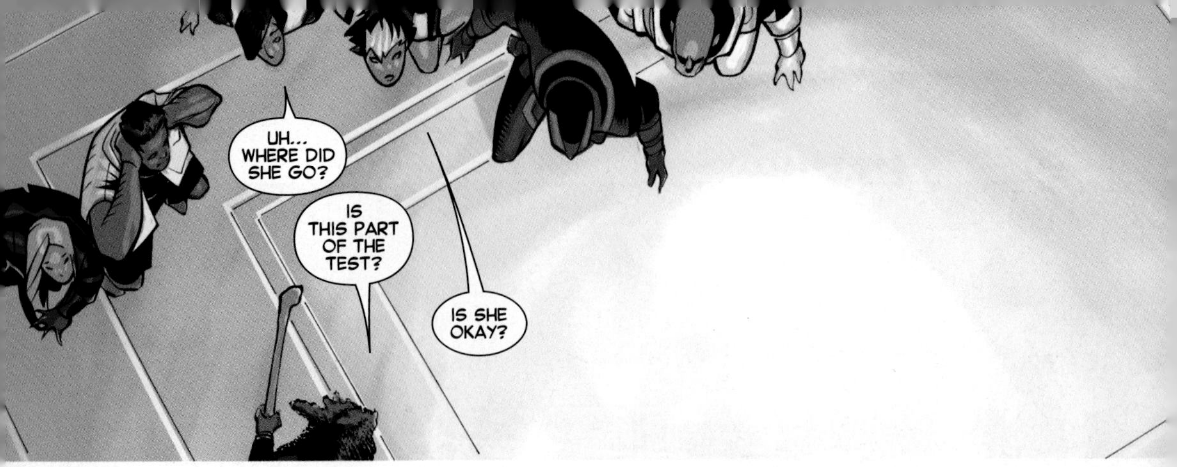
UH... WHERE DID SHE GO?
IS THIS PART OF THE TEST?
IS SHE OKAY?

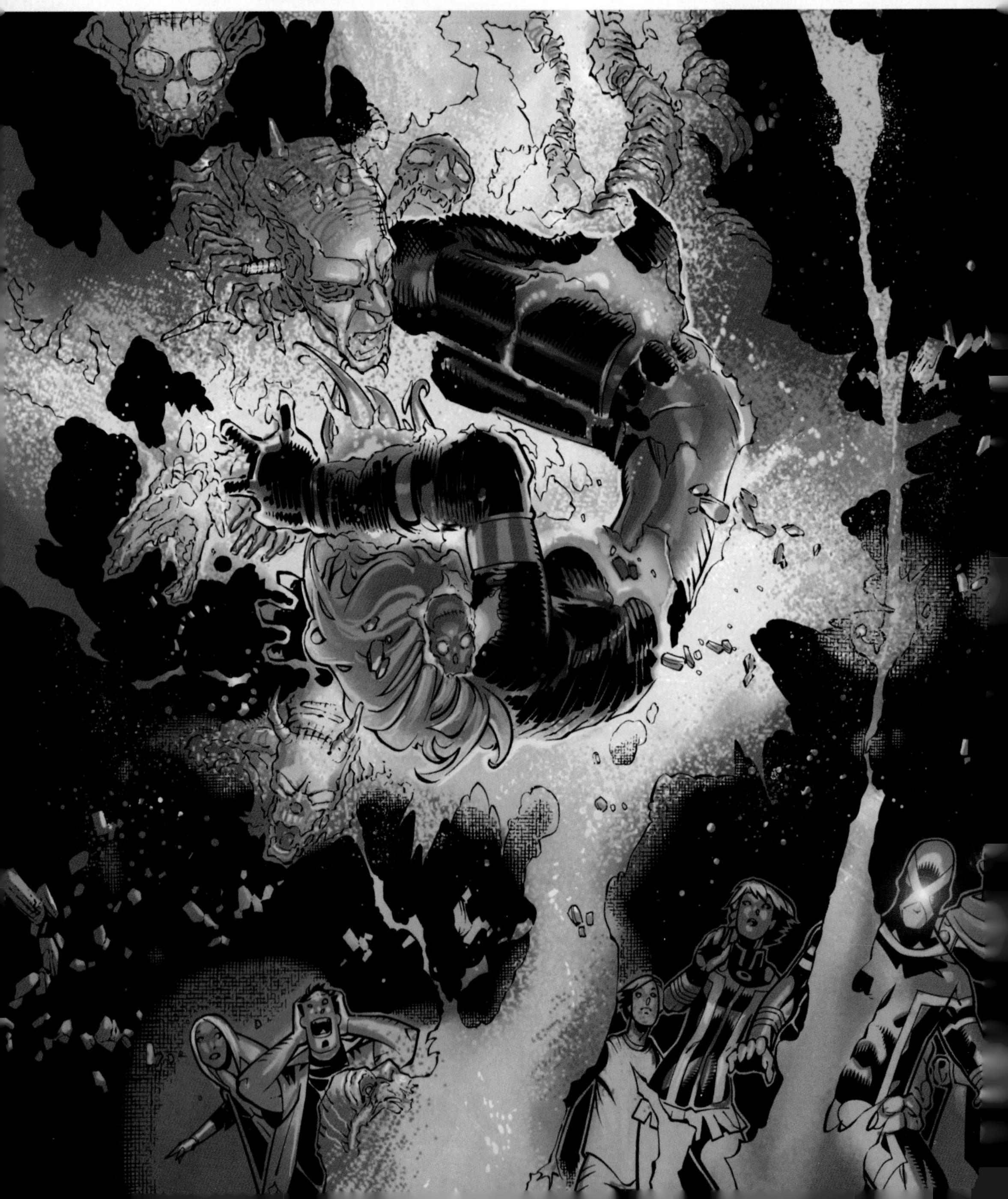

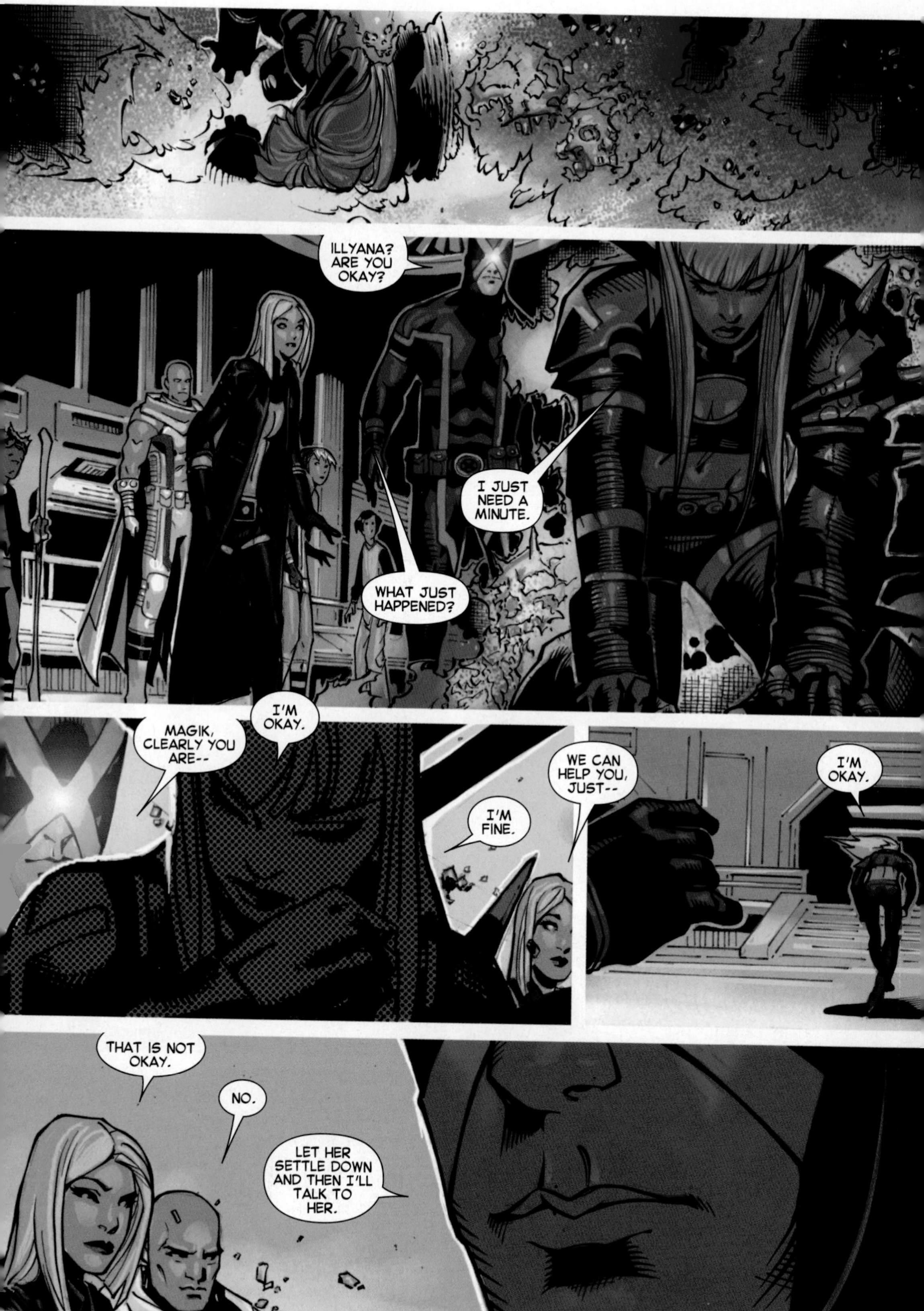
ILLYANA? ARE YOU OKAY?
I JUST NEED A MINUTE.
WHAT JUST HAPPENED?
MAGIK, CLEARLY YOU ARE--
I'M OKAY.
WE CAN HELP YOU, JUST--
I'M FINE.
I'M OKAY.
THAT IS NOT OKAY.
NO.
LET HER SETTLE DOWN AND THEN I'LL TALK TO HER.

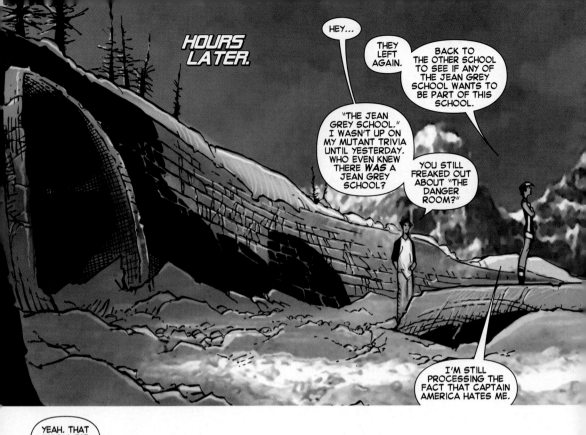

HOURS LATER.

HEY...

THEY LEFT AGAIN.

BACK TO THE OTHER SCHOOL TO SEE IF ANY OF THE JEAN GREY SCHOOL WANTS TO BE PART OF THIS SCHOOL.

"THE JEAN GREY SCHOOL." I WASN'T UP ON MY MUTANT TRIVIA UNTIL YESTERDAY. WHO EVEN KNEW THERE WAS A JEAN GREY SCHOOL?

YOU STILL FREAKED OUT ABOUT "THE DANGER ROOM?"

I'M STILL PROCESSING THE FACT THAT CAPTAIN AMERICA HATES ME.

YEAH. THAT WAS A BIT MUCH. THE AVENGERS!

I'M WORRIED THAT OUR TEACHERS HAVE MORE PROBLEMS THAN WE DO.

I'M WAITING FOR THEM TO DECIDE TO BE COMPLETELY HONEST WITH US.

FULL DISCLOSURE.

I THINK I'M GOING TO NEED IT IF I'M STAYING.

I THINK I'M GOING TO NEED PROOF THAT SCOTT SUMMERS IS A GOOD MAN.

I THINK HE IS A GOOD MAN. I JUST THINK HE--I DON'T KNOW--

I DON'T KNOW.

THERE'S SOMETHING ABOUT HIM THAT I-- I REALLY LIKE...

AND SOMETHING ABOUT HIM...

THAT SCARES THE HELL OUT OF YOU.

RIGHT.

THEY'RE BACK.

STUDENTS...

I'M HAPPY TO SAY WE HAVE SOME N BLOOD HERE THE NEW XAVI SCHOOL.

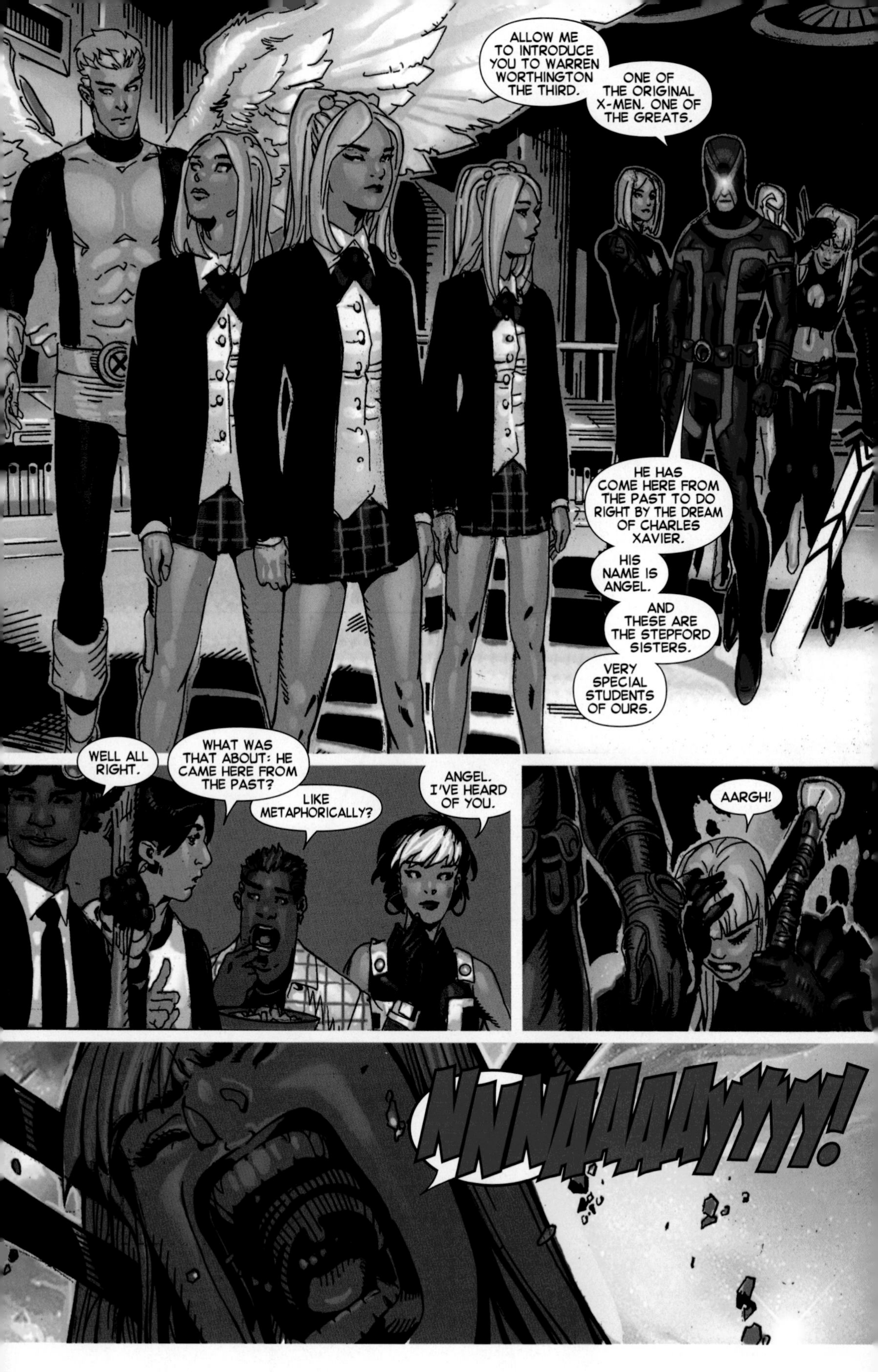
ALLOW ME TO INTRODUCE YOU TO WARREN WORTHINGTON THE THIRD.
ONE OF THE ORIGINAL X-MEN. ONE OF THE GREATS.
HE HAS COME HERE FROM THE PAST TO DO RIGHT BY THE DREAM OF CHARLES XAVIER.
HIS NAME IS ANGEL.
AND THESE ARE THE STEPFORD SISTERS.
VERY SPECIAL STUDENTS OF OURS.
WELL ALL RIGHT.
WHAT WAS THAT ABOUT: HE CAME HERE FROM THE PAST?
LIKE METAPHORICALLY?
ANGEL. I'VE HEARD OF YOU.
AARGH!
NNNAAAAYYYY!

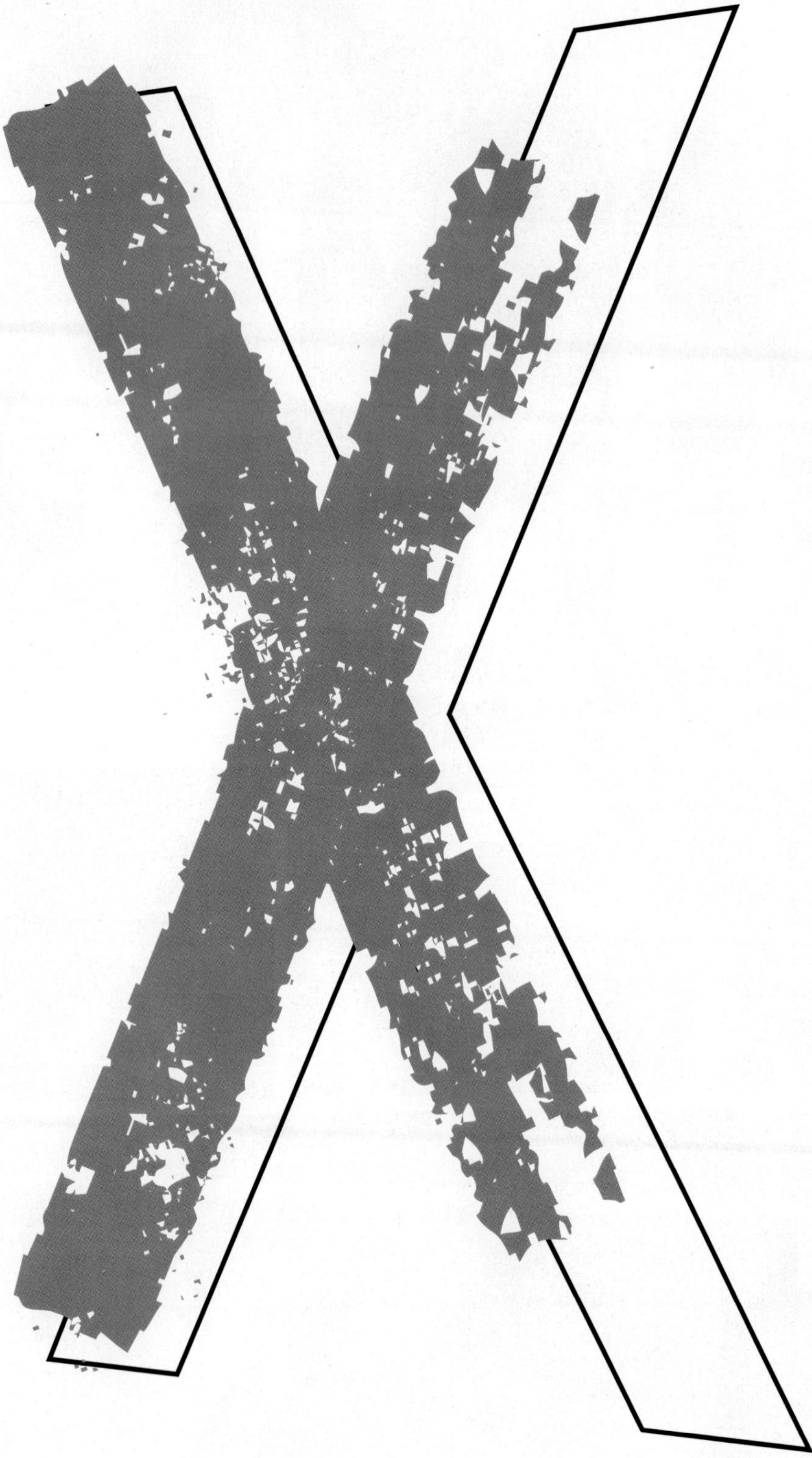

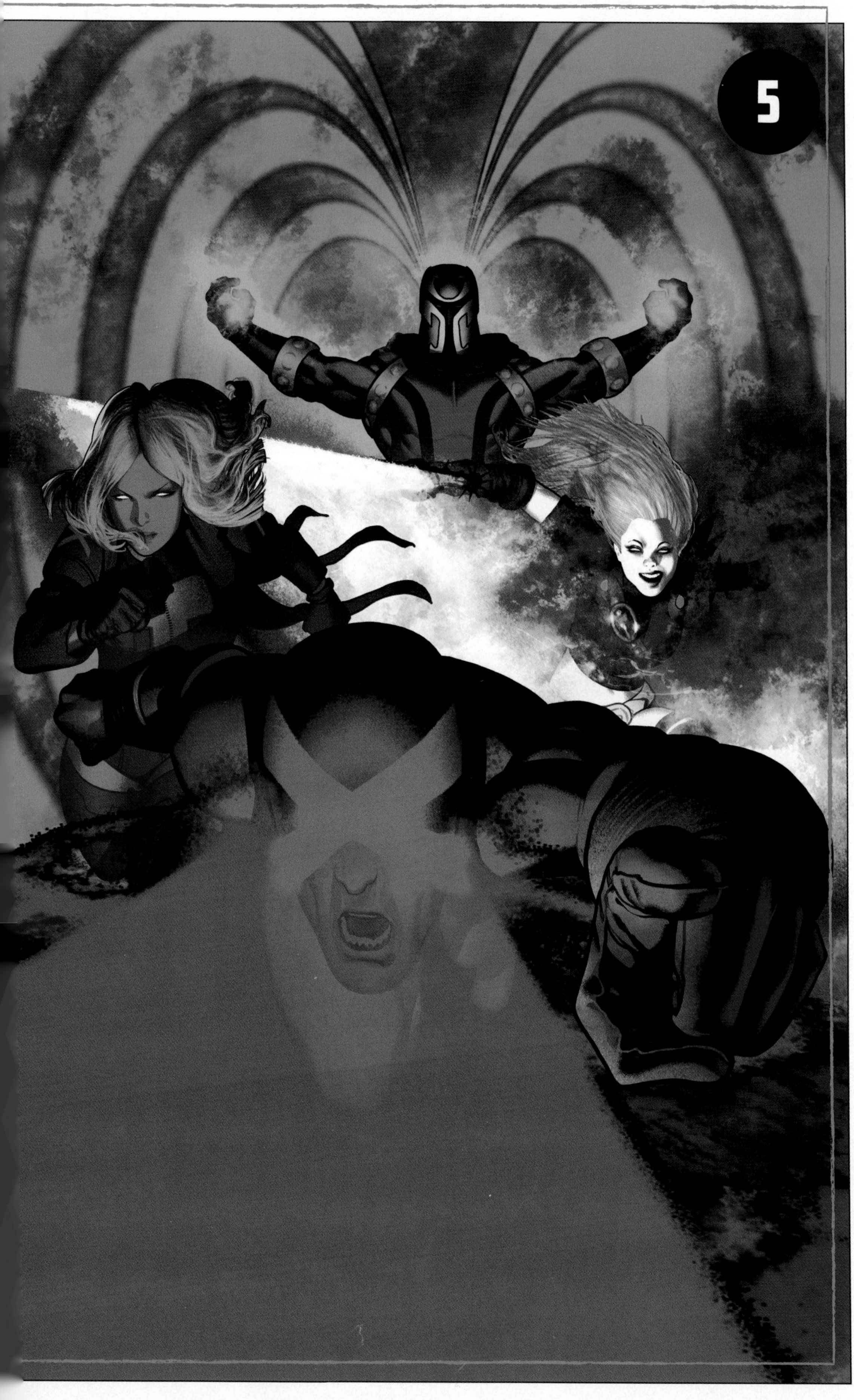
5

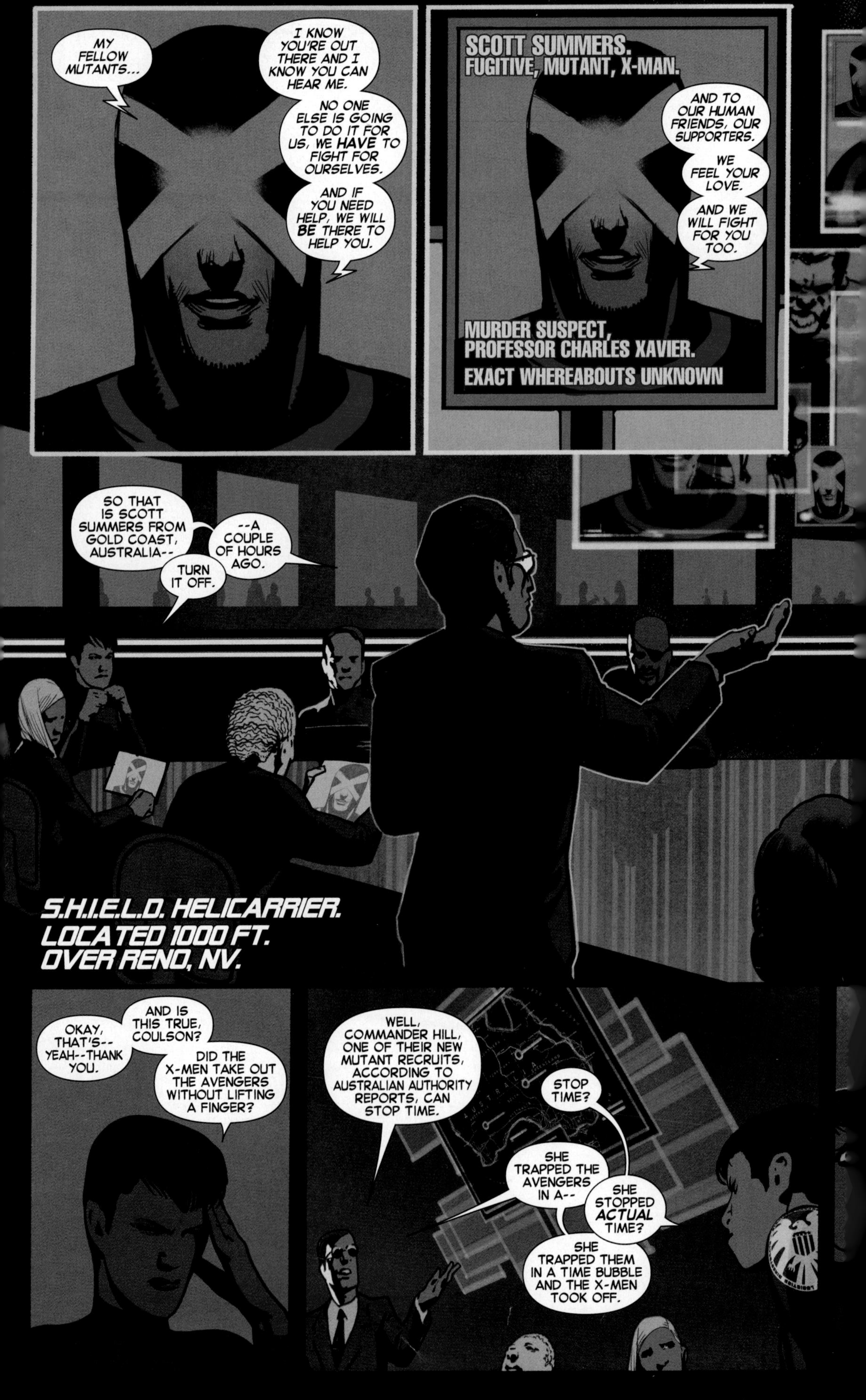
MY FELLOW MUTANTS...
I KNOW YOU'RE OUT THERE AND I KNOW YOU CAN HEAR ME.
NO ONE ELSE IS GOING TO DO IT FOR US, WE HAVE TO FIGHT FOR OURSELVES.
AND IF YOU NEED HELP, WE WILL BE THERE TO HELP YOU.
SCOTT SUMMERS.
FUGITIVE, MUTANT, X-MAN.
AND TO OUR HUMAN FRIENDS, OUR SUPPORTERS.
WE FEEL YOUR LOVE.
AND WE WILL FIGHT FOR YOU TOO.
MURDER SUSPECT, PROFESSOR CHARLES XAVIER.
EXACT WHEREABOUTS UNKNOWN
SO THAT IS SCOTT SUMMERS FROM GOLD COAST, AUSTRALIA--
--A COUPLE OF HOURS AGO.
TURN IT OFF.
S.H.I.E.L.D. HELICARRIER. LOCATED 1000 FT. OVER RENO, NV.
OKAY, THAT'S-- YEAH--THANK YOU.
AND IS THIS TRUE, COULSON?
DID THE X-MEN TAKE OUT THE AVENGERS WITHOUT LIFTING A FINGER?
WELL, COMMANDER HILL, ONE OF THEIR NEW MUTANT RECRUITS, ACCORDING TO AUSTRALIAN AUTHORITY REPORTS, CAN STOP TIME.
STOP TIME?
SHE TRAPPED THE AVENGERS IN A--
SHE STOPPED ACTUAL TIME?
SHE TRAPPED THEM IN A TIME BUBBLE AND THE X-MEN TOOK OFF.

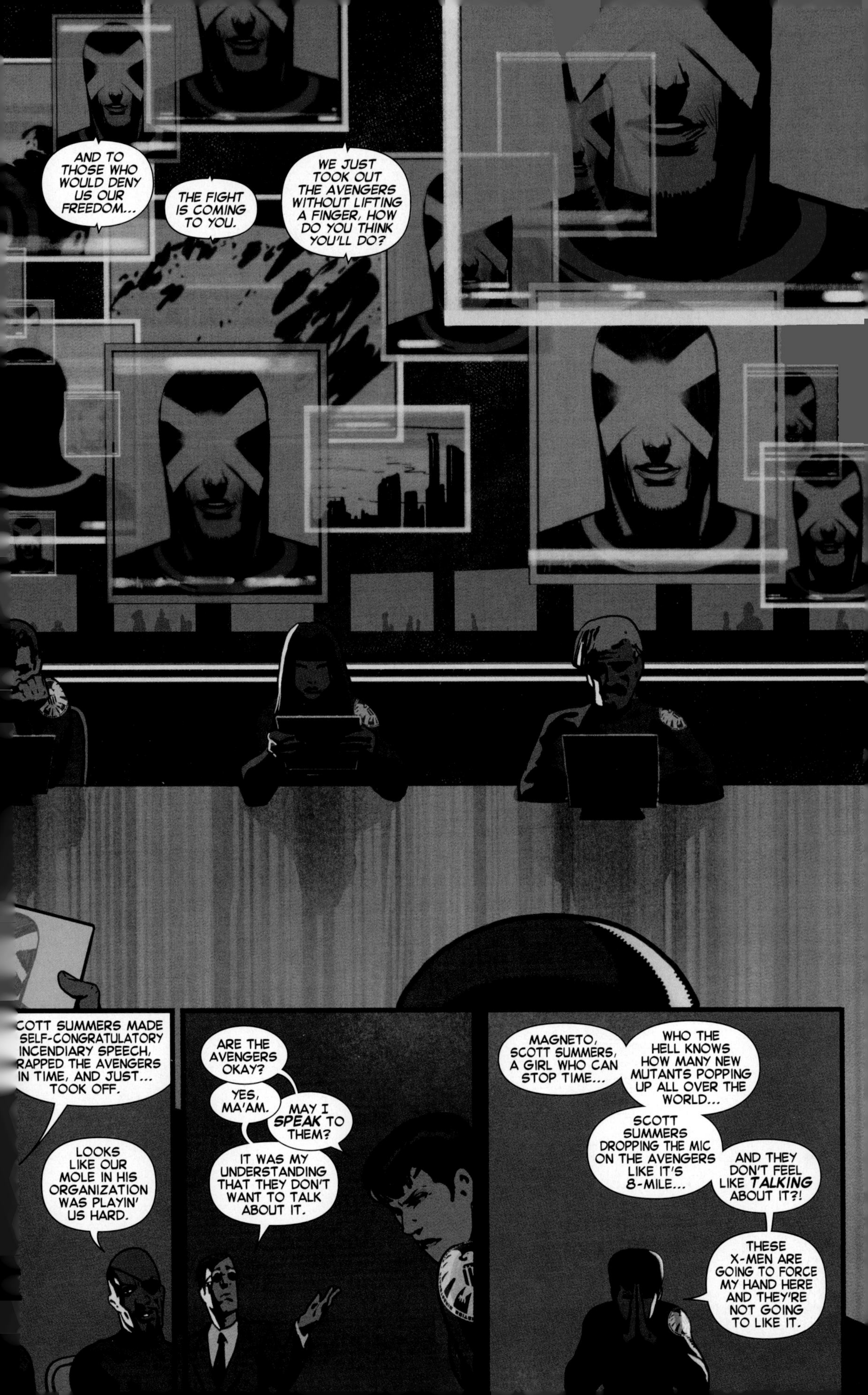
AND TO THOSE WHO WOULD DENY US OUR FREEDOM...
THE FIGHT IS COMING TO YOU.
WE JUST TOOK OUT THE AVENGERS WITHOUT LIFTING A FINGER, HOW DO YOU THINK YOU'LL DO?
SCOTT SUMMERS MADE A SELF-CONGRATULATORY INCENDIARY SPEECH, TRAPPED THE AVENGERS IN TIME, AND JUST... TOOK OFF.
LOOKS LIKE OUR MOLE IN HIS ORGANIZATION WAS PLAYIN' US HARD.
ARE THE AVENGERS OKAY?
YES, MA'AM.
MAY I SPEAK TO THEM?
IT WAS MY UNDERSTANDING THAT THEY DON'T WANT TO TALK ABOUT IT.
MAGNETO, SCOTT SUMMERS, A GIRL WHO CAN STOP TIME...
WHO THE HELL KNOWS HOW MANY NEW MUTANTS POPPING UP ALL OVER THE WORLD...
SCOTT SUMMERS DROPPING THE MIC ON THE AVENGERS LIKE IT'S 8-MILE...
AND THEY DON'T FEEL LIKE TALKING ABOUT IT?!
THESE X-MEN ARE GOING TO FORCE MY HAND HERE AND THEY'RE NOT GOING TO LIKE IT.

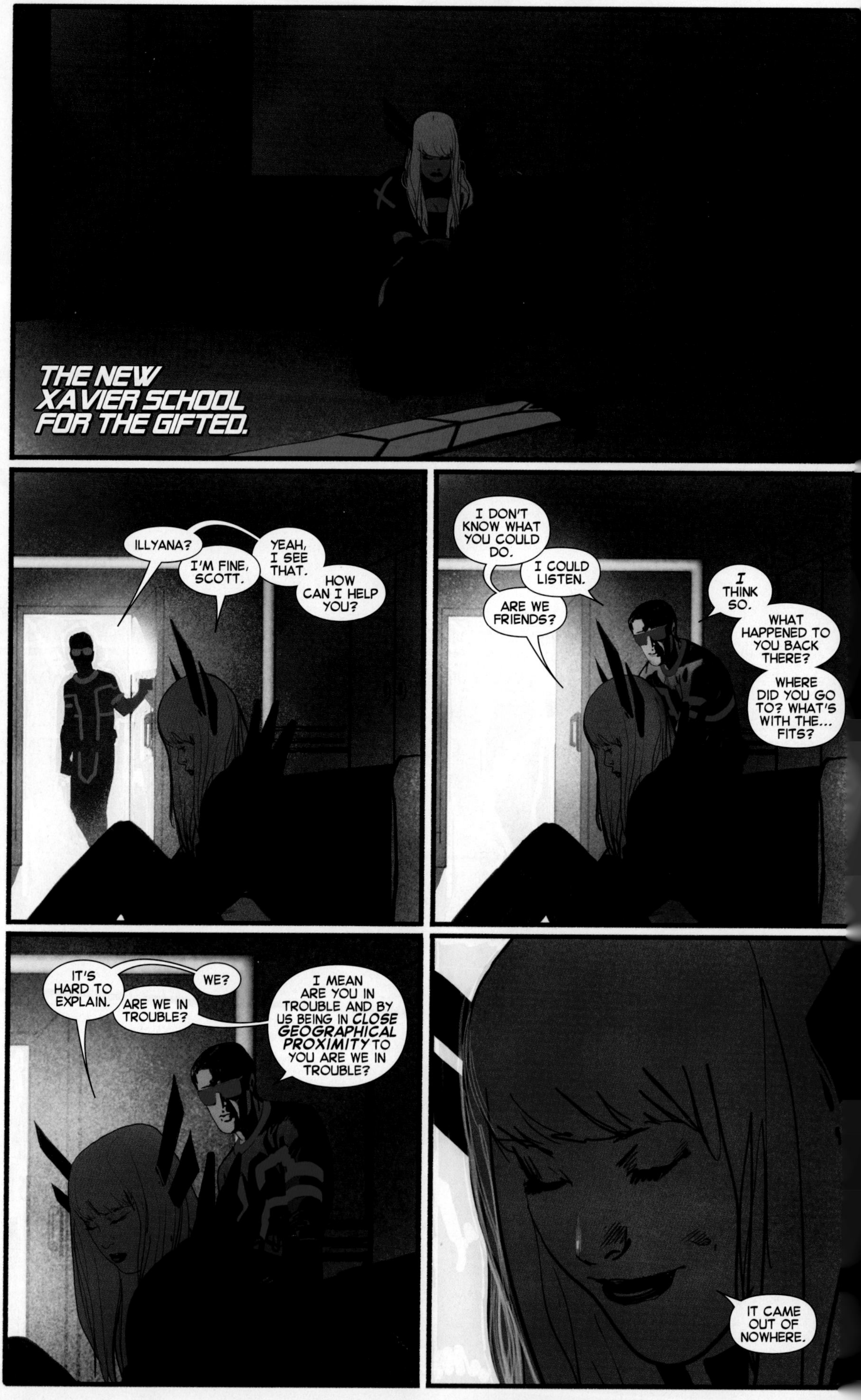
THE NEW XAVIER SCHOOL FOR THE GIFTED.
ILLYANA?
I'M FINE, SCOTT.
YEAH, I SEE THAT.
HOW CAN I HELP YOU?
I DON'T KNOW WHAT YOU COULD DO.
I COULD LISTEN.
ARE WE FRIENDS?
I THINK SO.
WHAT HAPPENED TO YOU BACK THERE?
WHERE DID YOU GO TO? WHAT'S WITH THE... FITS?
IT'S HARD TO EXPLAIN.
WE?
ARE WE IN TROUBLE?
I MEAN ARE YOU IN TROUBLE AND BY US BEING IN CLOSE GEOGRAPHICAL PROXIMITY TO YOU ARE WE IN TROUBLE?
IT CAME OUT OF NOWHERE.

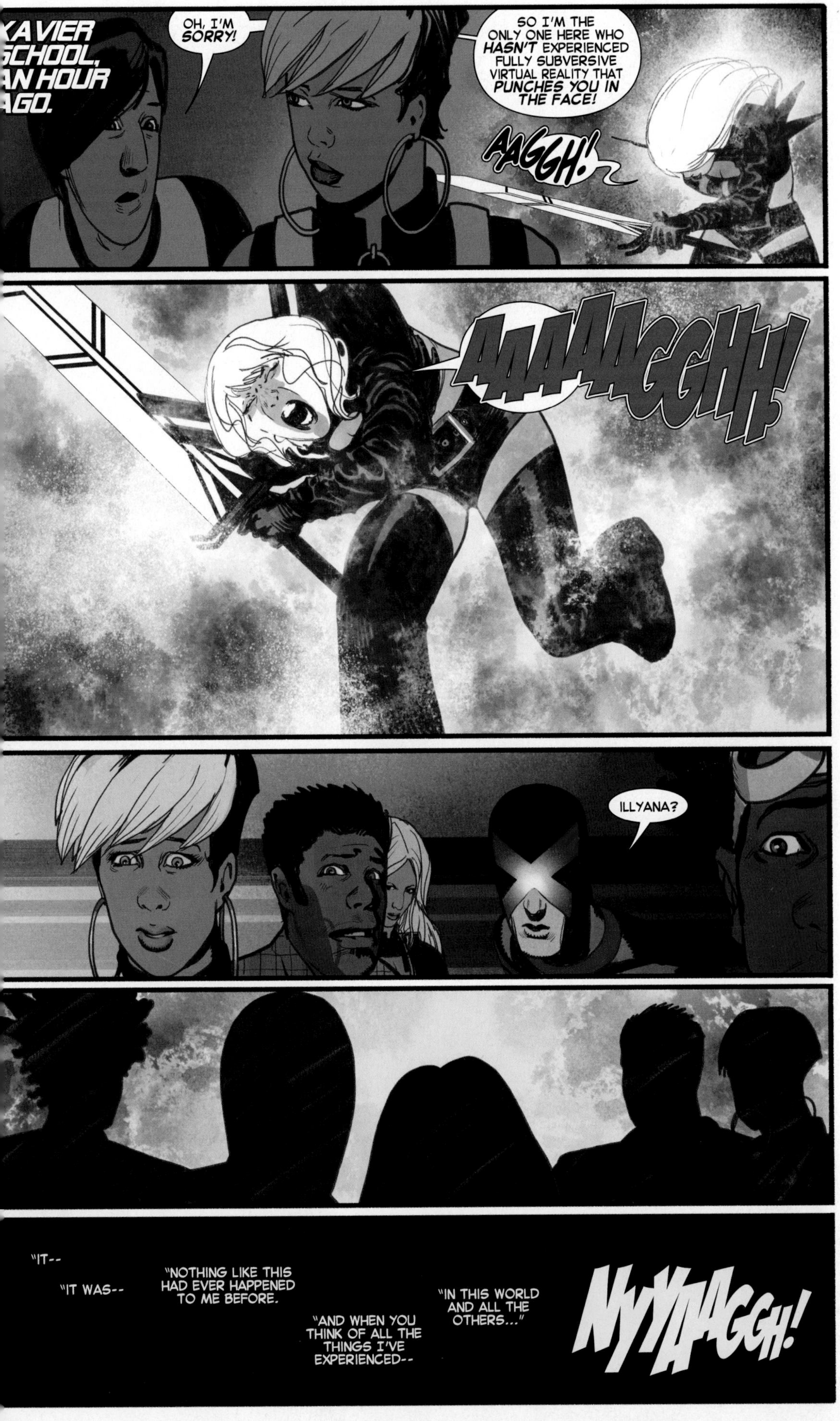
XAVIER SCHOOL, AN HOUR AGO.
OH, I'M SORRY!
SO I'M THE ONLY ONE HERE WHO HASN'T EXPERIENCED FULLY SUBVERSIVE VIRTUAL REALITY THAT PUNCHES YOU IN THE FACE!
AAGGH!
AAAAAAGGHH!
ILLYANA?
"IT--
"IT WAS--
"NOTHING LIKE THIS HAD EVER HAPPENED TO ME BEFORE.
"AND WHEN YOU THINK OF ALL THE THINGS I'VE EXPERIENCED--
"IN THIS WORLD AND ALL THE OTHERS..."
NYYAAGGH!

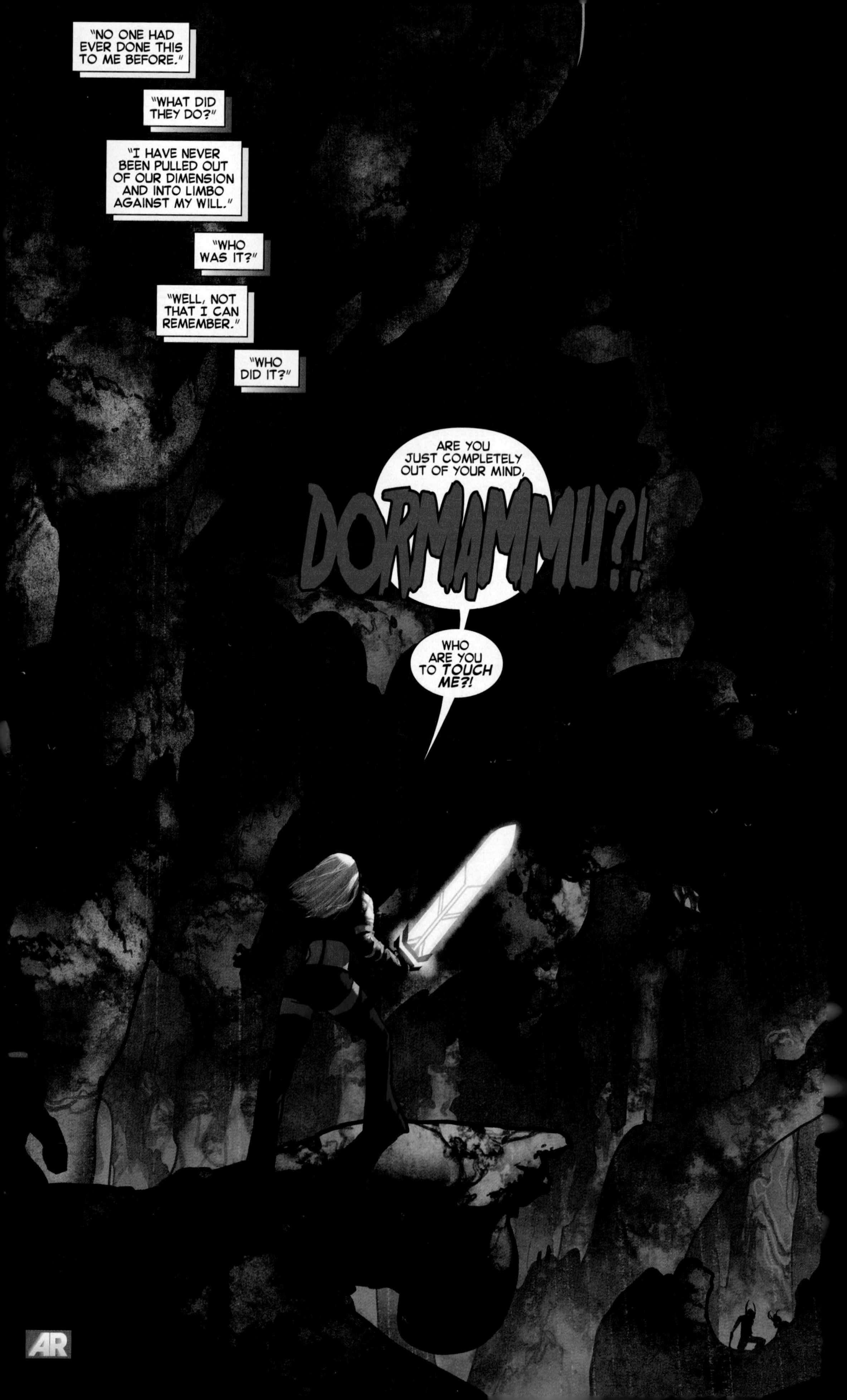
"NO ONE HAD EVER DONE THIS TO ME BEFORE."
"WHAT DID THEY DO?"
"I HAVE NEVER BEEN PULLED OUT OF OUR DIMENSION AND INTO LIMBO AGAINST MY WILL."
"WHO WAS IT?"
"WELL, NOT THAT I CAN REMEMBER."
"WHO DID IT?"
ARE YOU JUST COMPLETELY OUT OF YOUR MIND, DORMAMMU?!
WHO ARE YOU TO *TOUCH ME?!*
AR

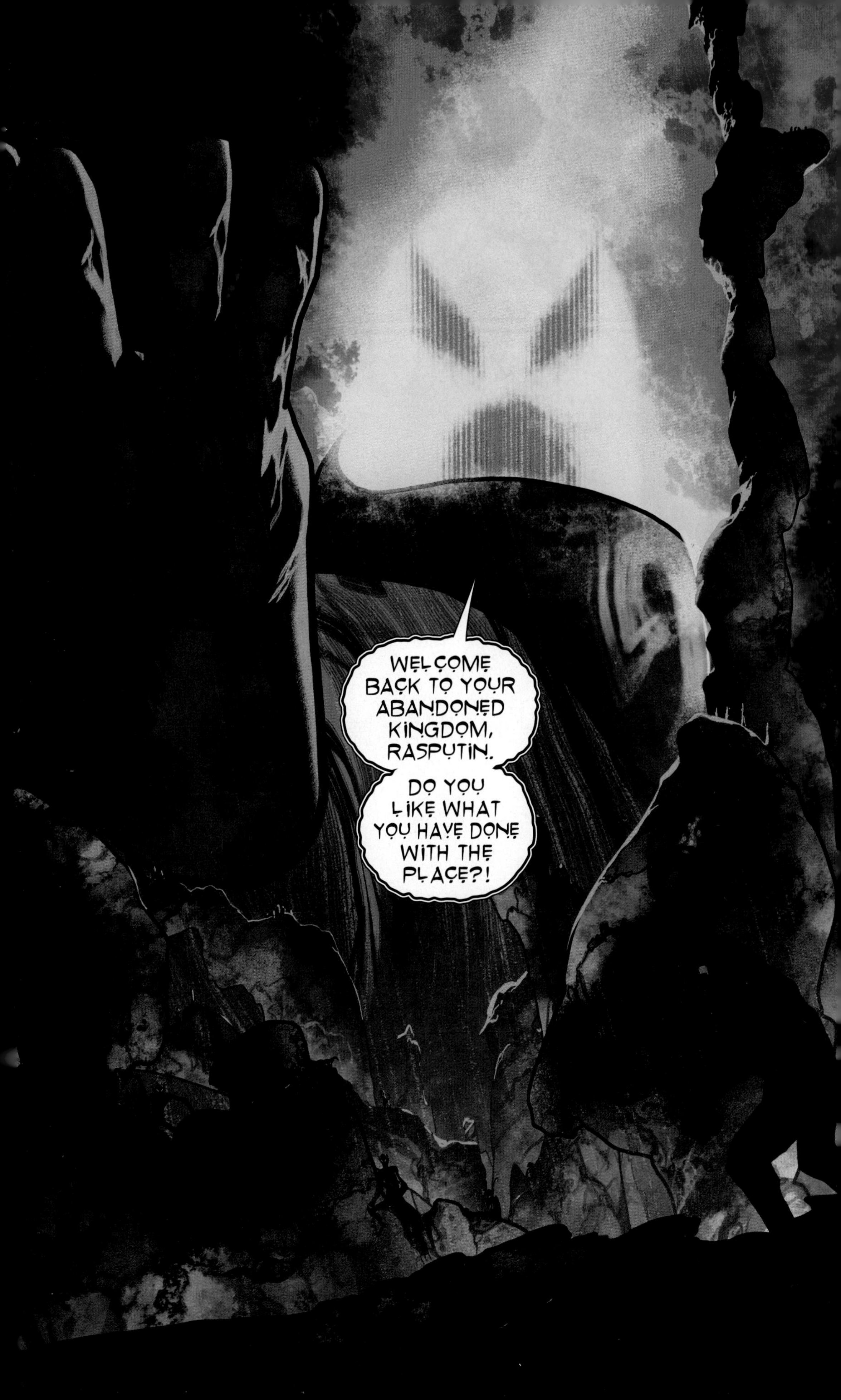
WELCOME BACK TO YOUR ABANDONED KINGDOM, RASPUTIN.
DO YOU LIKE WHAT YOU HAVE DONE WITH THE PLACE?!

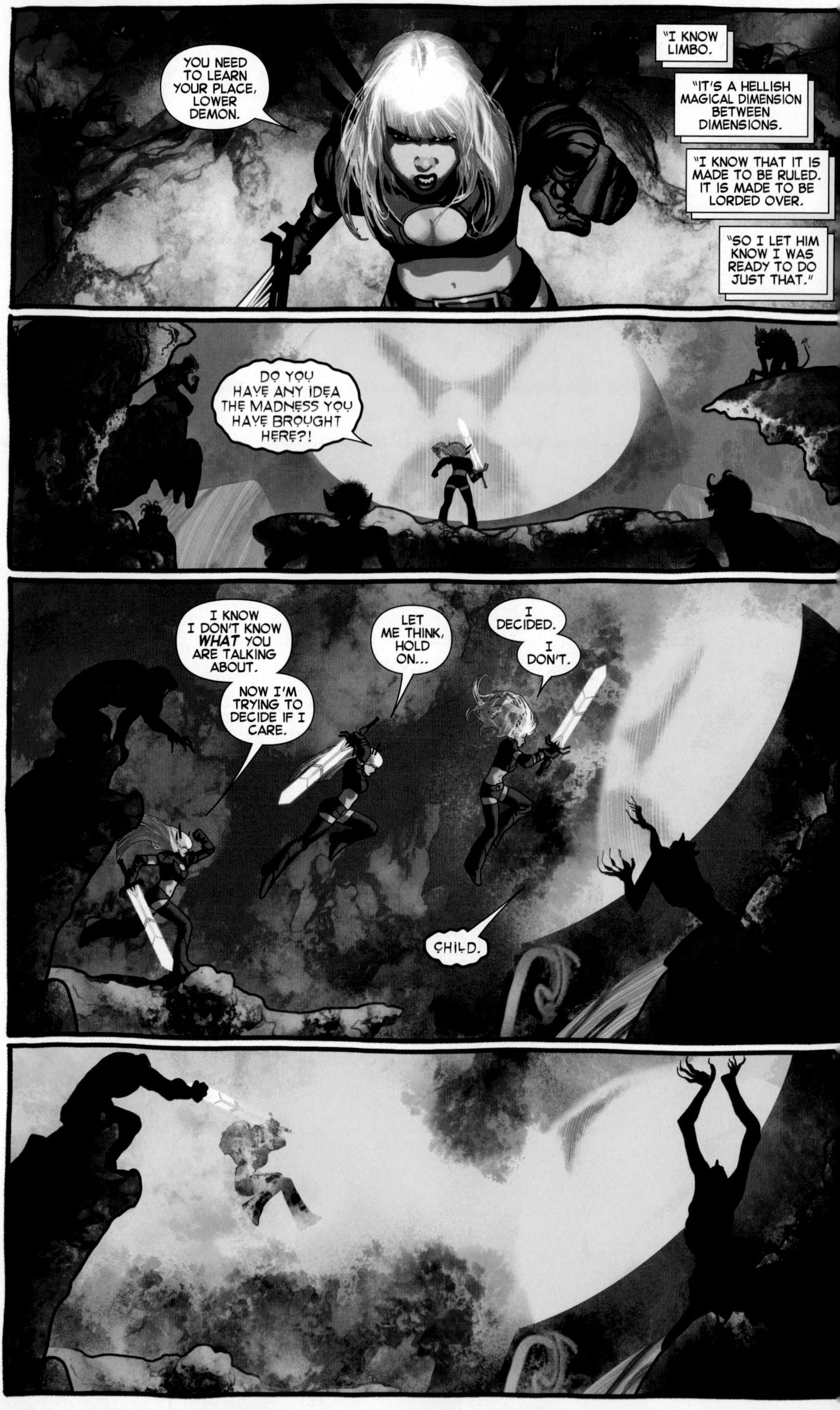
"I KNOW LIMBO.
"IT'S A HELLISH MAGICAL DIMENSION BETWEEN DIMENSIONS.
"I KNOW THAT IT IS MADE TO BE RULED. IT IS MADE TO BE LORDED OVER.
"SO I LET HIM KNOW I WAS READY TO DO JUST THAT."
YOU NEED TO LEARN YOUR PLACE, LOWER DEMON.
DO YOU HAVE ANY IDEA THE MADNESS YOU HAVE BROUGHT HERE?!
I KNOW I DON'T KNOW WHAT YOU ARE TALKING ABOUT.
NOW I'M TRYING TO DECIDE IF I CARE.
LET ME THINK, HOLD ON...
I DECIDED.
I DON'T.
CHILD.

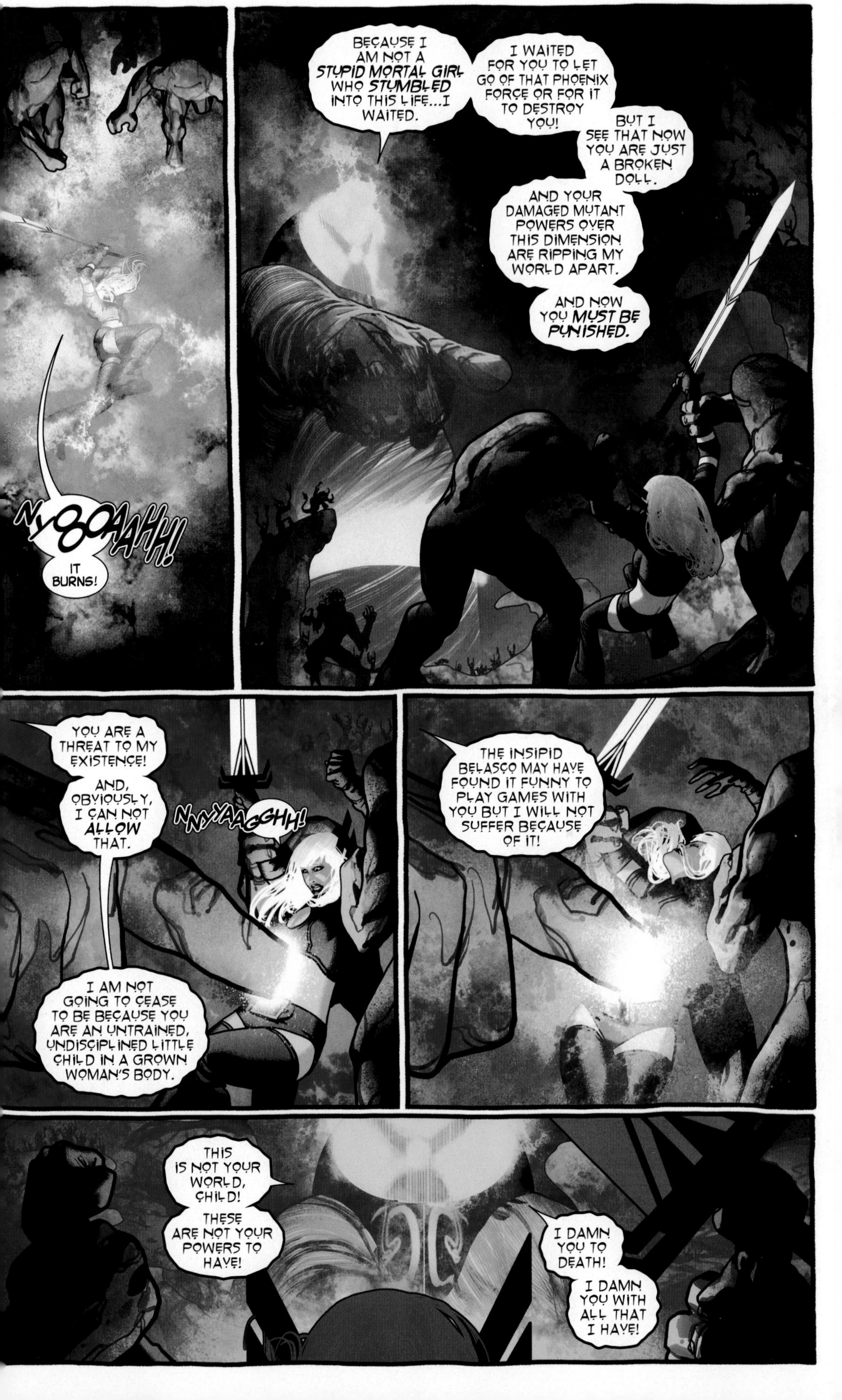
NyBOAAHH!
IT BURNS!
BECAUSE I AM NOT A STUPID MORTAL GIRL WHO STUMBLED INTO THIS LIFE...I WAITED.
I WAITED FOR YOU TO LET GO OF THAT PHOENIX FORCE OR FOR IT TO DESTROY YOU!
BUT I SEE THAT NOW YOU ARE JUST A BROKEN DOLL.
AND YOUR DAMAGED MUTANT POWERS OVER THIS DIMENSION ARE RIPPING MY WORLD APART.
AND NOW YOU MUST BE PUNISHED.
YOU ARE A THREAT TO MY EXISTENCE!
AND, OBVIOUSLY, I CAN NOT ALLOW THAT.
NNYYAAGGHH!
I AM NOT GOING TO CEASE TO BE BECAUSE YOU ARE AN UNTRAINED, UNDISCIPLINED LITTLE CHILD IN A GROWN WOMAN'S BODY.
THE INSIPID BELASCO MAY HAVE FOUND IT FUNNY TO PLAY GAMES WITH YOU BUT I WILL NOT SUFFER BECAUSE OF IT!
THIS IS NOT YOUR WORLD, CHILD!
THESE ARE NOT YOUR POWERS TO HAVE!
I DAMN YOU TO DEATH!
I DAMN YOU WITH ALL THAT I HAVE!

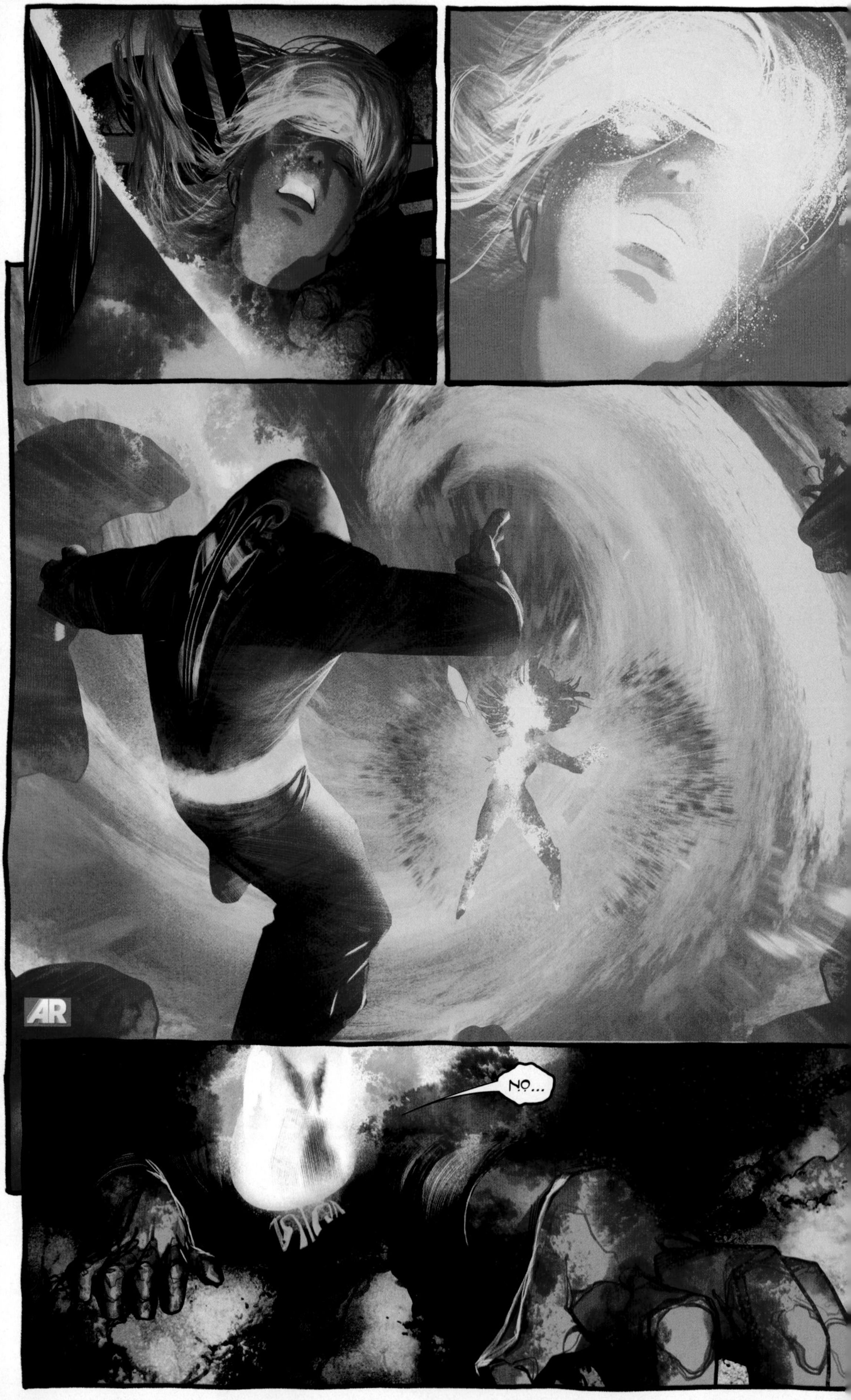
NO....

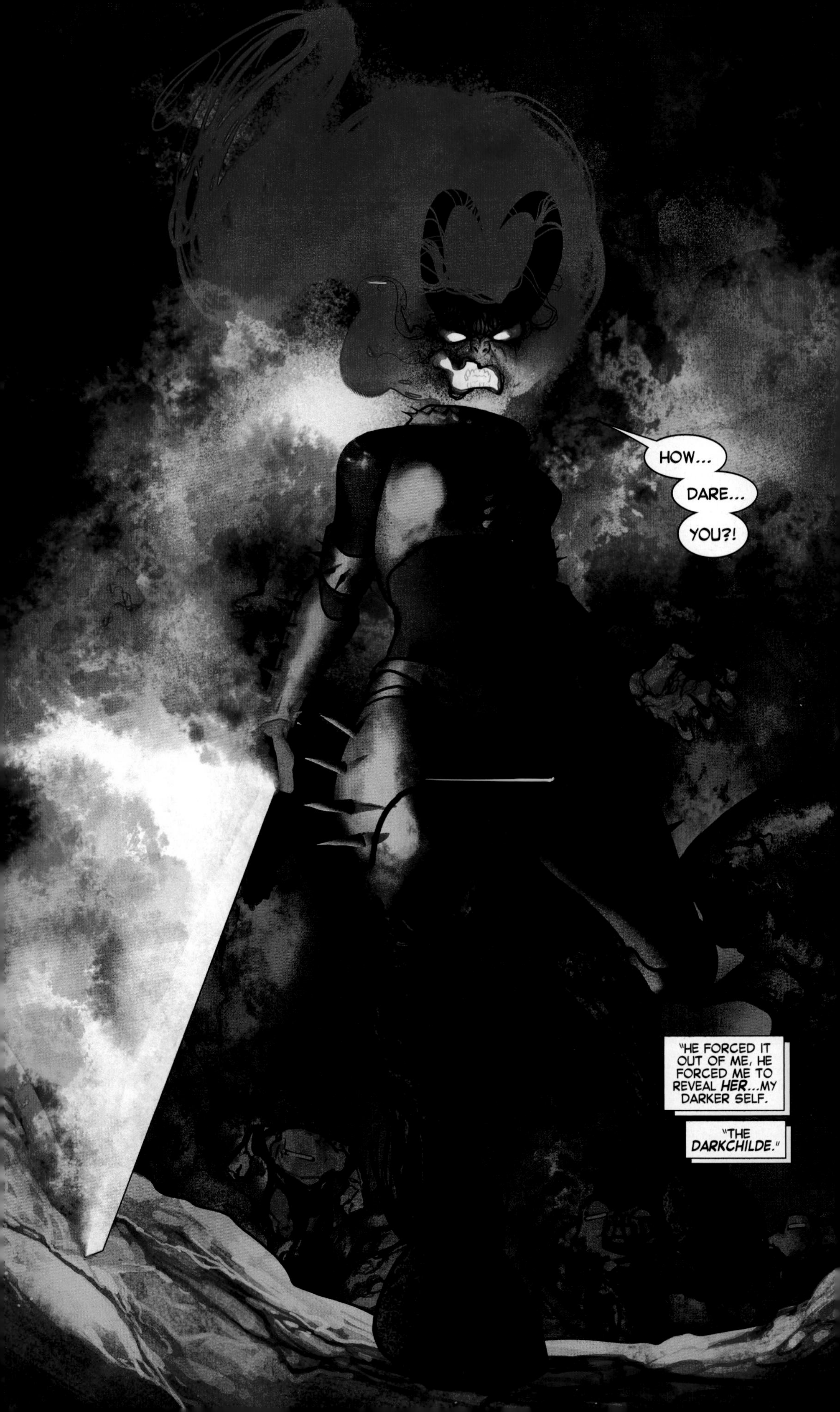
HOW...
DARE...
YOU?!
"HE FORCED IT OUT OF ME, HE FORCED ME TO REVEAL HER...MY DARKER SELF.
"THE DARKCHILDE."

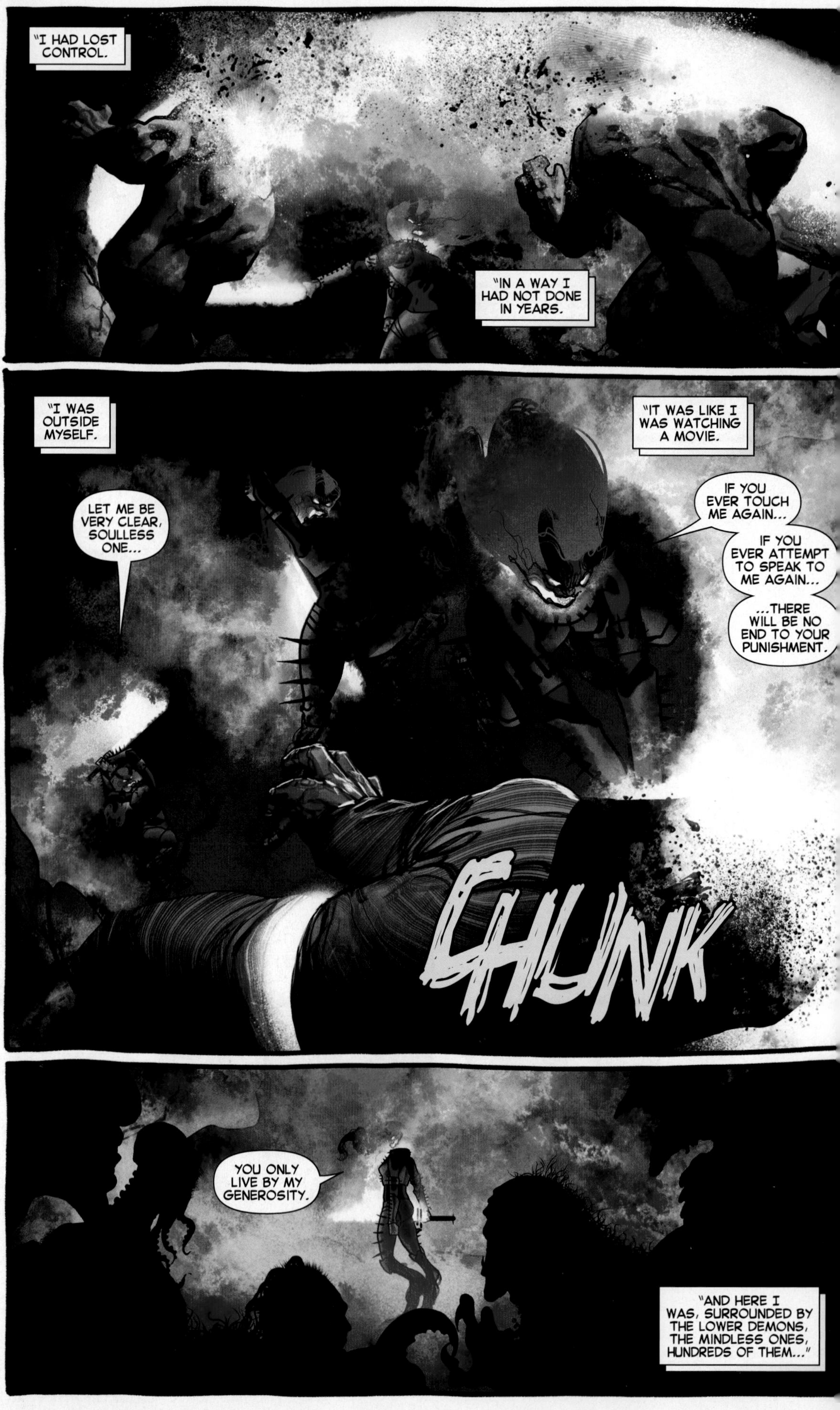
"I HAD LOST CONTROL.
"IN A WAY I HAD NOT DONE IN YEARS.
"I WAS OUTSIDE MYSELF.
"IT WAS LIKE I WAS WATCHING A MOVIE.
LET ME BE VERY CLEAR, SOULLESS ONE...
IF YOU EVER TOUCH ME AGAIN...
IF YOU EVER ATTEMPT TO SPEAK TO ME AGAIN...
...THERE WILL BE NO END TO YOUR PUNISHMENT.
CHUNK
YOU ONLY LIVE BY MY GENEROSITY.
"AND HERE I WAS, SURROUNDED BY THE LOWER DEMONS, THE MINDLESS ONES, HUNDREDS OF THEM..."

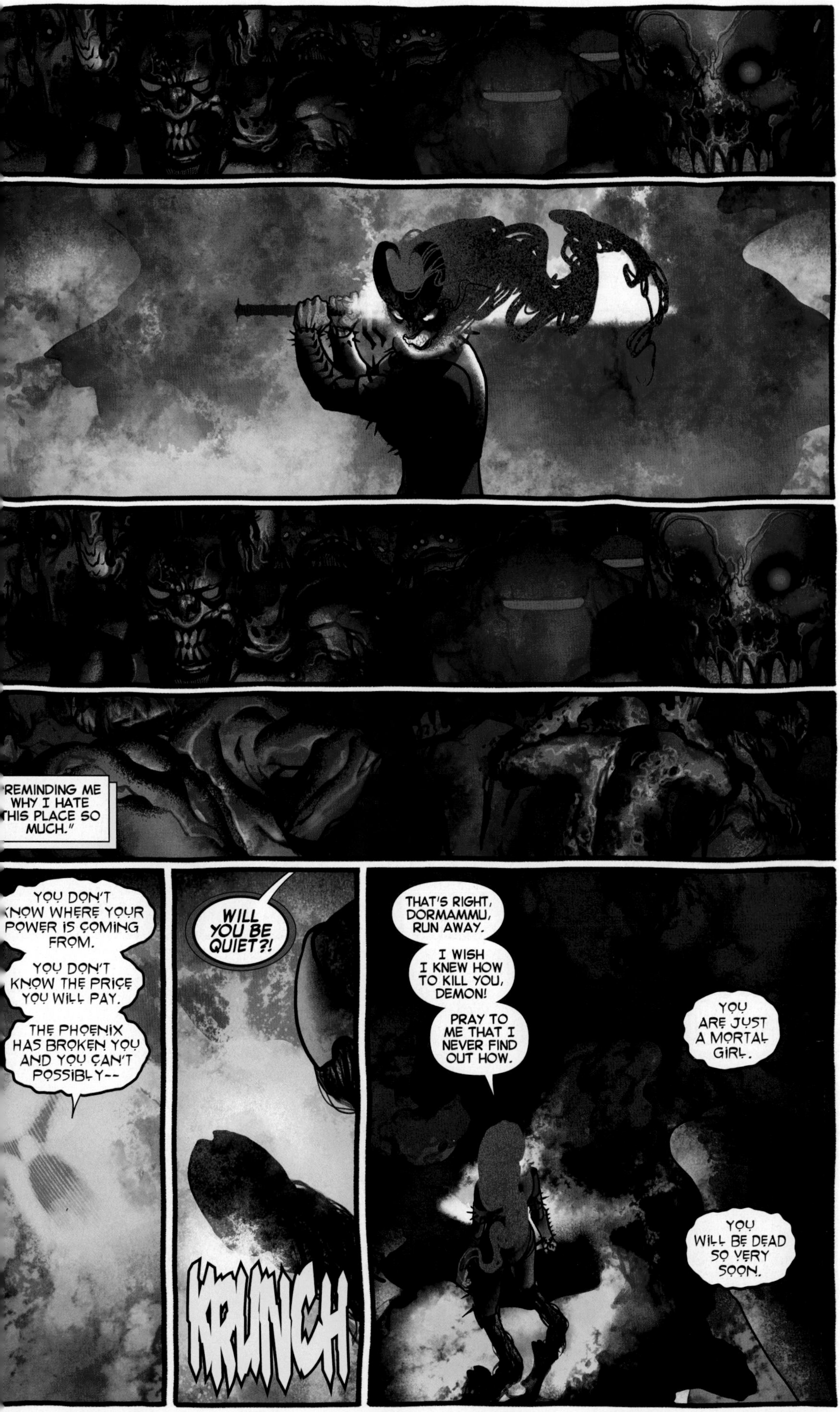

"REMINDING ME WHY I HATE THIS PLACE SO MUCH."
YOU DON'T KNOW WHERE YOUR POWER IS COMING FROM.
YOU DON'T KNOW THE PRICE YOU WILL PAY.
THE PHOENIX HAS BROKEN YOU AND YOU CAN'T POSSIBLY--
WILL YOU BE QUIET?!
KRUNCH
THAT'S RIGHT, DORMAMMU, RUN AWAY.
I WISH I KNEW HOW TO KILL YOU, DEMON!
PRAY TO ME THAT I NEVER FIND OUT HOW.
YOU ARE JUST A MORTAL GIRL.
YOU WILL BE DEAD SO VERY SOON.

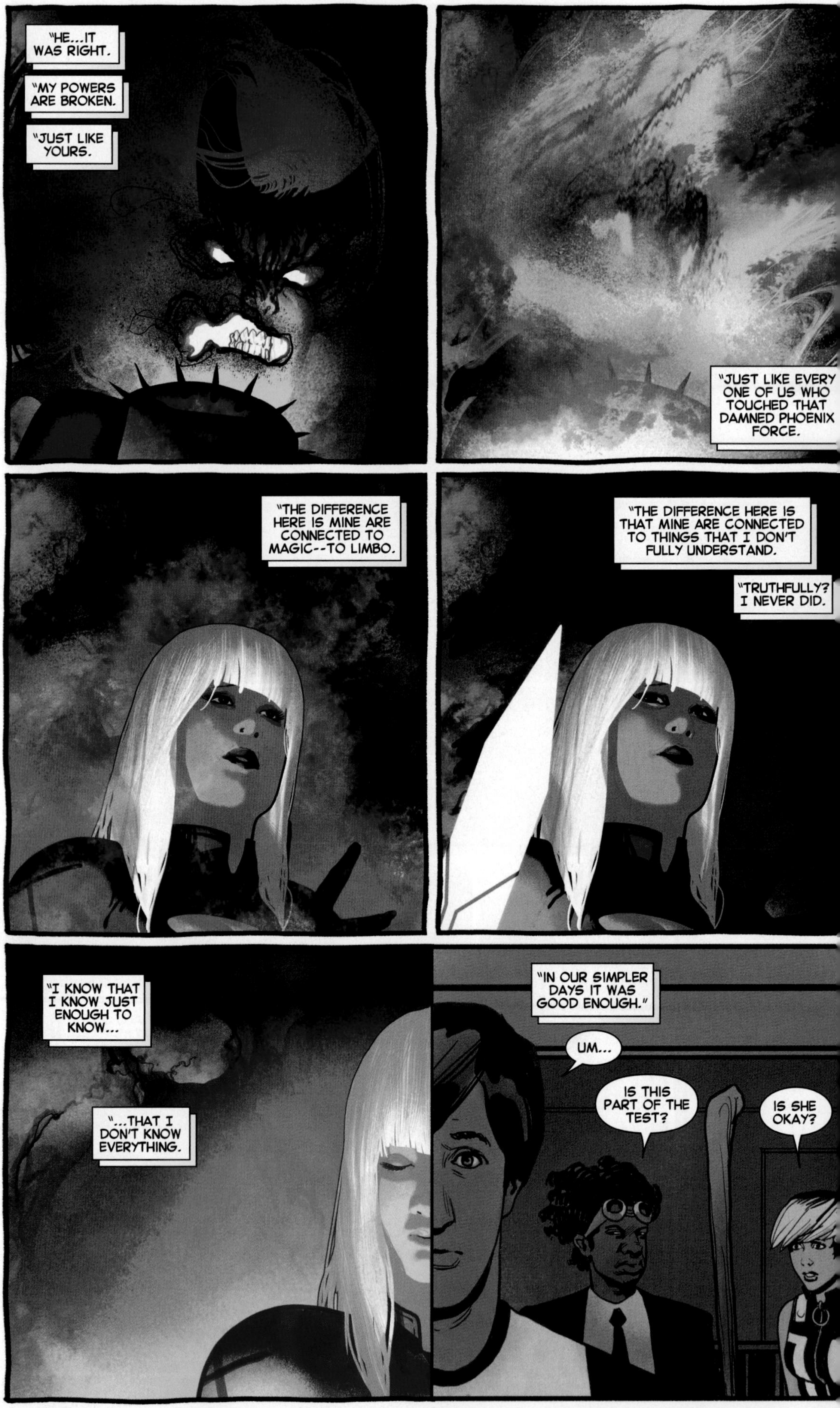
"HE...IT WAS RIGHT.
"MY POWERS ARE BROKEN.
"JUST LIKE YOURS.
"JUST LIKE EVERY ONE OF US WHO TOUCHED THAT DAMNED PHOENIX FORCE.
"THE DIFFERENCE HERE IS MINE ARE CONNECTED TO MAGIC--TO LIMBO.
"THE DIFFERENCE HERE IS THAT MINE ARE CONNECTED TO THINGS THAT I DON'T FULLY UNDERSTAND.
"TRUTHFULLY? I NEVER DID.
"I KNOW THAT I KNOW JUST ENOUGH TO KNOW...
"...THAT I DON'T KNOW EVERYTHING.
"IN OUR SIMPLER DAYS IT WAS GOOD ENOUGH."
UM...
IS THIS PART OF THE TEST?
IS SHE OKAY?

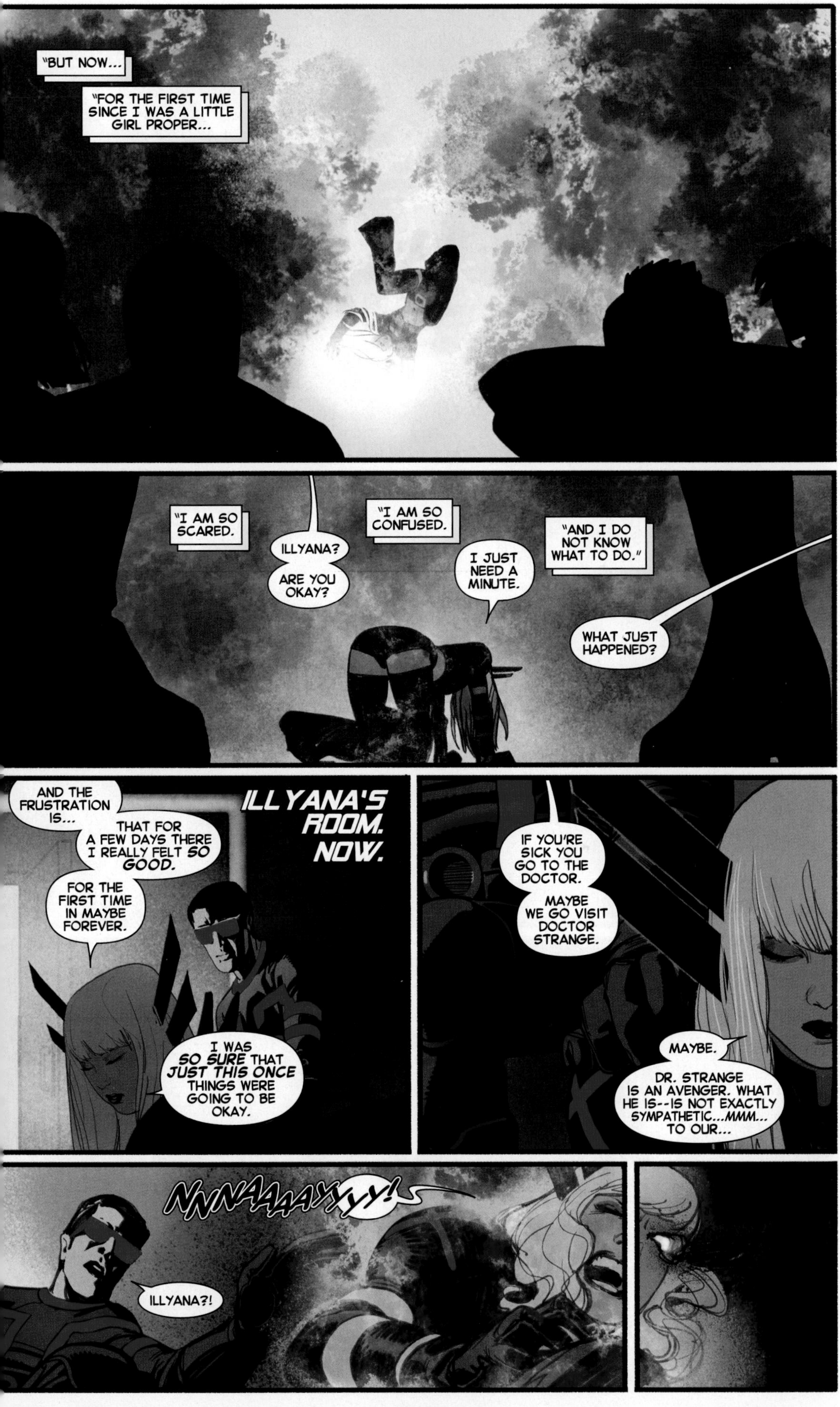

"BUT NOW...
"FOR THE FIRST TIME SINCE I WAS A LITTLE GIRL PROPER...
"I AM SO SCARED.
ILLYANA?
ARE YOU OKAY?
"I AM SO CONFUSED.
I JUST NEED A MINUTE.
"AND I DO NOT KNOW WHAT TO DO."
WHAT JUST HAPPENED?
ILLYANA'S ROOM. NOW.
AND THE FRUSTRATION IS...
THAT FOR A FEW DAYS THERE I REALLY FELT SO GOOD.
FOR THE FIRST TIME IN MAYBE FOREVER.
I WAS SO SURE THAT JUST THIS ONCE THINGS WERE GOING TO BE OKAY.
IF YOU'RE SICK YOU GO TO THE DOCTOR.
MAYBE WE GO VISIT DOCTOR STRANGE.
MAYBE.
DR. STRANGE IS AN AVENGER. WHAT HE IS--IS NOT EXACTLY SYMPATHETIC...MMM... TO OUR...
NNNAAAAAYYYYY!
ILLYANA?!

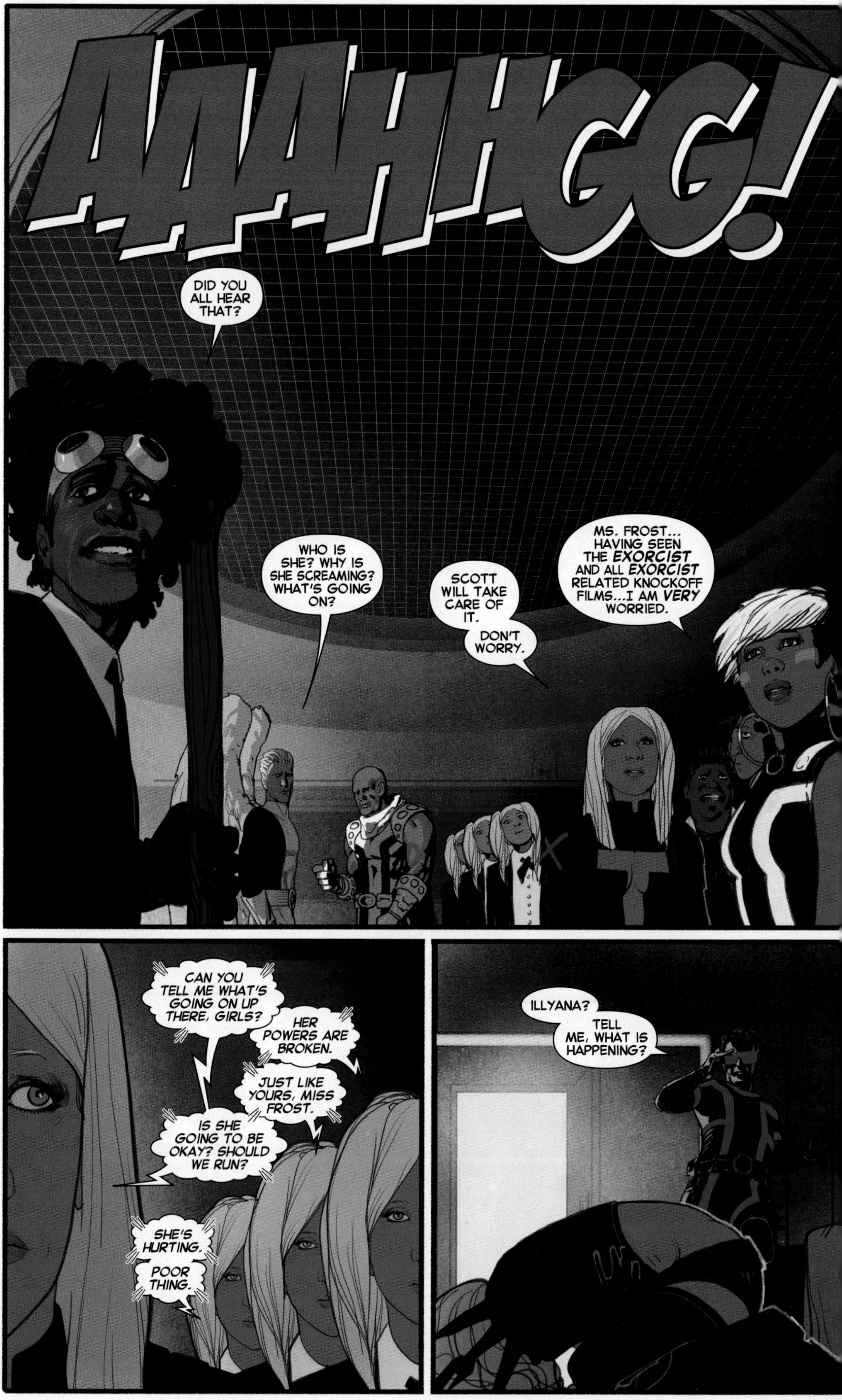
AAAHHGG!
DID YOU ALL HEAR THAT?
WHO IS SHE? WHY IS SHE SCREAMING? WHAT'S GOING ON?
SCOTT WILL TAKE CARE OF IT.
DON'T WORRY.
MS. FROST... HAVING SEEN THE EXORCIST AND ALL EXORCIST RELATED KNOCKOFF FILMS...I AM VERY WORRIED.
CAN YOU TELL ME WHAT'S GOING ON UP THERE, GIRLS?
HER POWERS ARE BROKEN.
JUST LIKE YOURS, MISS FROST.
IS SHE GOING TO BE OKAY? SHOULD WE RUN?
SHE'S HURTING.
POOR THING.
ILLYANA?
TELL ME, WHAT IS HAPPENING?

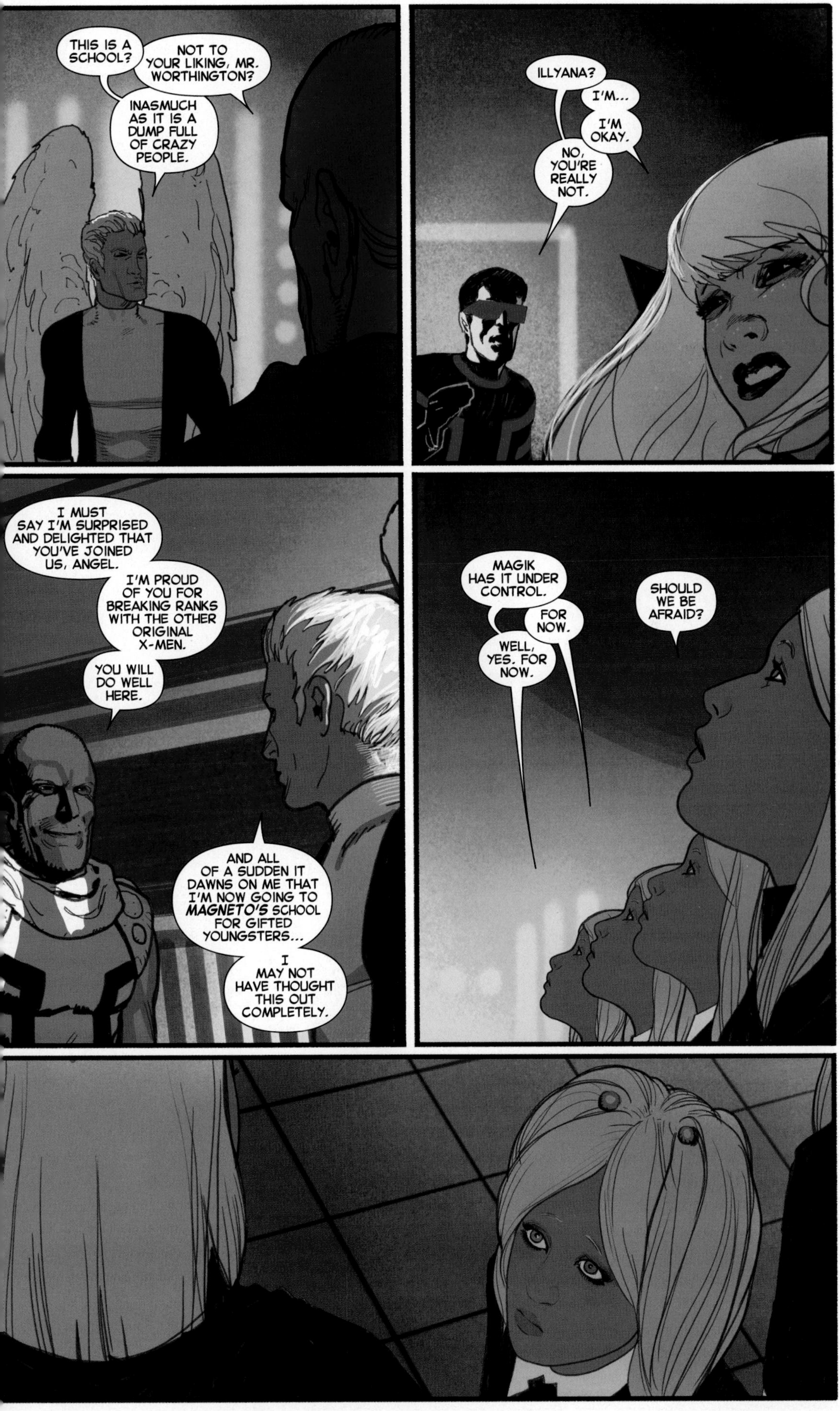
THIS IS A SCHOOL?
NOT TO YOUR LIKING, MR. WORTHINGTON?
INASMUCH AS IT IS A DUMP FULL OF CRAZY PEOPLE.
ILLYANA?
I'M...
I'M OKAY.
NO, YOU'RE REALLY NOT.
I MUST SAY I'M SURPRISED AND DELIGHTED THAT YOU'VE JOINED US, ANGEL.
I'M PROUD OF YOU FOR BREAKING RANKS WITH THE OTHER ORIGINAL X-MEN.
YOU WILL DO WELL HERE.
AND ALL OF A SUDDEN IT DAWNS ON ME THAT I'M NOW GOING TO MAGNETO'S SCHOOL FOR GIFTED YOUNGSTERS...
I MAY NOT HAVE THOUGHT THIS OUT COMPLETELY.
MAGIK HAS IT UNDER CONTROL.
FOR NOW.
WELL, YES. FOR NOW.
SHOULD WE BE AFRAID?

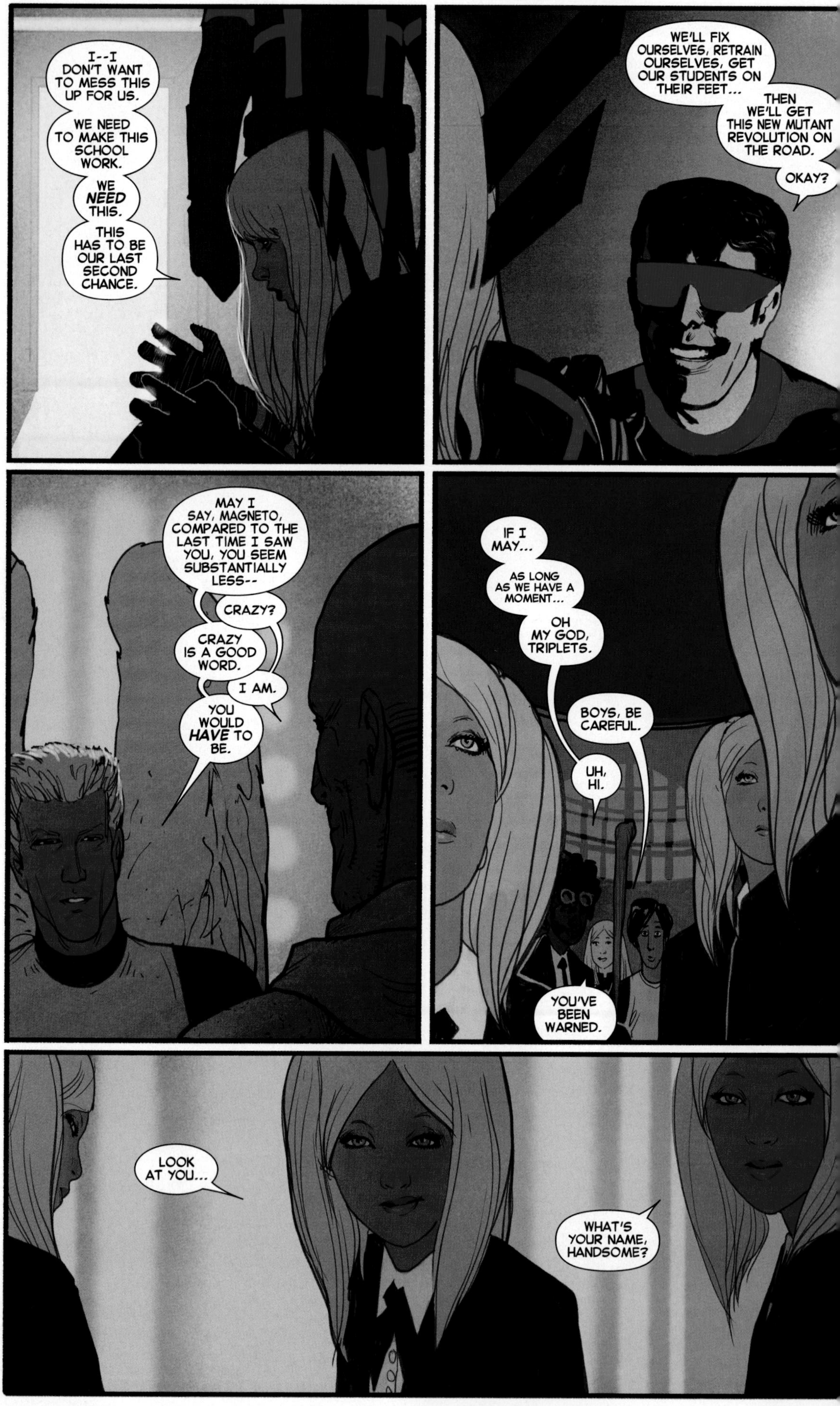

I--I DON'T WANT TO MESS THIS UP FOR US.
WE NEED TO MAKE THIS SCHOOL WORK.
WE *NEED* THIS.
THIS HAS TO BE OUR LAST SECOND CHANCE.
WE'LL FIX OURSELVES, RETRAIN OURSELVES, GET OUR STUDENTS ON THEIR FEET...
THEN WE'LL GET THIS NEW MUTANT REVOLUTION ON THE ROAD.
OKAY?
MAY I SAY, MAGNETO, COMPARED TO THE LAST TIME I SAW YOU, YOU SEEM SUBSTANTIALLY LESS--
CRAZY?
CRAZY IS A GOOD WORD.
I AM.
YOU WOULD *HAVE* TO BE.
IF I MAY...
AS LONG AS WE HAVE A MOMENT...
OH MY GOD, TRIPLETS.
BOYS, BE CAREFUL.
UH, HI.
YOU'VE BEEN WARNED.
LOOK AT YOU...
WHAT'S YOUR NAME, HANDSOME?

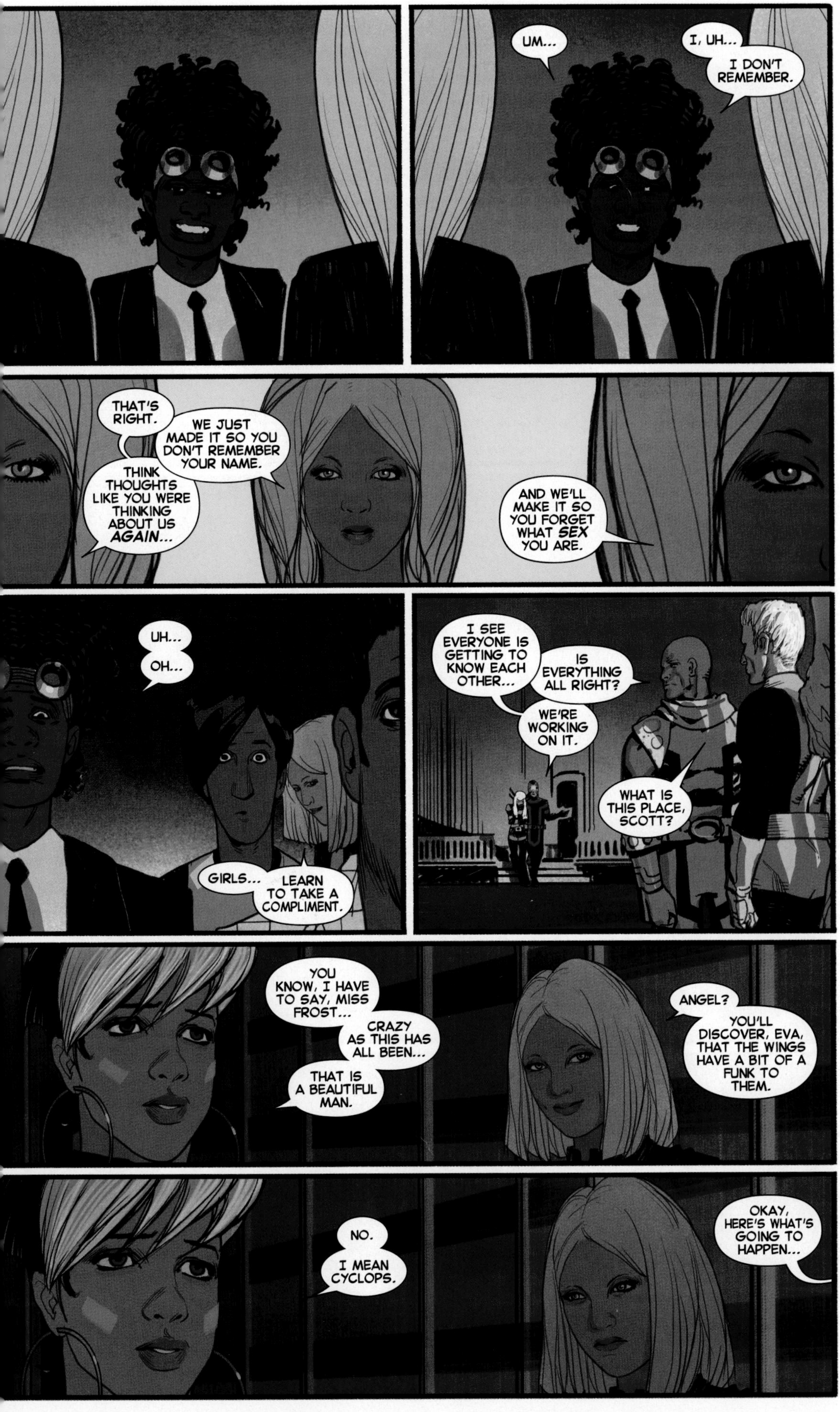
UM...
I, UH...
I DON'T REMEMBER.
THAT'S RIGHT.
WE JUST MADE IT SO YOU DON'T REMEMBER YOUR NAME.
THINK THOUGHTS LIKE YOU WERE THINKING ABOUT US *AGAIN*...
AND WE'LL MAKE IT SO YOU FORGET WHAT *SEX* YOU ARE.
UH...
OH...
GIRLS...
LEARN TO TAKE A COMPLIMENT.
I SEE EVERYONE IS GETTING TO KNOW EACH OTHER...
IS EVERYTHING ALL RIGHT?
WE'RE WORKING ON IT.
WHAT IS THIS PLACE, SCOTT?
YOU KNOW, I HAVE TO SAY, MISS FROST...
CRAZY AS THIS HAS ALL BEEN...
THAT IS A BEAUTIFUL MAN.
ANGEL?
YOU'LL DISCOVER, EVA, THAT THE WINGS HAVE A BIT OF A FUNK TO THEM.
NO.
I MEAN CYCLOPS.
OKAY, HERE'S WHAT'S GOING TO HAPPEN...

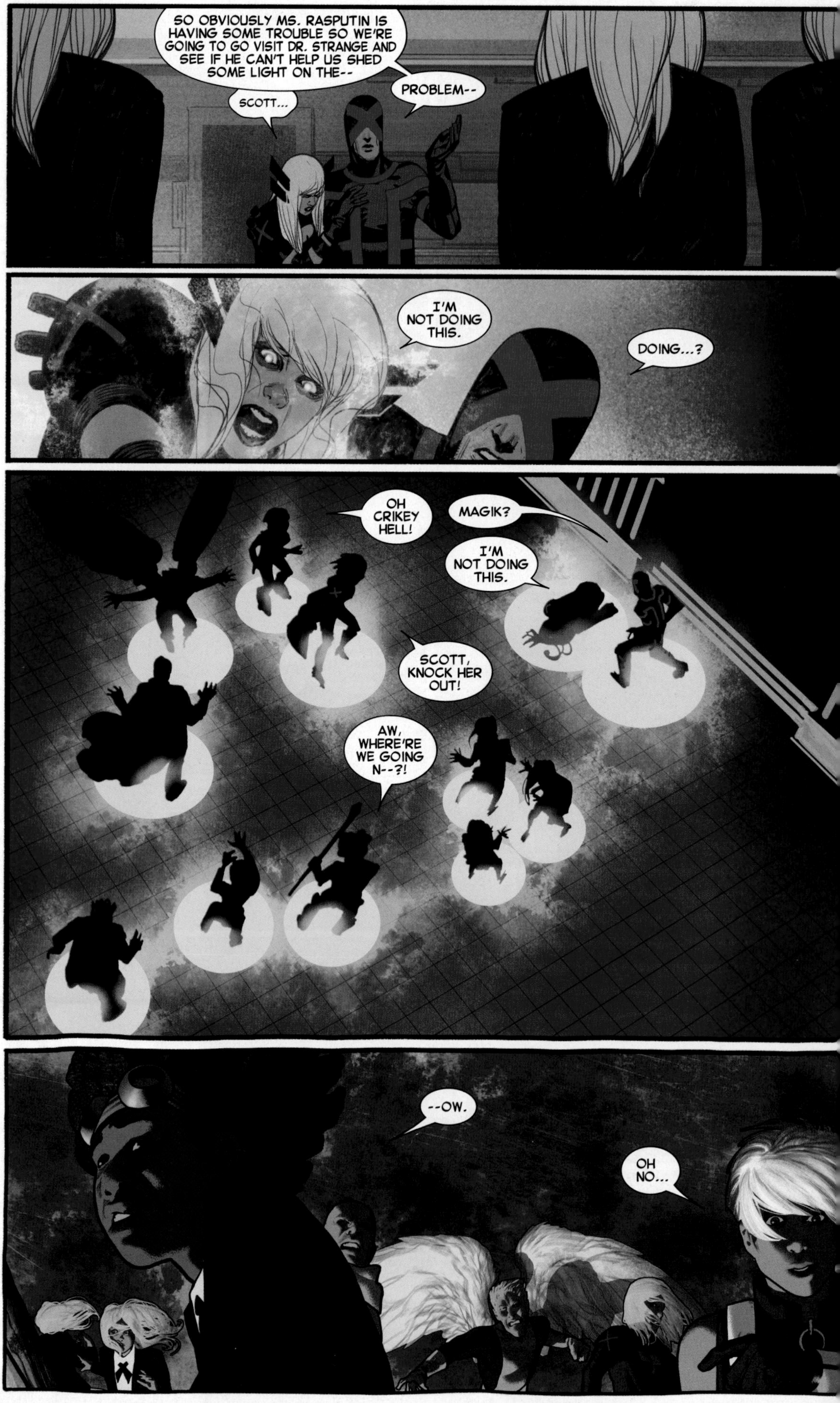
SO OBVIOUSLY MS. RASPUTIN IS HAVING SOME TROUBLE SO WE'RE GOING TO GO VISIT DR. STRANGE AND SEE IF HE CAN'T HELP US SHED SOME LIGHT ON THE--
SCOTT...
PROBLEM--
I'M NOT DOING THIS.
DOING...?
OH CRIKEY HELL!
MAGIK?
I'M NOT DOING THIS.
SCOTT, KNOCK HER OUT!
AW, WHERE'RE WE GOING N--?!
--OW.
OH NO...

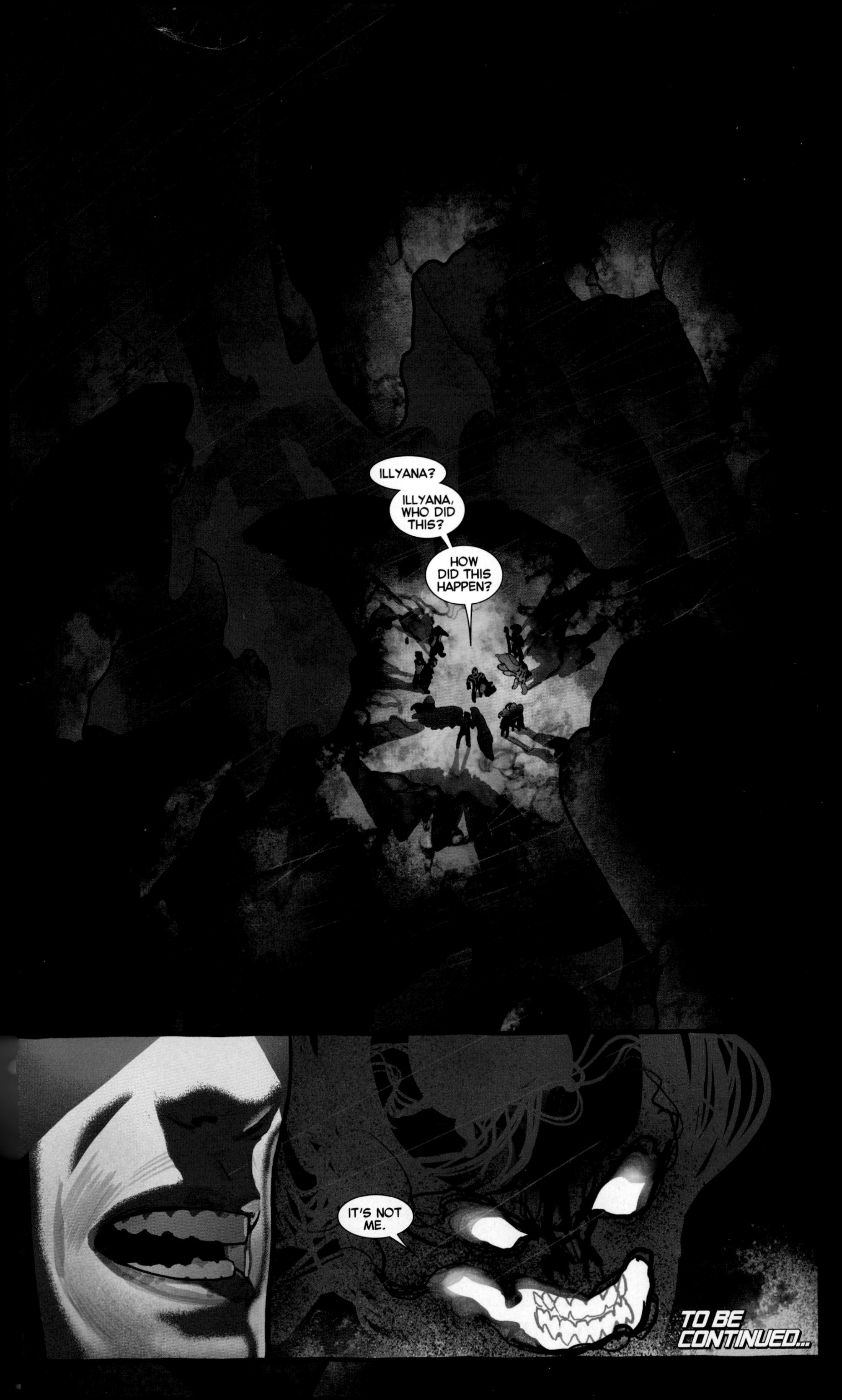
ILLYANA?
ILLYANA, WHO DID THIS?
HOW DID THIS HAPPEN?
IT'S NOT ME.
TO BE CONTINUED...

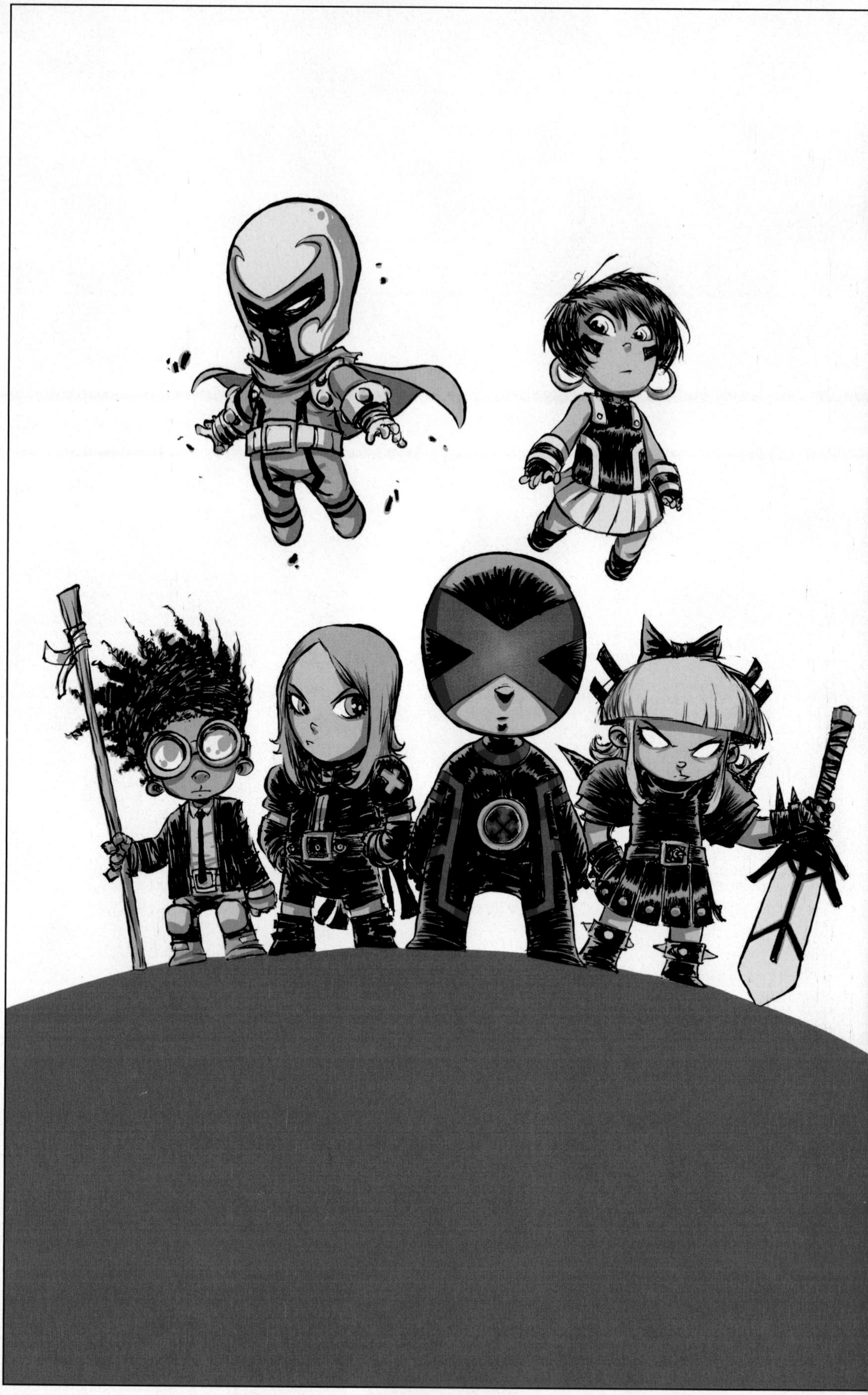

UNCANNY X-MEN #1 YOUNG VARIANT

BY SKOTTIE YOUNG

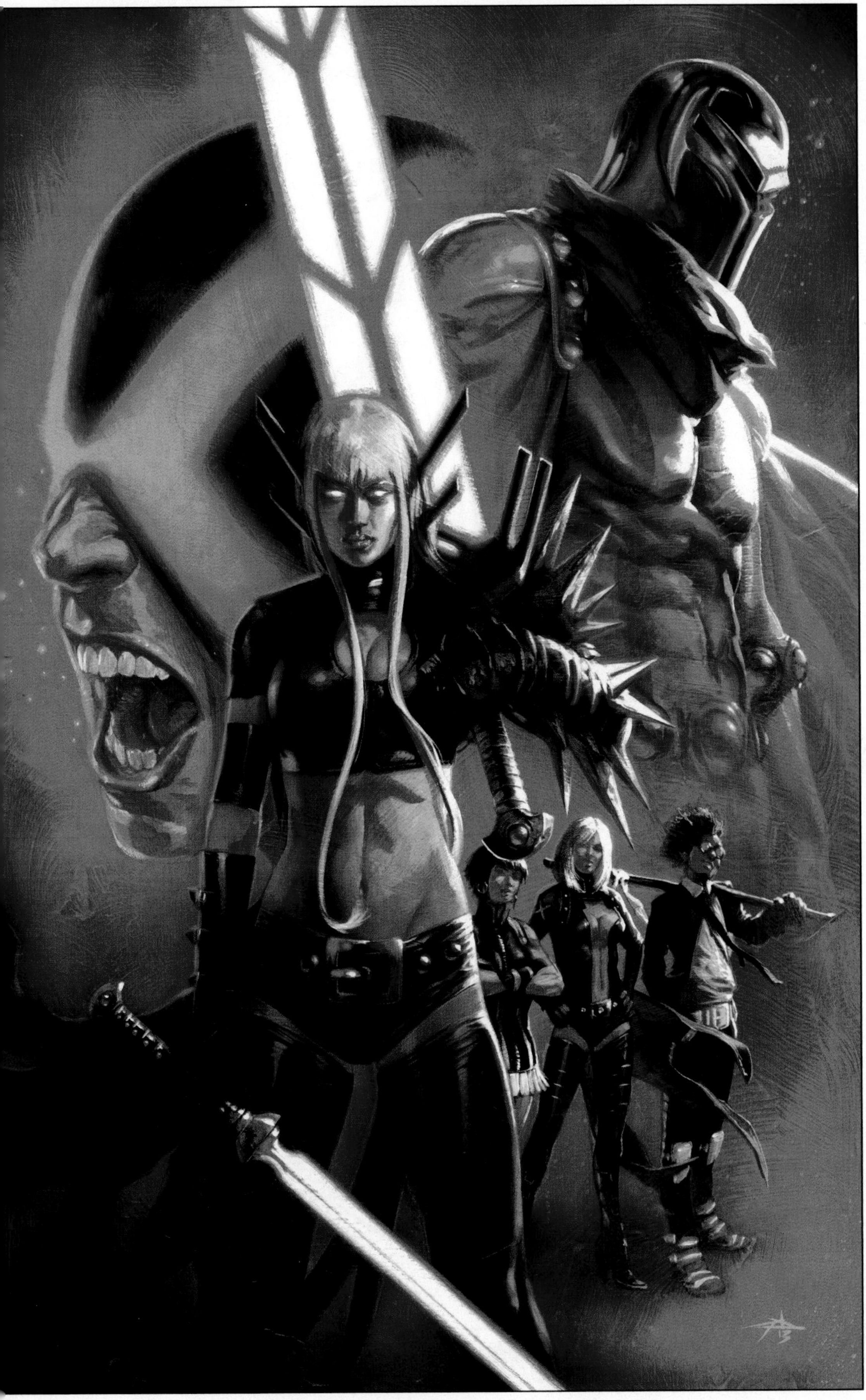

UNCANNY X-MEN #1 VARIANT
BY GABRIELE DELL'OTTO

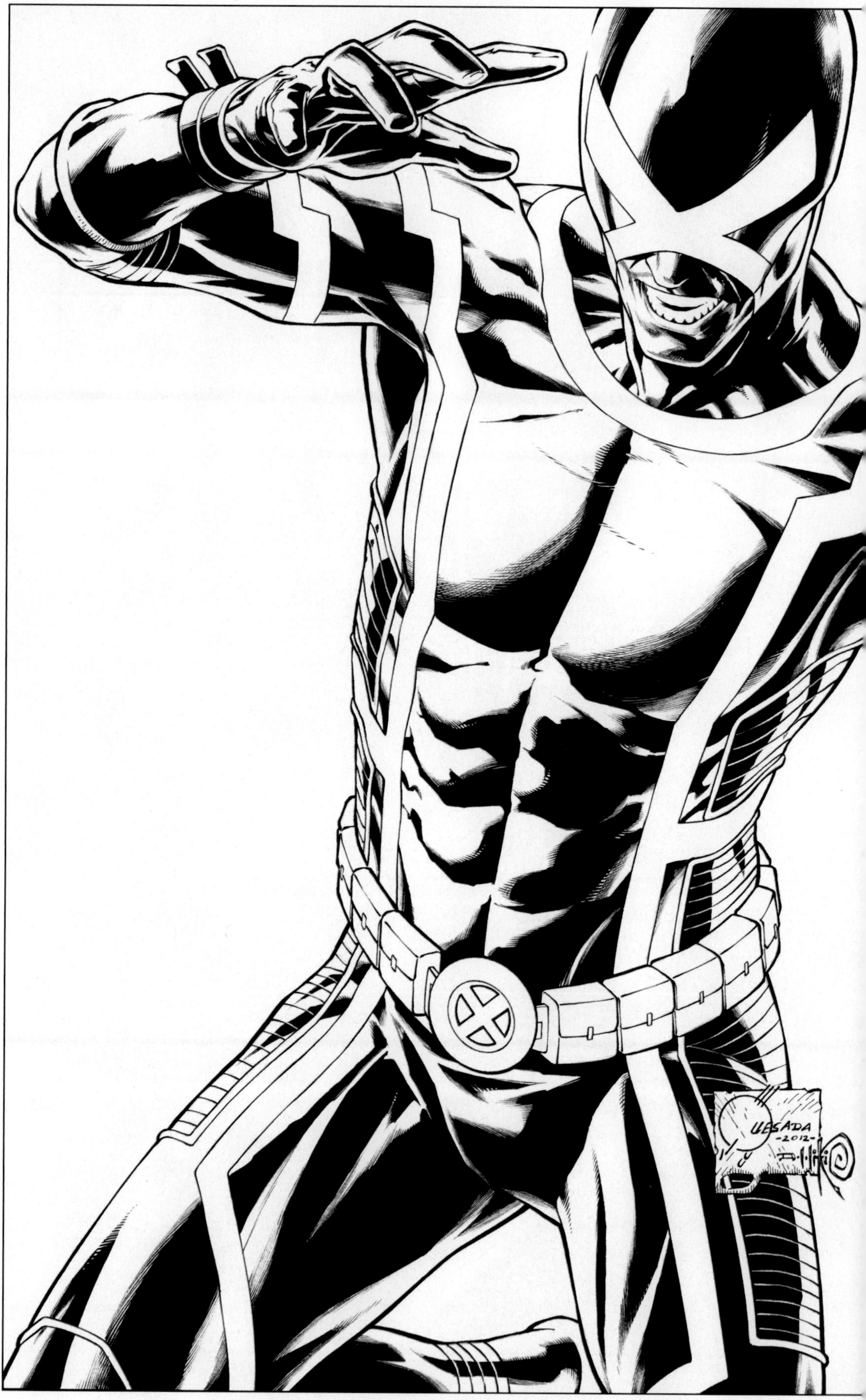

UNCANNY X-MEN #1 SKETCH VARIANT

BY JOE QUESADA & DANNY MIKI

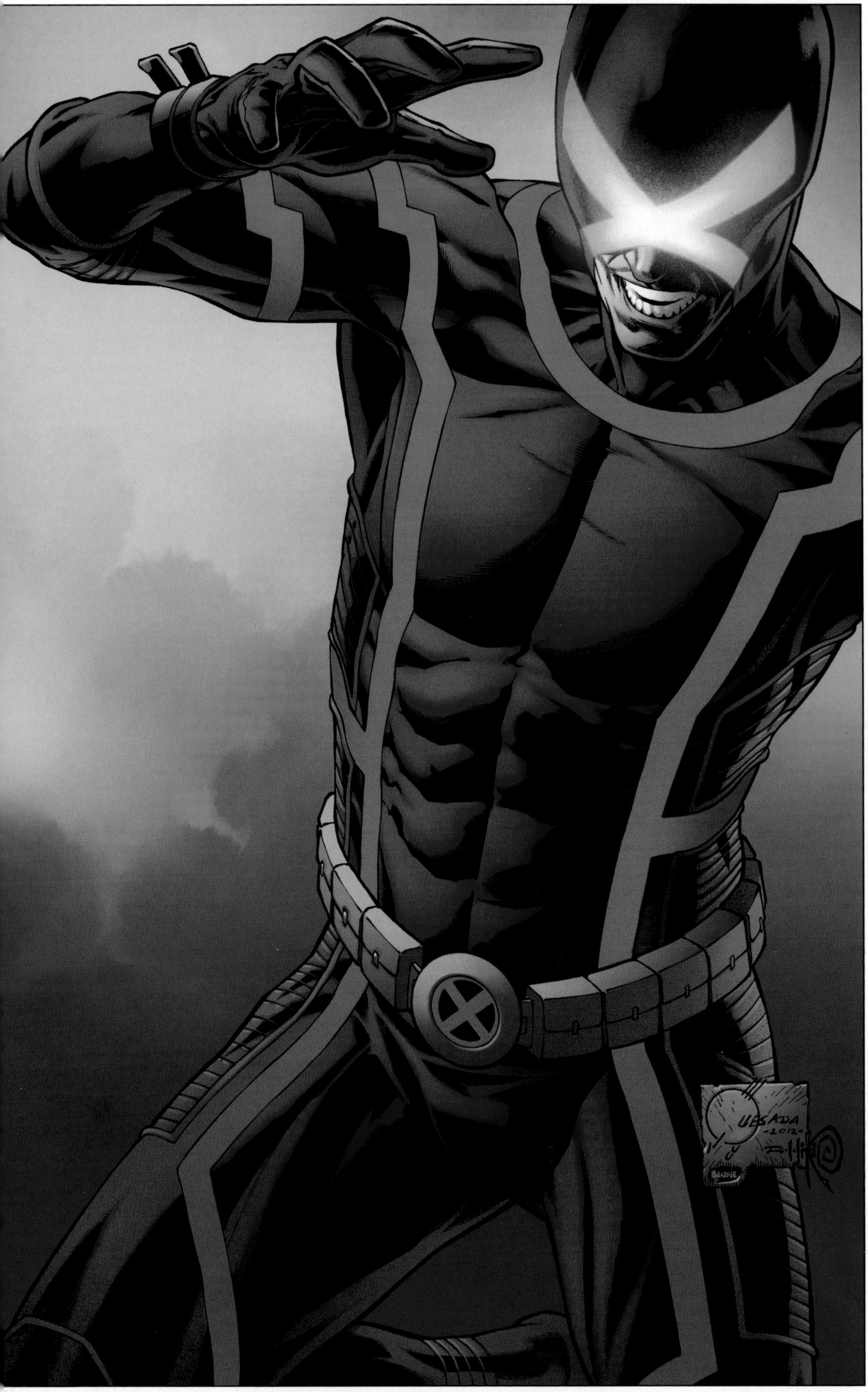
QUESADA
-2012-
ISANOVE

UNCANNY X-MEN #1 VARIANT
BY JOE QUESADA, DANNY MIKI & RICHARD ISANOVE

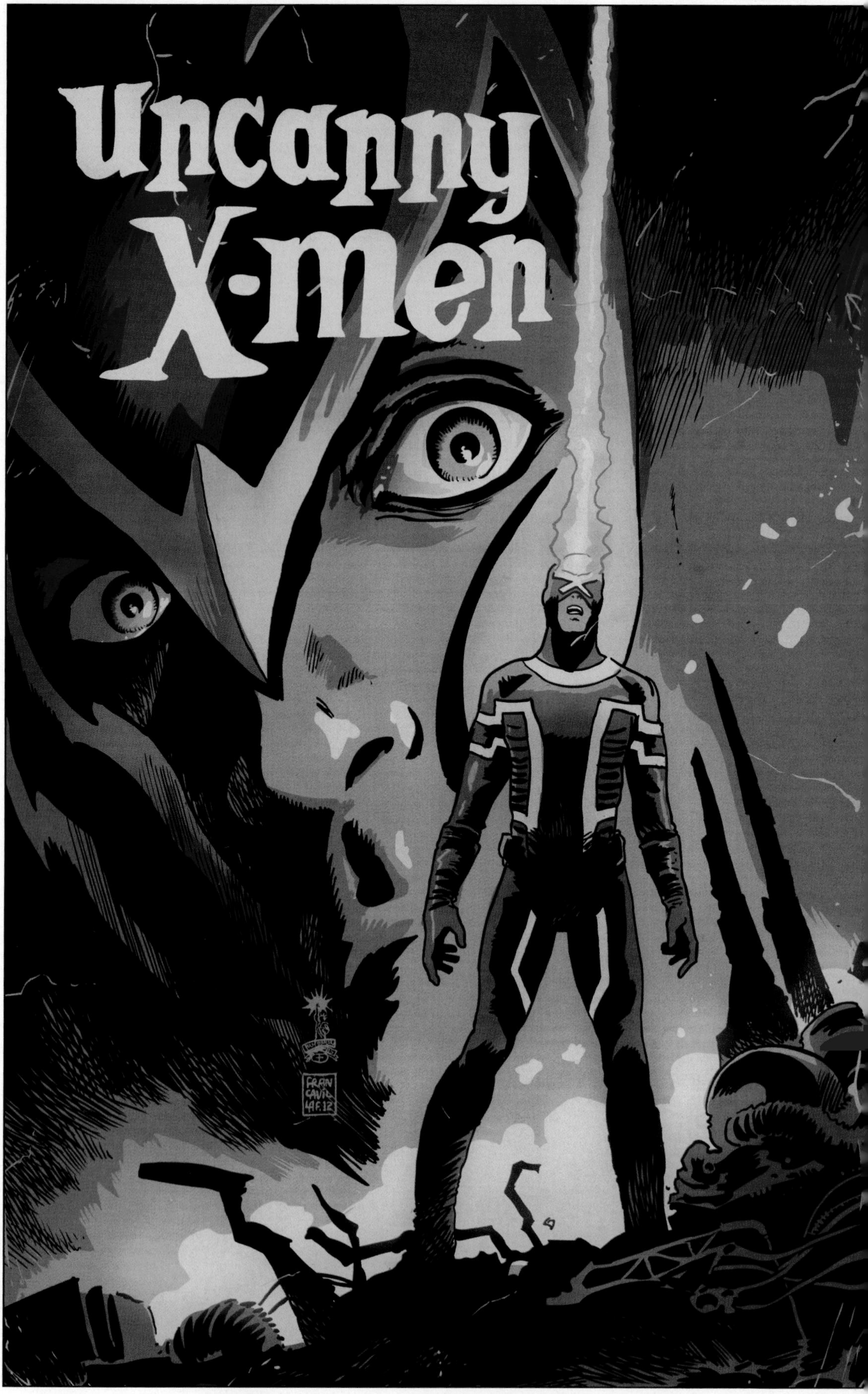
Uncanny
X-Men

UNCANNY X-MEN #1 HASTINGS VARIANT
BY FRANCESCO FRANCAVILLA

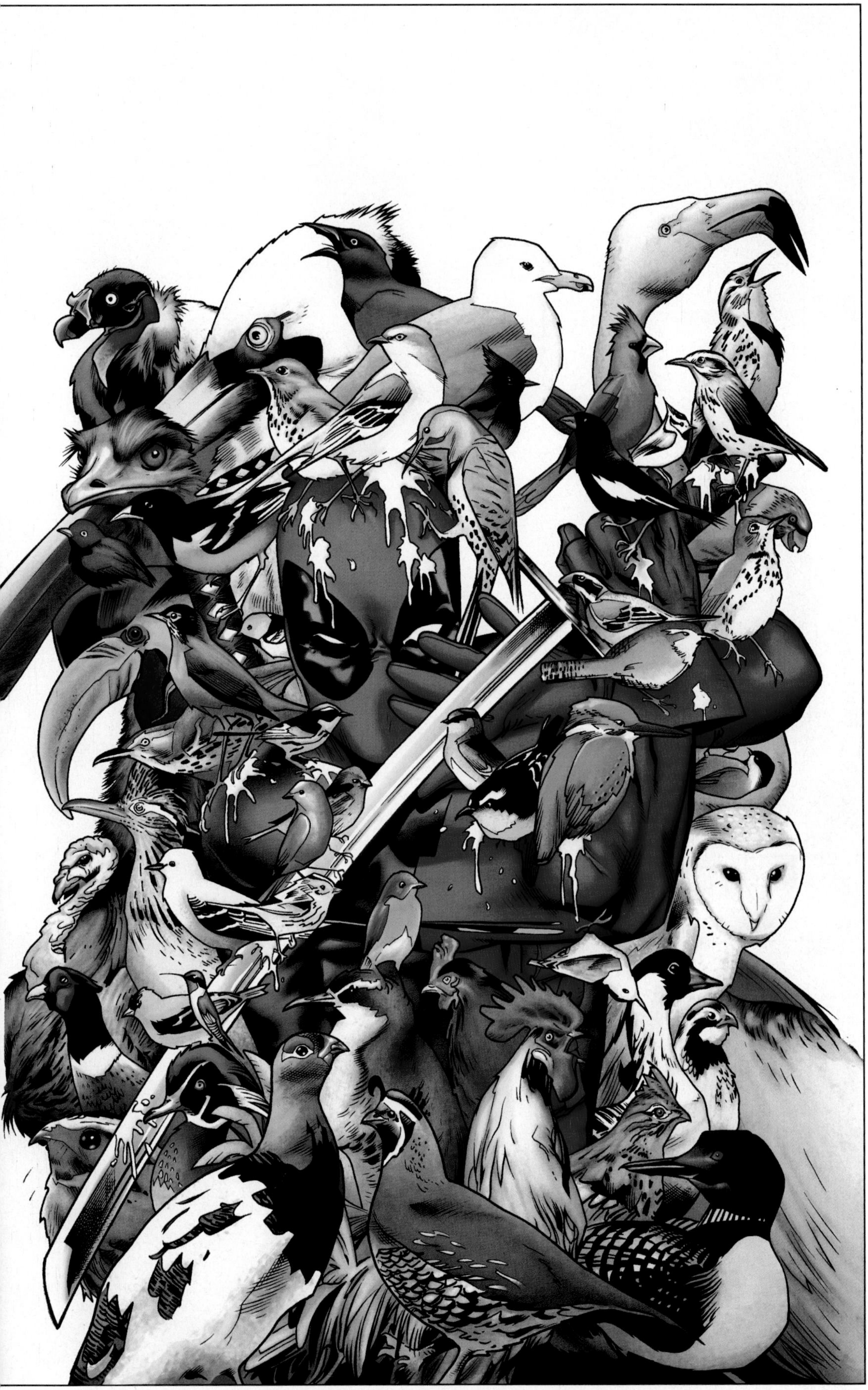

UNCANNY X-MEN #1 DEADPOOL 53 STATE BIRD VARIANT
BY STUART IMMONEN & MORRY HOLLOWELL

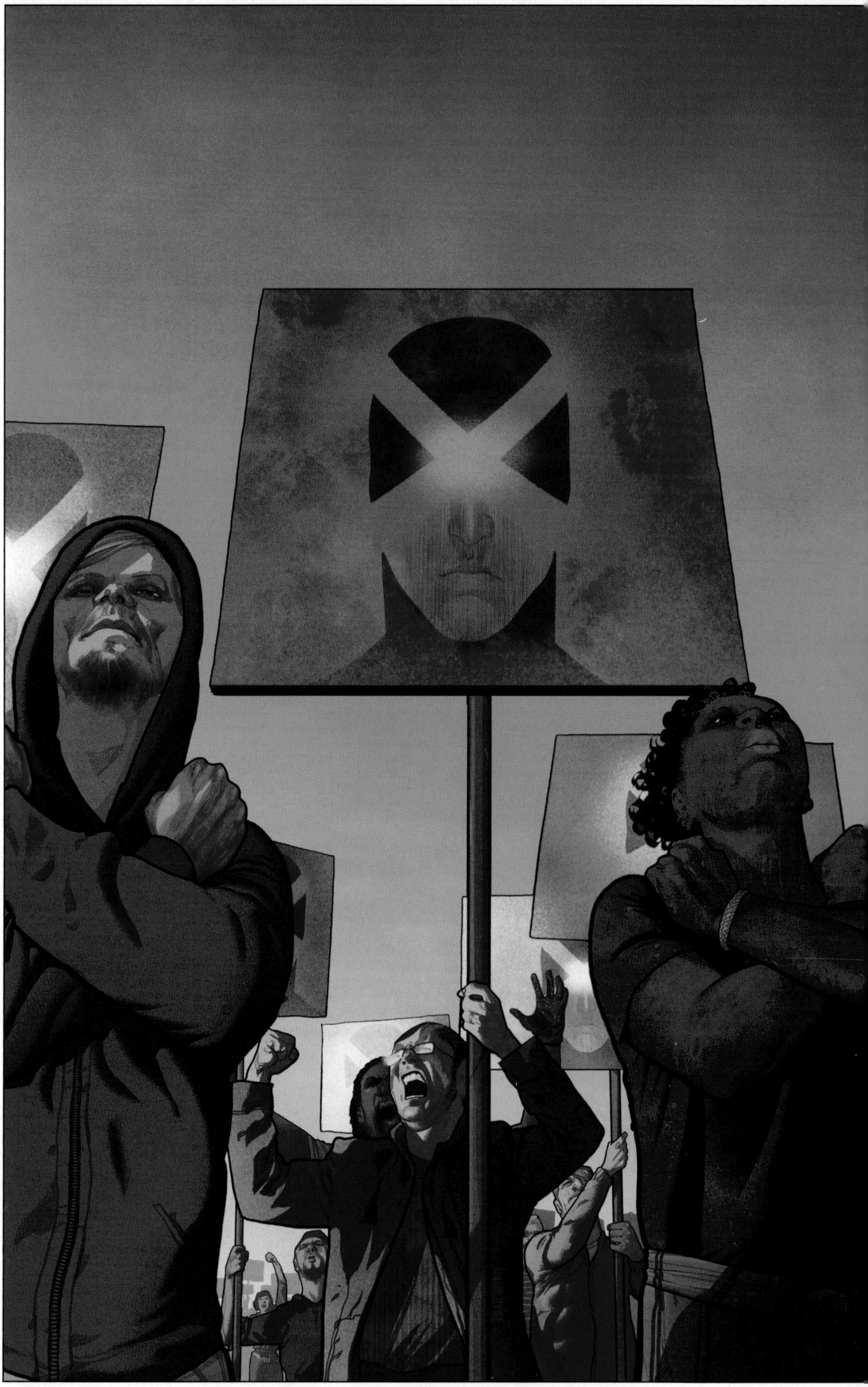

UNCANNY X-MEN #2 VARIANT
BY FRAZER IRVING

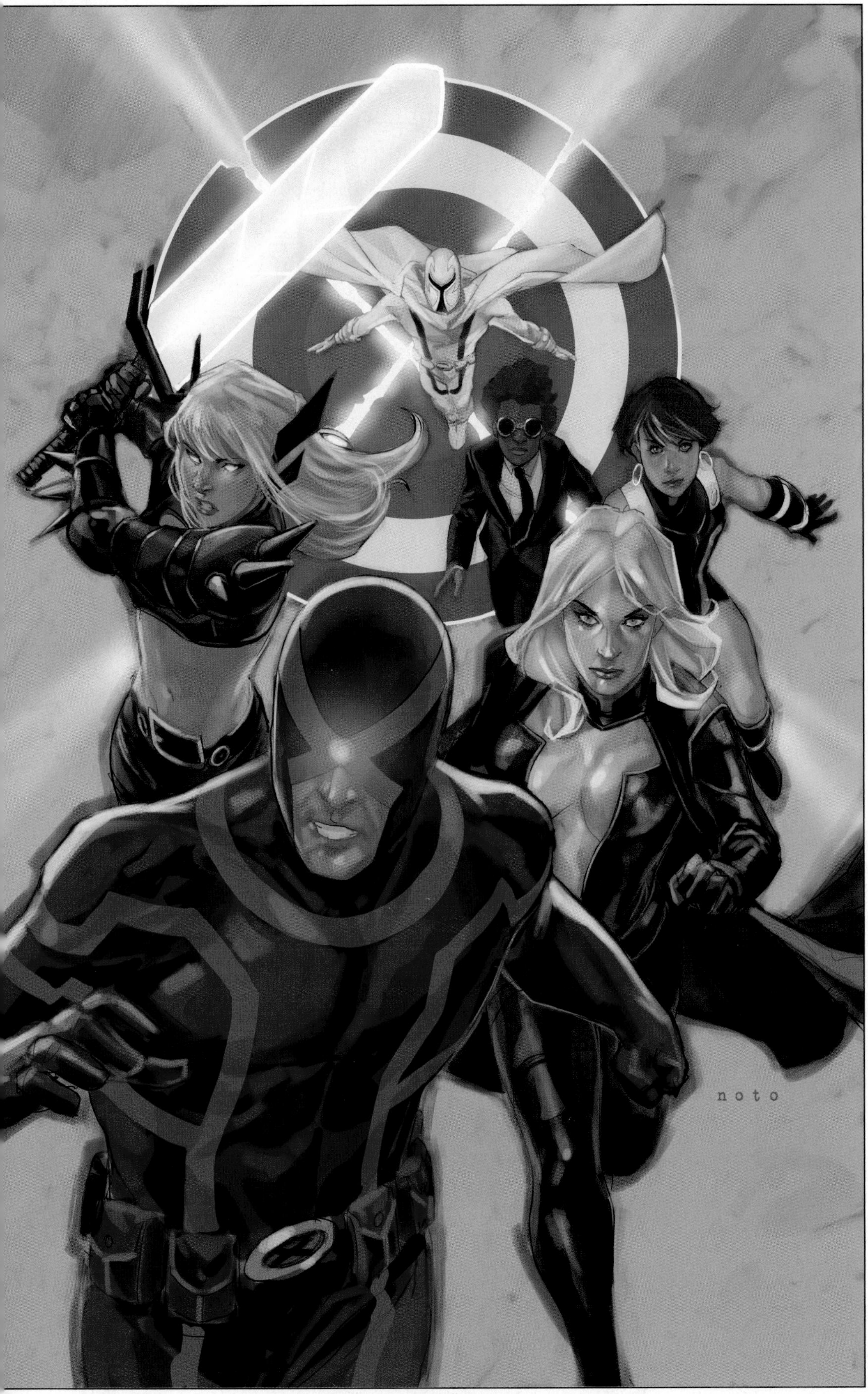
noto

UNCANNY X-MEN #3 VARIANT

BY PHIL NOTO

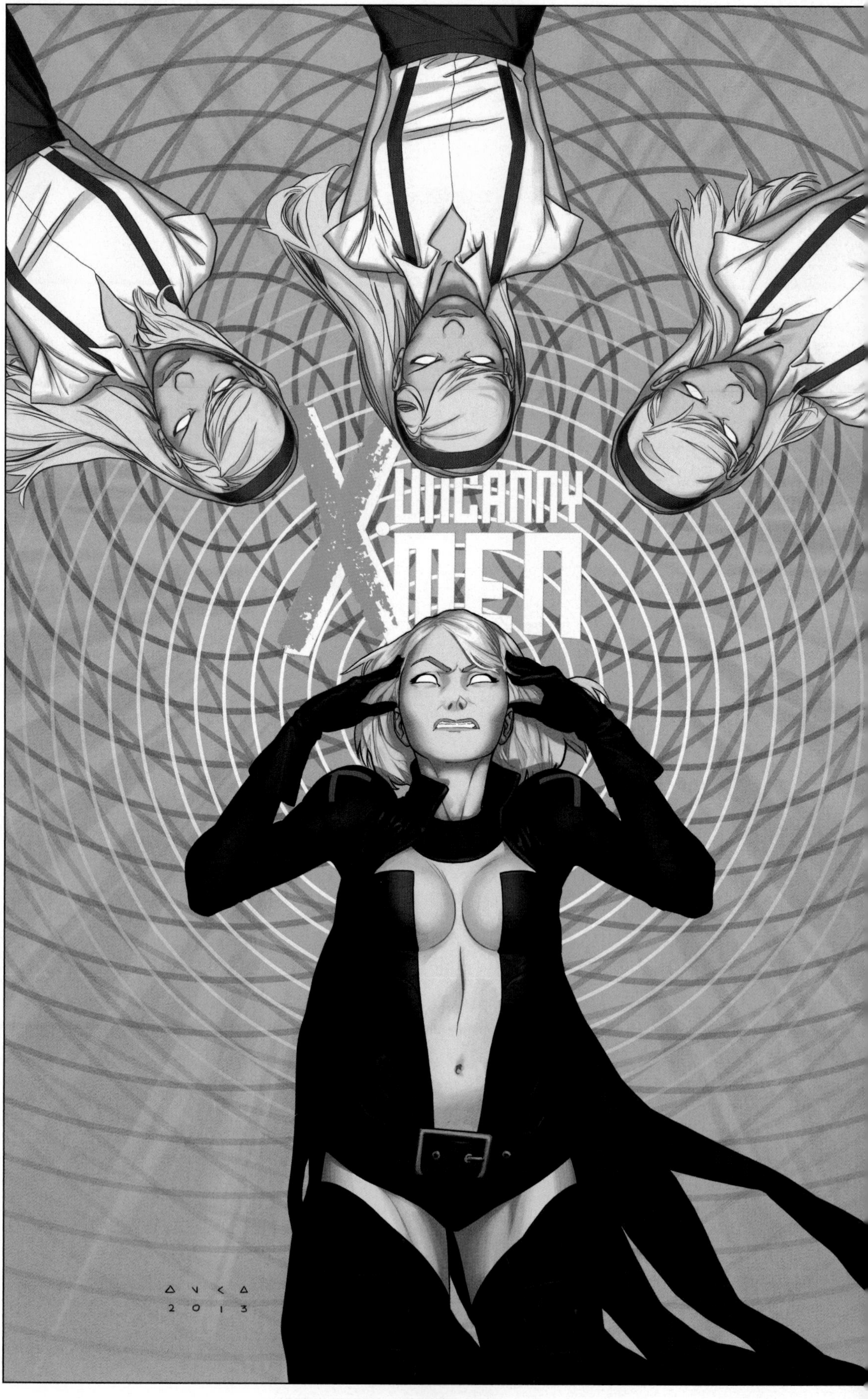
UNCANNY
X-MEN
ANKA
2013

UNCANNY X-MEN #4 VARIANT
BY KRIS ANKA

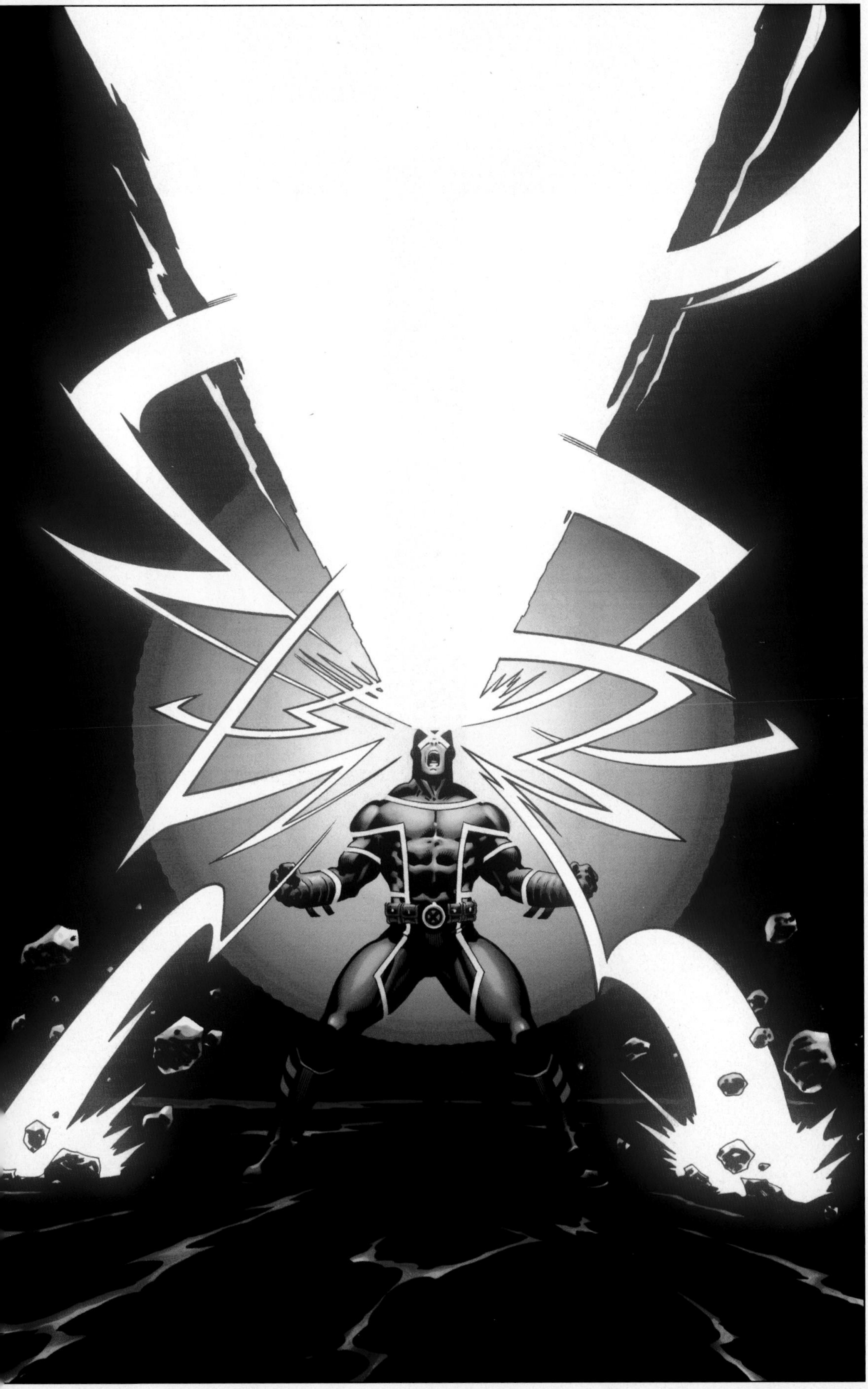

UNCANNY X-MEN #5 VARIANT
BY ED McGUINNESS & MORRY HOLLOWELL

CHARACTER DESIGNS BY
CHRIS BACHALO

CYCLOPS

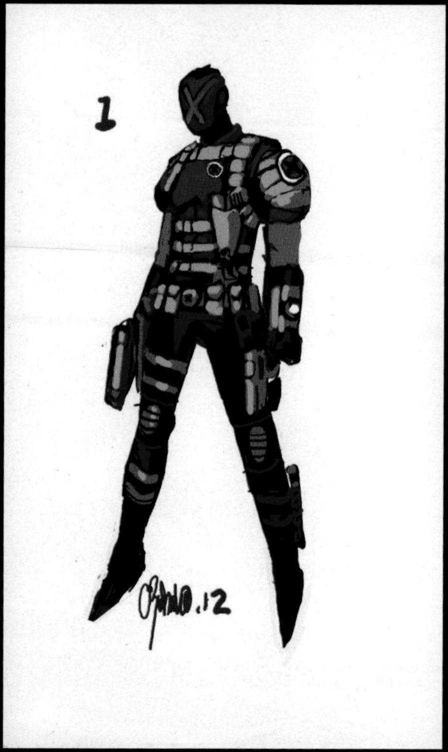
1
Bachalo.12

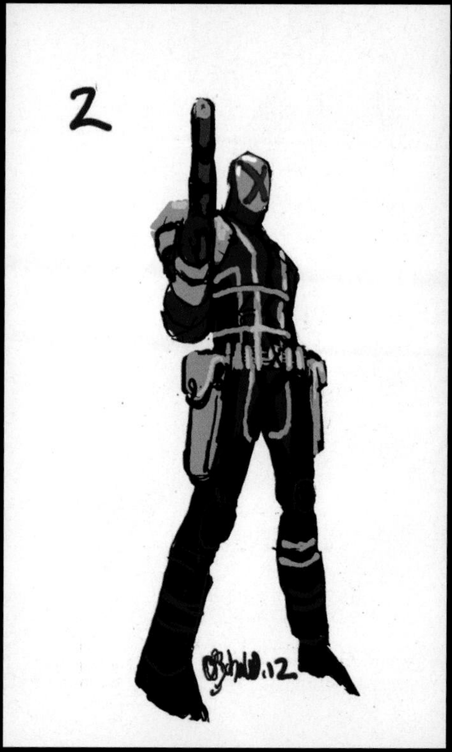
2
Bachalo.12

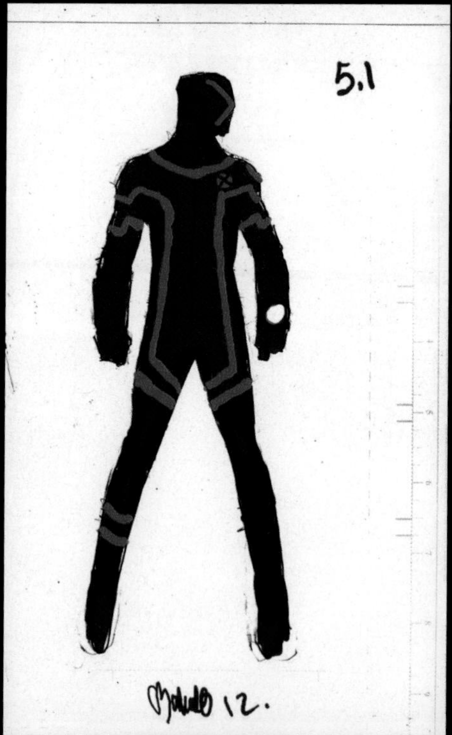
5.1
Bachalo 12.

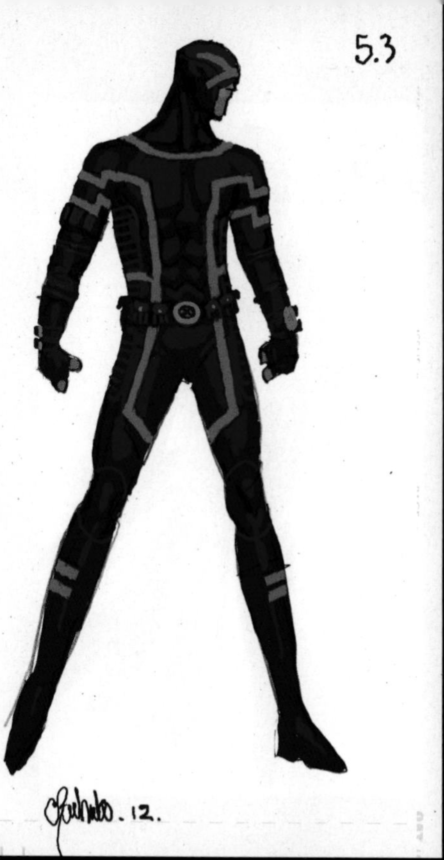
5.3

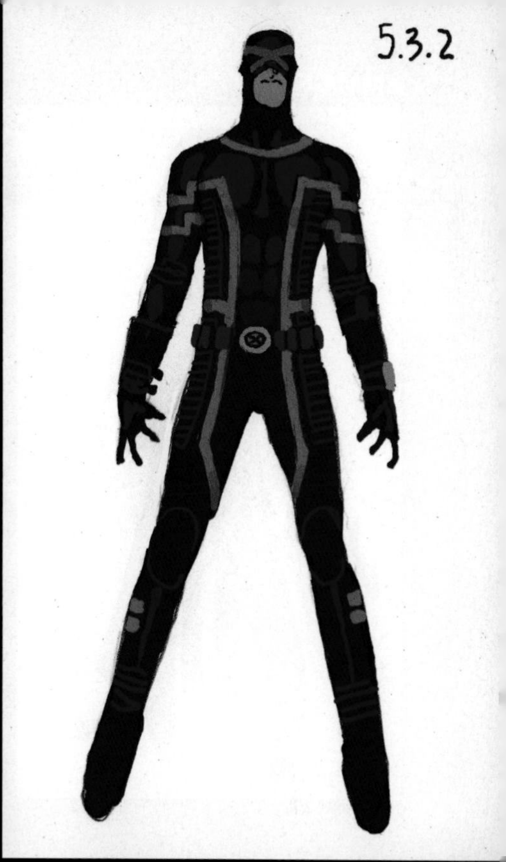
5.3.2

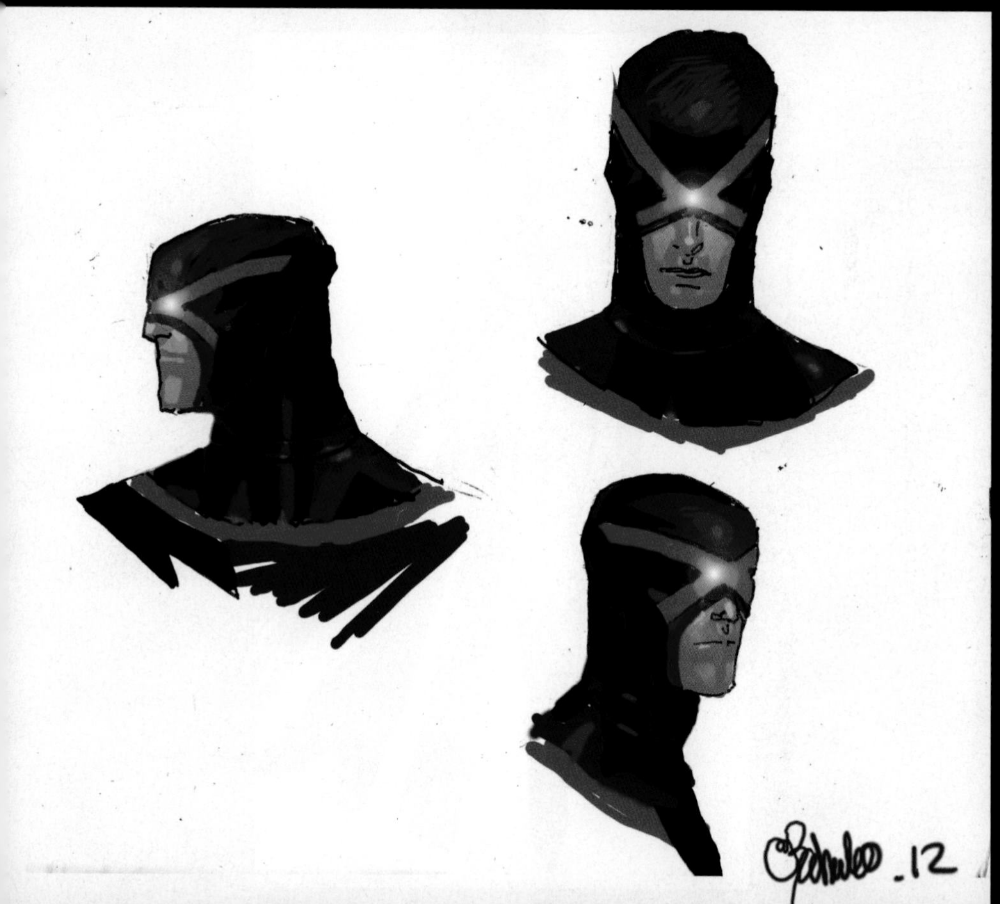

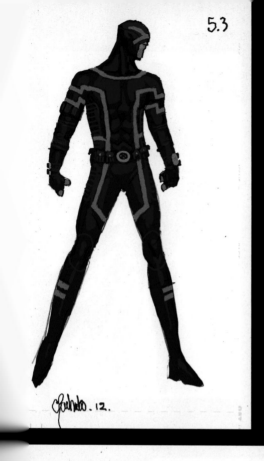

EMMA FROST

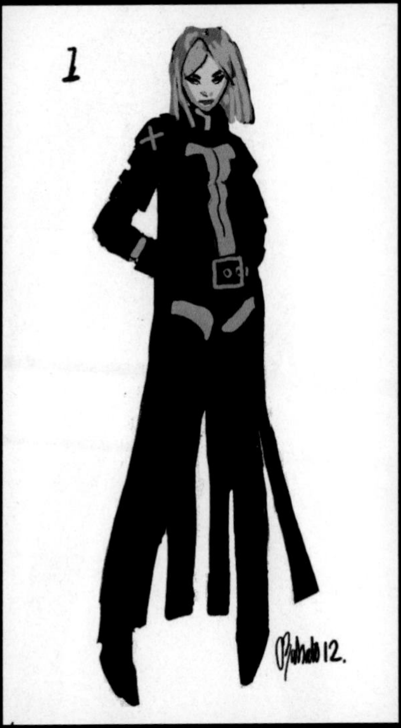
1

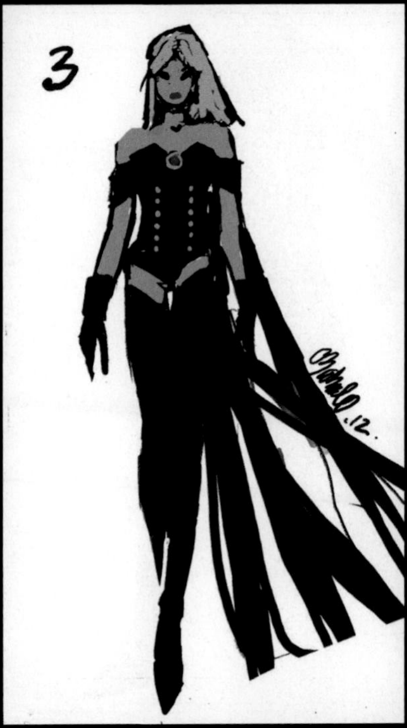
3

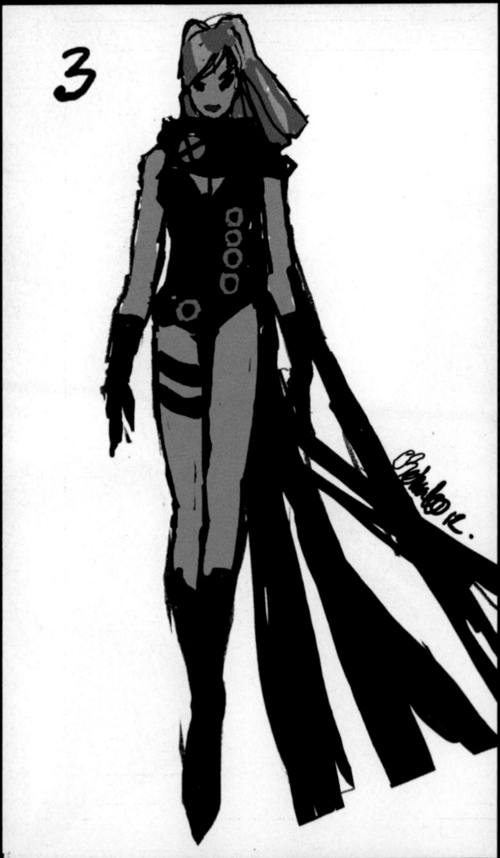
3

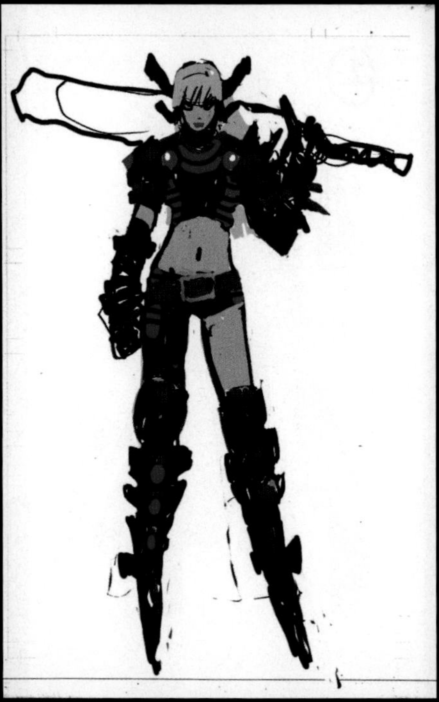

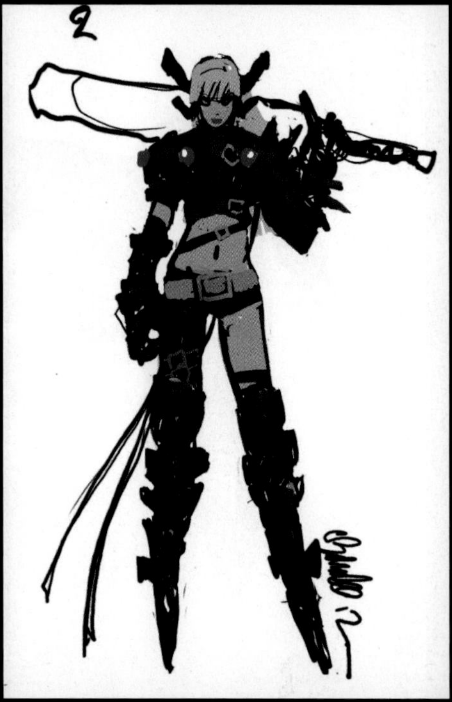
2

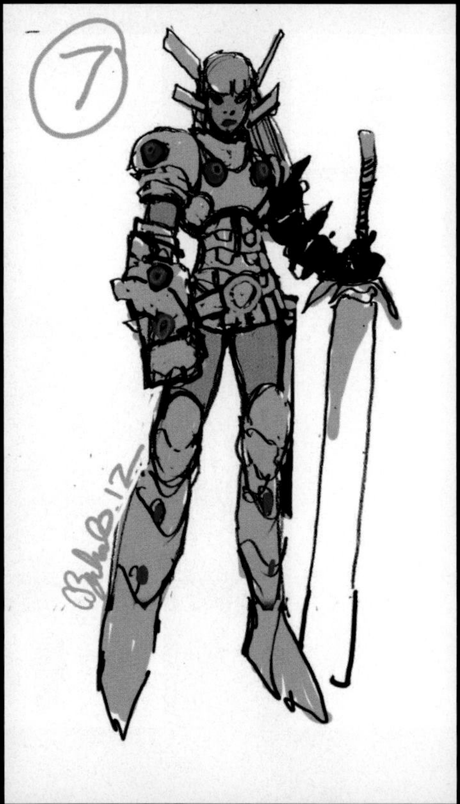
7

MAGNETO

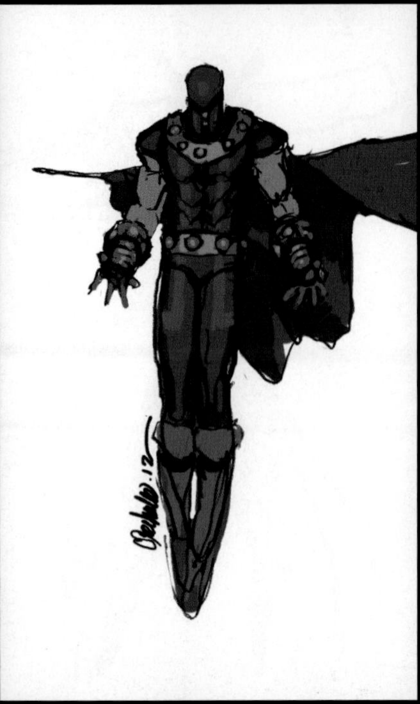

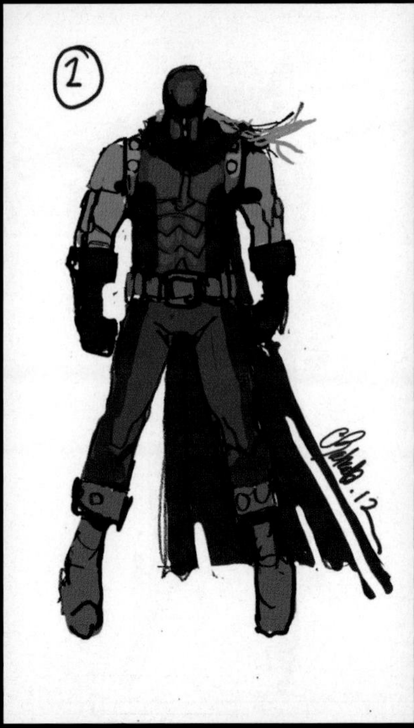
2

TRIAGE

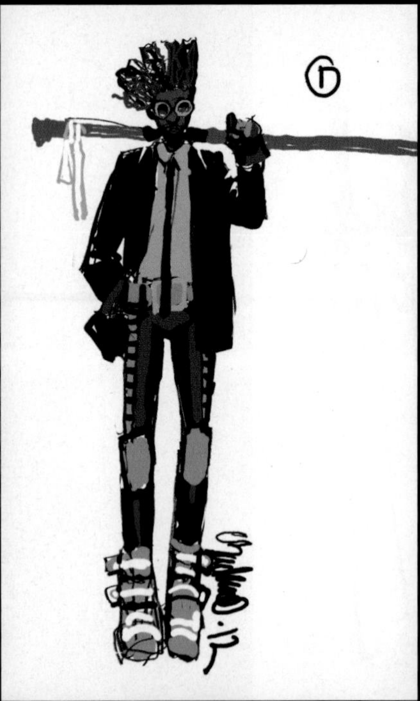
6

TEMPUS

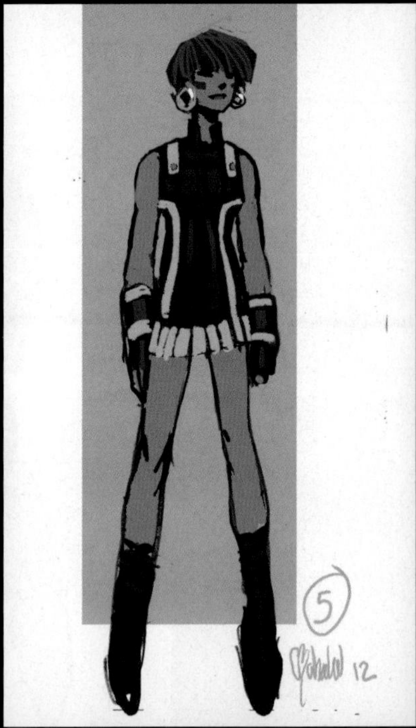
5

COVER SKETCHES BY

CHRIS BACHALO

#1

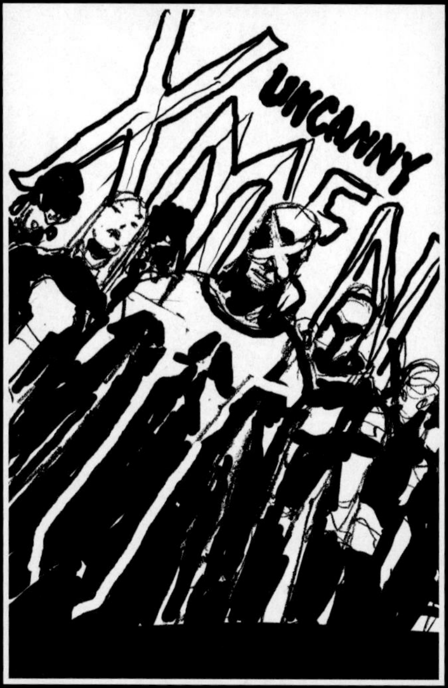
UNCANNY

#2

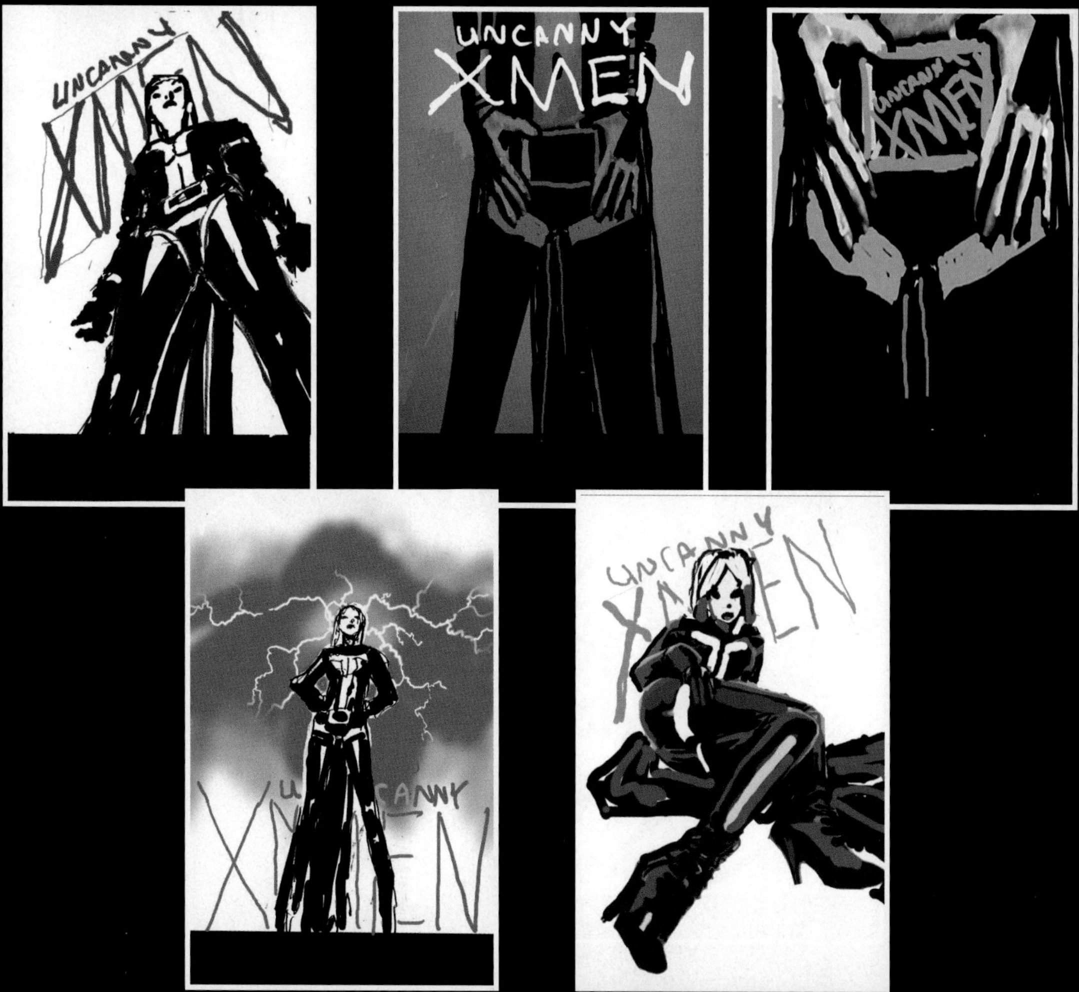
UNCANNY
XMEN

#3

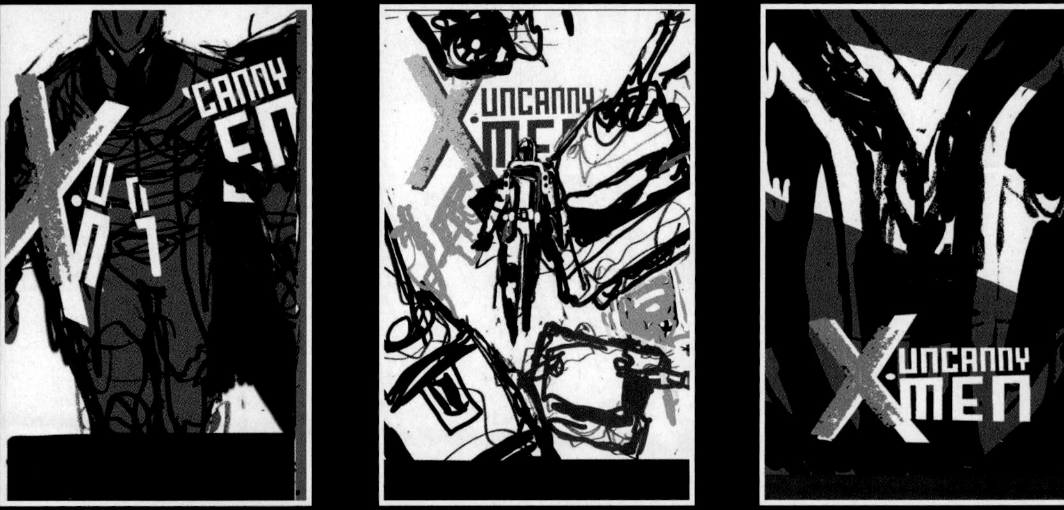
X UNCANNY MEN

#4

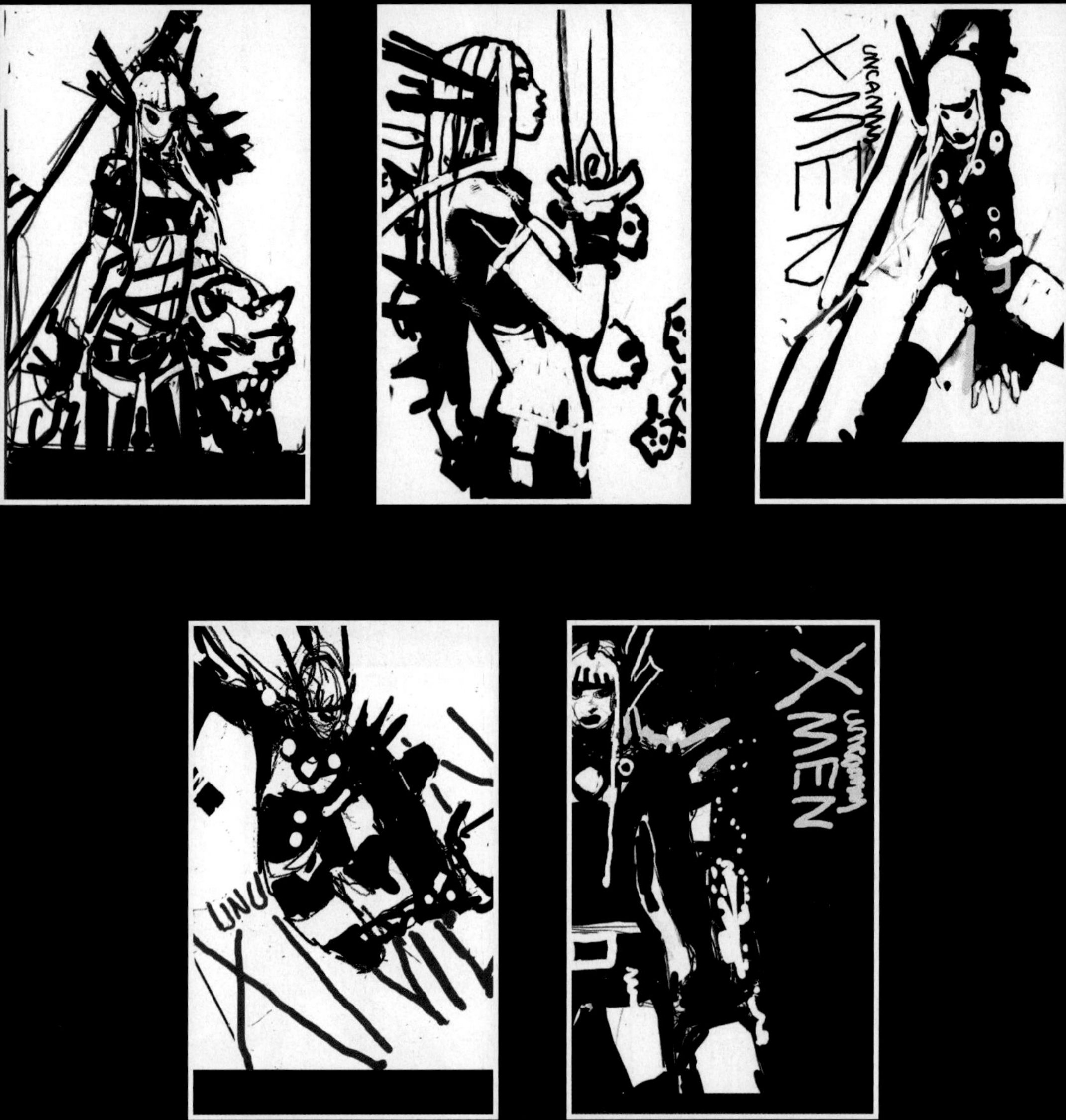
X MEN

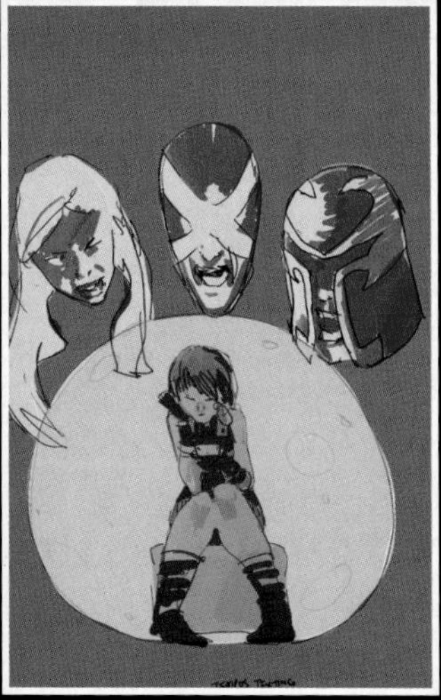
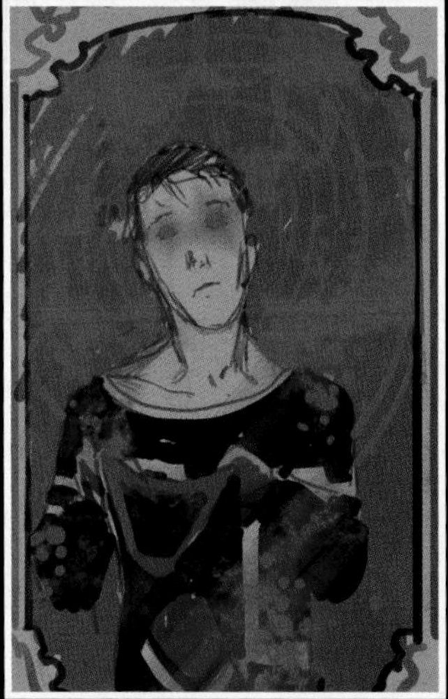
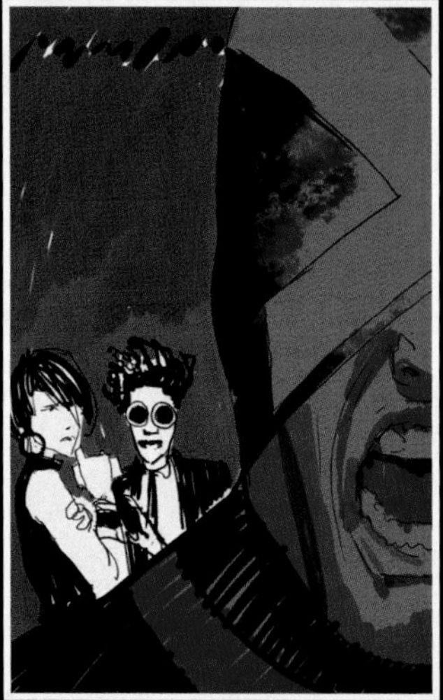
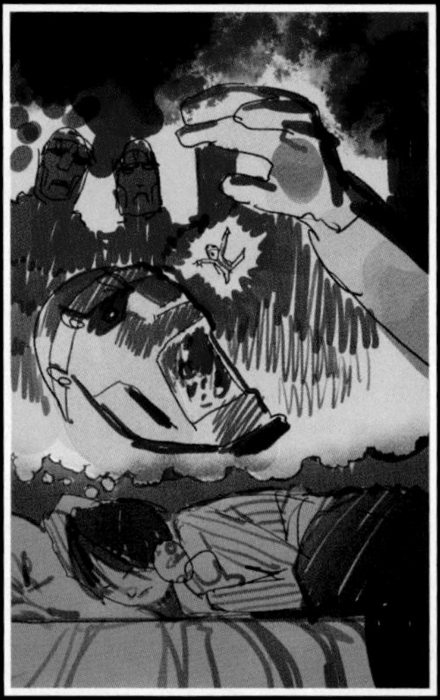
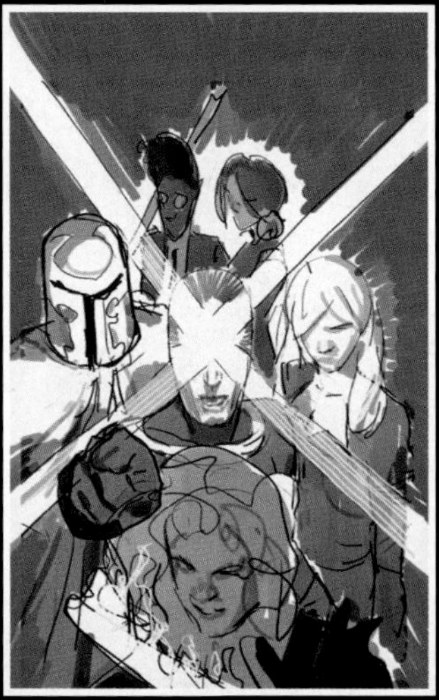
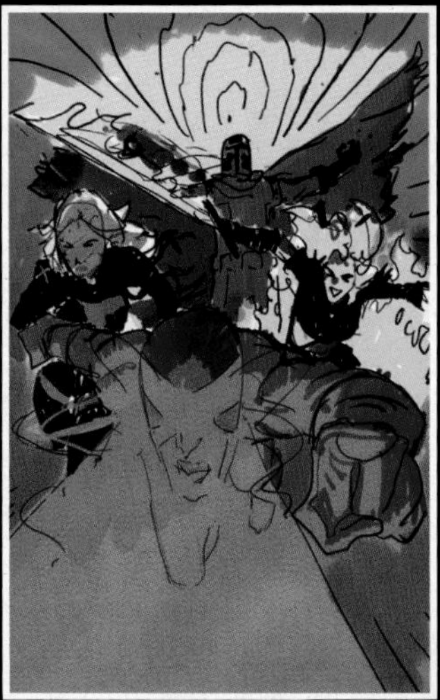
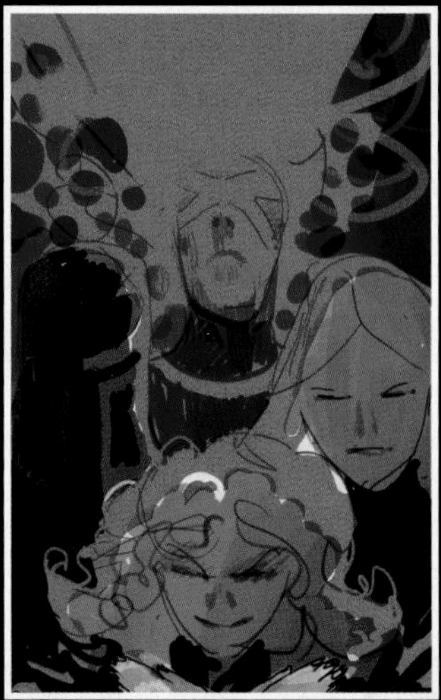

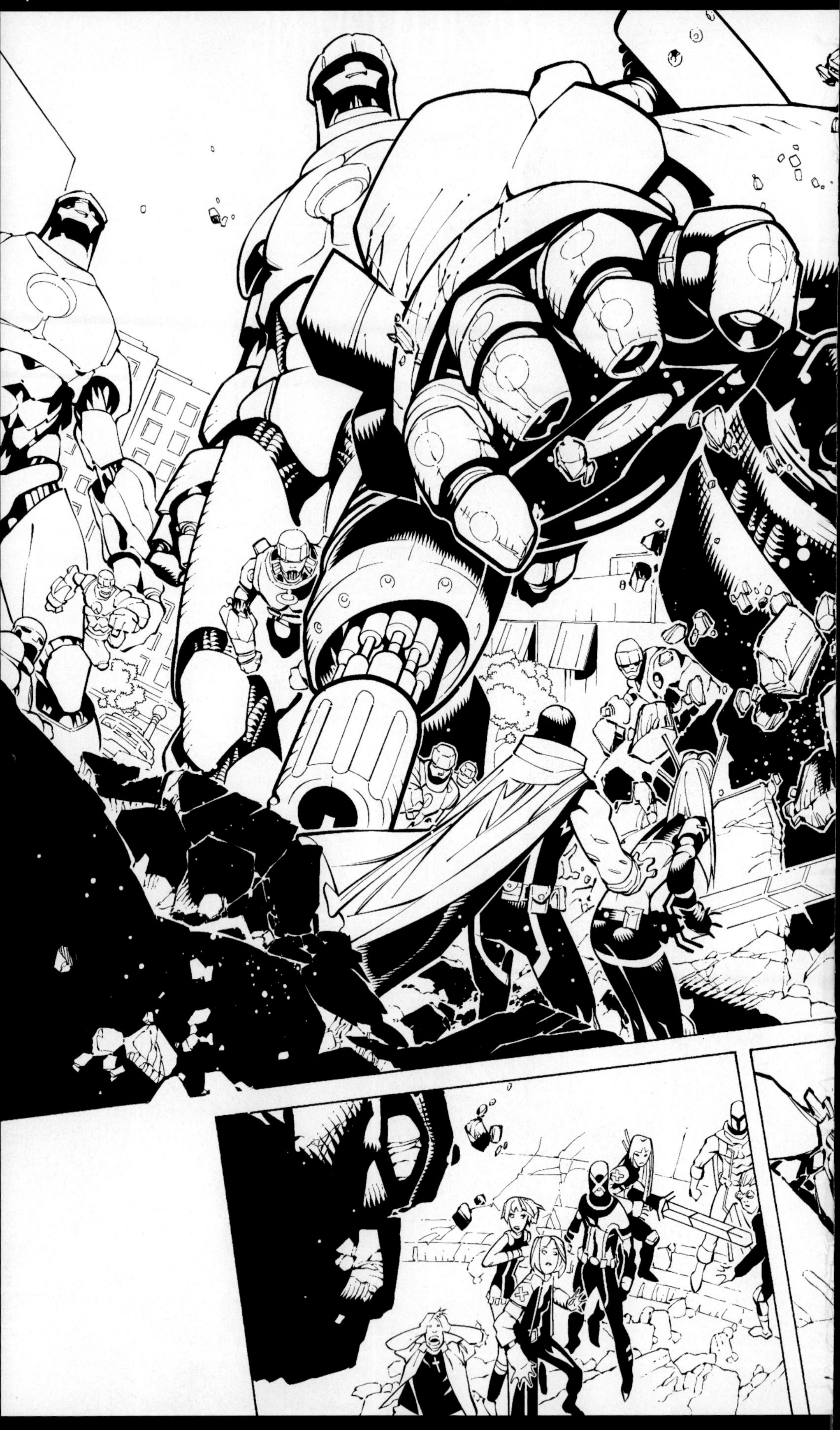

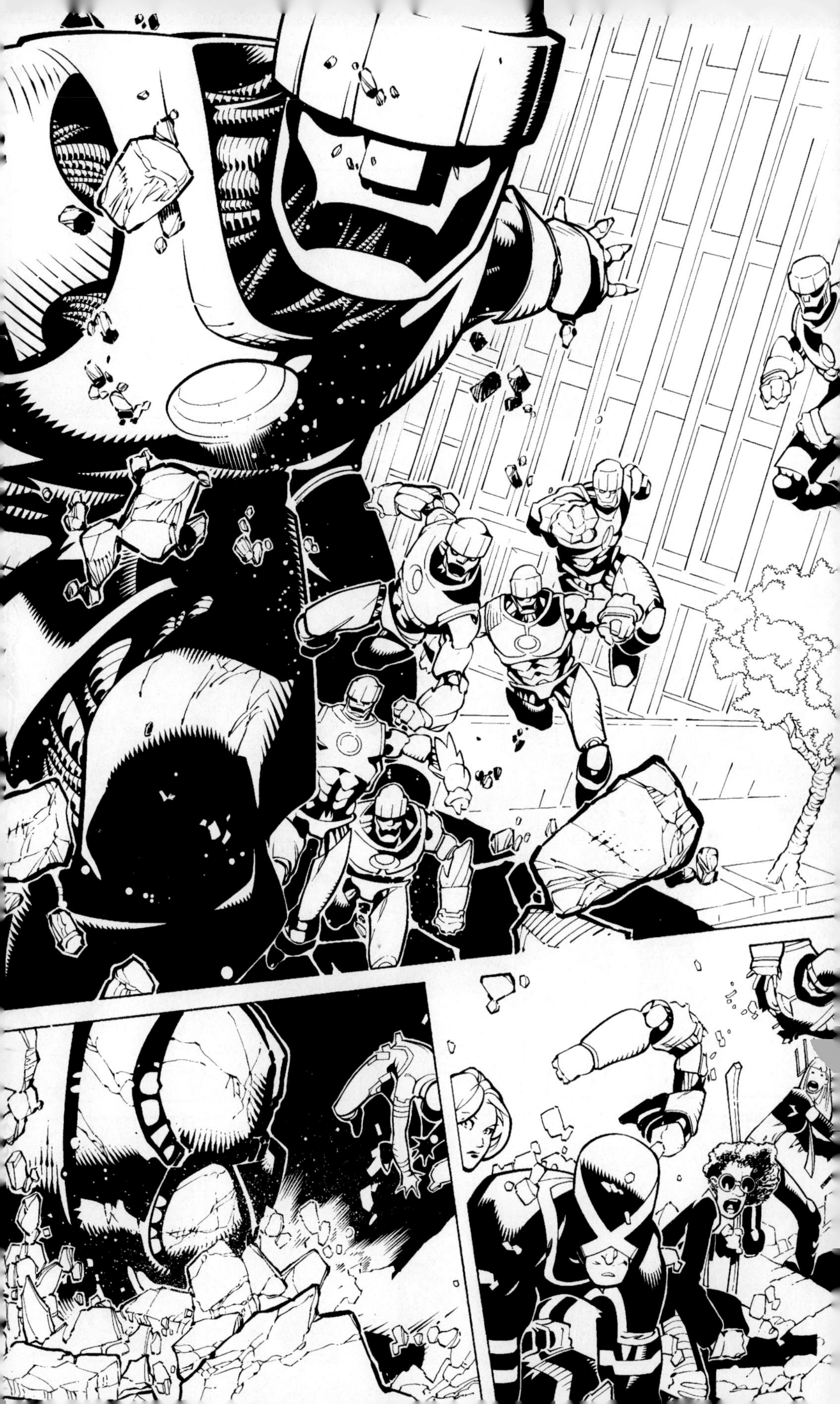

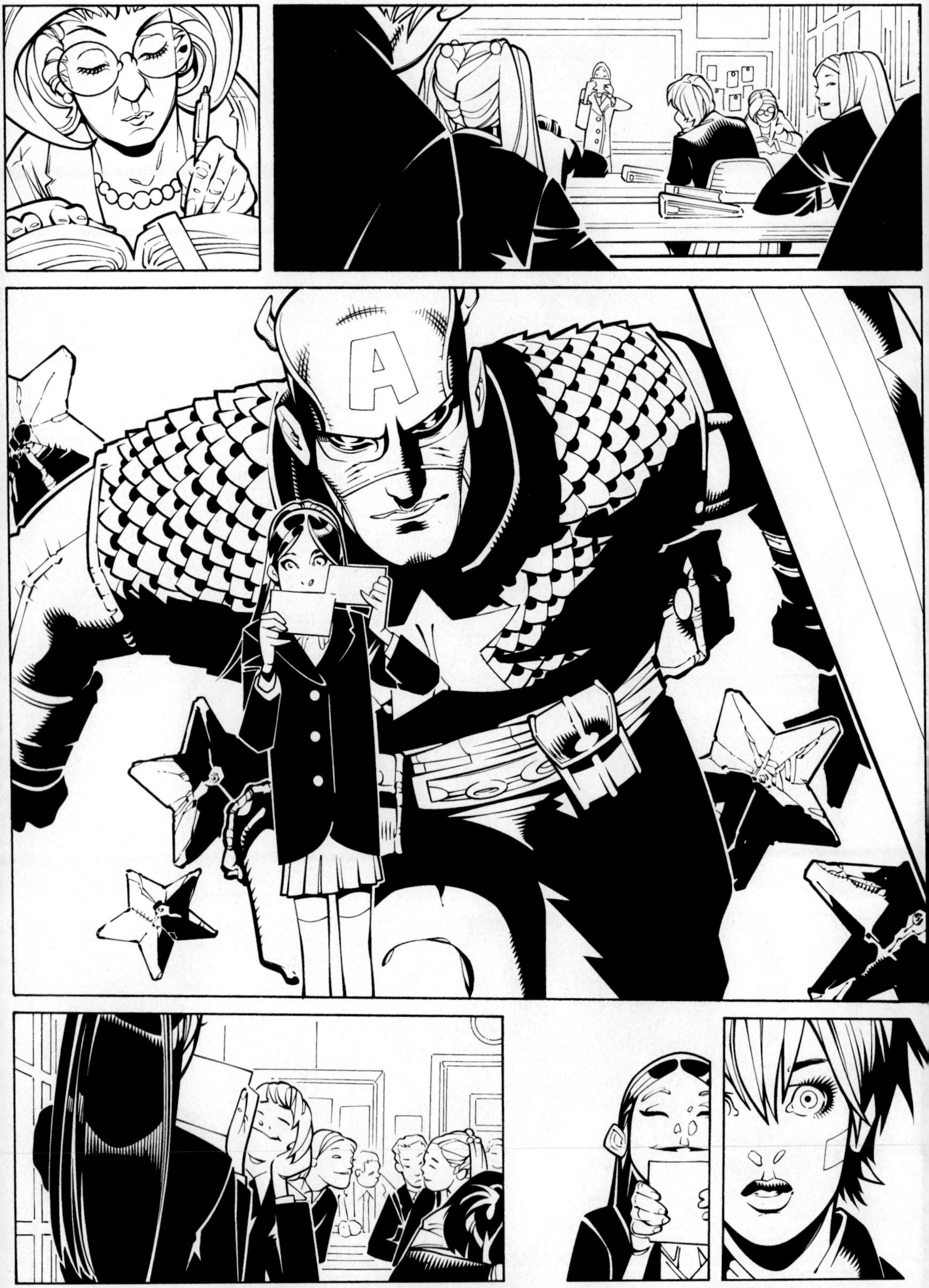

TO ACCESS THE FREE MARVEL AUGMENTED REALITY APP THAT ENHANCES AND CHANGES THE WAY YOU EXPERIENCE COMICS:

1. Download the app for free via marvel.com/ARapp
2. Launch the app on your camera-enabled Apple iOS® or Android™ device*
3. Hold your mobile device's camera over any cover or panel with the AR graphi
4. Sit back and see the future of comics in action!

*Available on most camera-enabled Apple iOS® and Android™ devices. Content subject to change and availability.

UNCANNY X-MEN AR INDEX